Instant Pot Cookbook

550 Easy and Healthy Instant Pot Recipes That Anyone Can Cook, Even If You're A Newbie In The Kitchen

Liam Sandler

Table of Contents

Introduction

We live in such a busy world that we barley have any time left by the end of the day. We deal with so much during the day that sometimes we just don't have enough energy left to do something for us or to eat a delicious meal in the comfort of our homes. We all love good food but how can we enjoy it with minimum effort?

Many people all over the world started to search for ways to make tasty meals in less time. This is why a revolutionary kitchen tool was developed. It's called an instant pot and it has million of fans already.

The instant pot is an innovative tool that has literally changed the way people cook their meals. It allows you to cook tasty and succulent meals in a few minutes.

Add the dishes are so easy to make in this pot and they are all so flavored and rich.

You can cook each of your favorite meals as long as you follow the directions. You will be able to make your meals in a much more effective and healthy way.

Forget about spending long hours in the kitchen and about using so many pans, pots and cooking methods. Just gather your ingredients, heat up your instant pot and make sure you follow all the directions. That the key to your success in the kitchen.

These new recipes collection you are about to discover brings to you some of the best instant pot dishes in a very simple and clear manner. All the ingredients used here are simple and accessible ones and all the directions are very easy to follow.

Just sit back, relax and enjoy some amazing dishes made in one of the most useful kitchen tools: the instant pot. Enjoy cooking in a futuristic and fun way and have fun using this great tool!

Peanut Butter Oatmeal
*Prep time: 10 minutes | **Cooking time:** 12 minutes | Servings: 6*

Ingredients:
- 1 and ½ cups steel cut oats
- 3 tablespoons peanut butter
- 1 banana, peeled and sliced
- 4 cups water

Directions:
Put the oats and the water in your instant pot, put the lid on and cook on High for 12 minutes. Release the pressure naturally for 10 minutes, add the peanut butter and stir well everything. Divide the oatmeal into bowls, top each serving with banana slices and serve.

Nutrition: calories 172, fat 9, fiber 5, carbs 7, protein 10

Veggie Soufflé
*Prep time: 10 minutes | **Cooking time:** 25 minutes | Servings: 4*

Ingredients:
- ½ cup almond milk
- 6 eggs, whisked
- ½ cup cheddar cheese, grated
- 1 cup water
- 1 cup red bell pepper, chopped
- 1 carrot, grated
- 1 cup broccoli florets, chopped
- Cooking spray

Directions:
In a bowl, mix the eggs with the other ingredients except the cooking spray, cheese and the water and stir them well. Grease a soufflé dish with the cooking spray, pour the veggie mix inside and sprinkle the cheese on top. Put the water in the instant pot, lower the soufflé dish inside, put the lid on and cook on High for 25 minutes. Release the pressure naturally for 10 minutes, cool the soufflé down a bit, divide between plates and serve.

Nutrition: calories 200, fat 7, fiber 3, carbs 6, protein 9

Coconut Quinoa
*Prep time: 10 minutes | **Cooking time:** 1 minutes | Servings: 4*

Ingredients:
- 1 cup quinoa
- 2 cups coconut milk
- Zest of 1 lime, grated
- Juice of 1 lime
- 1 cup water
- 2 tablespoons coconut chips
- ¼ cup blueberries

Directions:
In your instant pot, combine the quinoa with the other ingredients except the coconut chips and the blueberries, put the lid on and cook on High for 1 minute. Release the pressure naturally for 10 minutes, stir the quinoa and divide it into bowls. Top each serving with blueberries and coconut chips and serve for breakfast.

Nutrition: calories 152, fat 1, fiber 2, carbs 6, protein 11

Mushroom Oatmeal

Prep time: 10 minutes | Cooking time: 20 minutes | Servings: 4

Ingredients:

- 4 tablespoons olive oil
- 1 cup steel cut oats
- 1 red onion, chopped
- 2 garlic cloves, minced
- 14 ounces chicken stock
- ½ cup water
- 1 tablespoon thyme, chopped
- 10 ounces white mushrooms, sliced
- ½ cup cheddar, grated
- A pinch of salt and black pepper

Directions:

Set the instant pot on Sauté mode, add half of the oil, heat it up, add the onion, stir and sauté for 3 minutes. Add garlic and the oats, toss and cook for 2 minutes more. Add the stock, water, salt, pepper and the thyme, toss again, put the lid on and cook on High for 10 minutes. Meanwhile, heat up a pan with the rest of the oil over medium-high heat, add the mushrooms and sauté them for 5 minutes. Release the pressure naturally for 10 minutes from the pot, add the mushrooms and toss. Divide the oatmeal into bowls, sprinkle the cheese on top and serve for breakfast.

Nutrition: calories 188, fat 8, fiber 3, carbs 7, protein 9

Turkey Frittata

Prep time: 5 minutes | Cooking time: 10 minutes | Servings: 4

Ingredients:

- 4 turkey bacon slices, chopped
- 1 red potato, peeled and grated
- 6 eggs, whisked
- A pinch of salt and black pepper
- 1 red bell pepper, chopped
- ¼ cup almond milk
- 1 small red onion, chopped
- ¼ cup cheddar cheese, grated
- 1 cup water

Directions:

Spread the bacon, potato, onion and bell pepper on the bottom of a ramekin. In a bowl, combine the eggs with the rest of the ingredients except the cheese and the water and whisk well. Pour this over the turkey and veggies mix, and sprinkle the cheese on top. Put the water in the instant pot, put the ramekin inside, put the lid on and cook on High for 10 minutes. Release the pressure fast for 5 minutes, divide the frittata between plates and serve for breakfast.

Nutrition: calories 191, fat 11, fiber 3, carbs 6, protein 7

Spinach Quiche

Prep time: 10 minutes | Cooking time: 20 minutes | Servings: 6

Ingredients:

- 12 eggs
- ½ cup almond milk
- 4 cups baby spinach, roughly torn
- 4 spring onions, chopped
- 1 cup tomato, cubed
- A pinch of salt and black pepper
- ¼ cup parmesan, grated
- 1 and ½ cups water

Directions:

In a bowl, combine the eggs with the milk, salt and pepper and whisk. Add the rest of the ingredients except the water and the parmesan and whisk again. Pour this into a quiche pan and sprinkle the parmesan on top. Put the water in the instant pot, add the pan inside, put the lid on and cook on High for 20 minutes. Release the pressure naturally for 10 minutes, divide the quiche between plates and serve for breakfast.

Nutrition: calories 200, fat 12, fiber 4, carbs 6, protein 8

Meat Pie

Prep time: 10 minutes | Cooking time: 30 minutes | Servings: 4

Ingredients:

- ½ cup almond milk
- A pinch of salt and black pepper
- 6 eggs, whisked
- 4 bacon slices, cooked and crumbled
- 1 cup pork sausage, ground
- 1 cup cheddar cheese, shredded
- 2 spring onions, chopped
- ½ cup ham, chopped
- 1 cup water

Ingredients:

In a bowl, combine the eggs with the milk, salt and pepper and whisk. Add the rest of the ingredients except the cheese and the water and whisk again. Pour this into a pie pan and sprinkle the cheese all over. Put the water in your instant pot, put the pie pan inside, cover the pan with tin foil, put the lid on and cook on High for 30 minutes. Release the pressure naturally for 10 minutes, divide the mix between plates and serve for breakfast.

Nutrition: calories 200, fat 12, fiber 5, carbs 7, protein 9

Lemon Steel Cut Oats

Prep time: 10 minutes | Cooking time: 13 minutes | Servings: 4

Ingredients:

- 1 cup steel cut oats
- 3 cups water
- ½ cup coconut cream
- 1 tablespoon avocado oil
- 2 tablespoons coconut sugar
- 1 tablespoon lemon zest, grated
- ¼ cup chia seeds
- 1 cup blueberries

Directions:

Set the instant pot on Sauté mode, add the oil, heat it up, add the oats and toast them for 3 minutes. Add all the other ingredients except the chia seeds and blueberries, toss, put the lid on and cook on High for 10 minutes. Release he pressure naturally for 10 minutes, add chia seeds and blueberries and mix everything. Divide into bowls and serve for breakfast.

Nutrition: calories 182, fat 10, fiber 5, carbs 8, protein 8

Cranberry Farro

Prep time: 10 minutes | Cooking time: 20 minutes | Servings: 4

Ingredients:

- 16 ounces farro
- ½ cup brown sugar
- 4 and ½ cups water
- 1 teaspoon lemon extract
- ½ cup cranberries

Directions:

In your instant pot, combine all the ingredients, toss, put the lid on and cook on High for 20 minutes. Release the pressure naturally for 10 minutes, divide the mix into bowls and serve for breakfast.

Nutrition: calories 165, fat 5, fiber 5, carbs 7, protein 10

Strawberries Oatmeal

Prep time: 20 minutes | Cooking time: 13 minutes | Servings: 4

Ingredients:

- 1 tablespoon avocado oil
- 1 cup steel cut oats
- ¼ cup heavy cream
- 4 cups water
- ¼ cup chia seeds
- 1 and ½ cups strawberries, sliced
- 3 tablespoons coconut sugar

Directions:

Set the instant pot on Sauté mode, add the oil, heat it up, add the oats and toast them for 3 minutes. Add the rest of the ingredients except the chia seeds and strawberries, put the lid on and cook on High for 10 minutes. Release the pressure naturally for 10 minutes, add the strawberries and the chia seeds and toss. Leave everything aside for 10 minutes more, divide into bowls and serve for breakfast.

Nutrition: calories 188, fat 6, fiber 4, carbs 6, protein 9

Peaches Oatmeal

Prep time: 10 minutes | Cooking time: 4 minutes | Servings: 4

Ingredients:

- 4 cups water
- 1 peach, stone removed and chopped
- 1 teaspoon vanilla extract
- 2 cups rolled oats
- ½ cup almonds, chopped
- 2 tablespoons flax meal

Directions:

In your instant pot, combine the oats with water, peach, and the vanilla, put the lid on and cook on High for 3 minutes. Release the pressure naturally for 10 minutes, add the almonds and flax meal, toss, divide into bowls and serve for breakfast.

Nutrition: calories 171, fat 8, fiber 4, carbs 6, protein 5

Egg Casserole

Prep time: 10 minutes | Cooking time: 20 minutes | Servings: 6

Ingredients:

- 32 ounces hash browns
- 2 cups turkey sausage, casings removed and ground
- 1 yellow onion, chopped
- 2 cups cheddar cheese, shredded
- 12 eggs, whisked
- 1 cup coconut milk
- A pinch of salt and black pepper
- Cooking spray

Directions:

Grease the instant pot with cooking spray and spread the hash browns, onion and turkey sausage on the bottom. In a bowl, mix the eggs with the rest of the ingredients, whisk and pour over the hash browns. Put the lid on and cook on High for 20 minutes. Release the pressure naturally for 10 minutes, divide into bowls and serve for breakfast.

Nutrition: calories 200, fat 8, fiber 4, carbs 6, protein 8

Quinoa Bowls

*Prep time: 10 minutes | **Cooking time:** 1 minutes | **Servings:** 6*

Ingredients:

- 1 and ½ cups quinoa
- 14 ounces coconut milk
- 1 and ½ cups water
- 2 tablespoons coconut sugar
- 2 teaspoons vanilla extract
- 1 teaspoon cinnamon powder
- 2 apples, cored and cubed

Directions:

In your instant pot, combine all the ingredients except the apples, toss, put the lid on and cook on High for 1 minute. Release the pressure naturally for 10 minutes, stir the quinoa, divide into bowls, sprinkle the apples on top and serve.

Nutrition: calories 200, fat 8, fiber 5, carbs 6, protein 10

Mushrooms and Sausage Mix

*Prep time: 10 minutes | **Cooking time:** 30 minutes | **Servings:** 6*

Ingredients:

- 2 cups almond milk
- 12 eggs, whisked
- ½ cup cheddar cheese, grated
- ½ cup feta cheese, crumbled
- A pinch of salt and black pepper
- 1 pound pork sausage, casings removed and chopped
- 2 cups spinach, chopped
- 1 cup red onion, chopped
- 1 cup white mushrooms, sliced
- 1 tablespoon olive oil

Directions:

Set the instant pot on Sauté mode, add the oil, heat it up, add the onion, stir and sauté for 3 minutes. Add the sausage, toss and brown for 2 minutes more. Add the mushrooms and the spinach, stir and brown for another 3 minutes. Add the eggs whisked with the milk, salt and pepper and spread. Sprinkle the cheddar and the feta cheese, put the lid on and cook on High for 20 minutes. Release the pressure naturally for 10 minutes, divide the mix between plates and serve for breakfast.

Nutrition: calories 200, fat 12, fiber 6, carbs 7, protein 9

Blackberries Pancake

*Prep time: 5 minutes | **Cooking time:** 15 minutes | **Servings:** 4*

Ingredients:

- 2 cups almond flour
- 2 teaspoons baking powder
- 1 teaspoon baking soda
- ¼ cup coconut sugar
- 2 eggs, whisked
- 1 and ½ cups almond milk
- 1 cup blackberries
- Cooking spray

Directions:

In a bowl, combine gradually all the ingredients except the cooking spray and whisk well. Grease the instant pot with the cooking spray, pour the pancake mix and spread well into the pot. Put the lid on and cook on High for 15 minutes. Release the pressure fast for 5 minutes, divide the pancake between plates and serve for breakfast.

Nutrition: calories 170, fat 10, fiber 4, carbs 7, protein 9

French Eggs

Prep time: 10 minutes | Cooking time: 2 minutes | Servings: 4

Ingredients:

- Cooking spray
- 2 tablespoons chives, chopped
- 4 eggs
- 4 tablespoons heavy cream
- A pinch of salt and black pepper
- 1 cup water

Directions:

Grease 4 ramekins with cooking spray and divide the cream in each. Crack an egg in each ramekin, sprinkle with salt, pepper and the chives. Put the water in the instant pot, add the trivet inside, add the ramekins in the pot, put the lid on and cook on High for 2 minutes. Release the pressure naturally for 10 minutes, and serve the eggs for breakfast.

Nutrition: calories 181, fat 11, fiber 2, carbs 6, protein 9

Buckwheat Porridge

Prep time: 20 minutes | Cooking time: 6 minutes | Servings: 4

Ingredients:

- 1 cup buckwheat
- ¼ cup raisins
- 3 cups almond milk
- 1 banana, peeled and sliced
- ½ teaspoon vanilla extract
- 1 teaspoon cinnamon powder

Directions:

In your instant pot, combine all the ingredients, put the lid on and cook on High for 6 minutes Release the pressure naturally for 20 minutes, divide the porridge into bowls and serve for breakfast.

Nutrition: calories 172, fat 8, fiber 2, carbs 7, protein 9

Zucchini Muffins

Prep time: 10 minutes | Cooking time: 8 minutes | Servings: 4

Ingredients:

- 2 eggs, whisked
- 1 cup coconut milk
- ½ cup avocado oil
- 2 teaspoons vanilla extract
- 3 tablespoons cocoa powder
- 1 cup almond flour
- 1 teaspoon cinnamon powder
- ½ teaspoon baking soda
- 1 cup zucchinis, grated
- 1 cup water
- 1/3 chocolate chips
- Cooking spray

Directions:

In a bowl, combine all the ingredients except the cooking spray and stir well. Divide this into 8 muffin tins. Put the racket in the pot, put the muffin tins inside, put the lid on and cook on High for 8 minutes. Release the pressure naturally for 10 minutes, divide the muffins between plates and serve for breakfast.

Nutrition: calories 188, fat 11, fiber 6, carbs 9, protein 7

Burrito Bowls

Prep time: 10 minutes | Cooking time: 7 minutes | Servings: 4

Ingredients:

- 3 tablespoons olive oil
- 6 eggs, whisked
- A pinch of salt and black pepper
- ½ pound pork sausage, cooked and crumbled
- ½ cup mild salsa
- ½ cup cheddar cheese, shredded
- ½ cup sour cream
- 1 avocado, peeled, pitted and cubed
- ¼ cup green onions, chopped

Directions:

Set the instant pot on Sauté mode, add the oil, heat it up, add the eggs, salt and pepper, and stir. Add the sausage, toss, put the lid on and cook on High for 7 minutes. Release the pressure naturally for 10 minutes, divide the mix into bowls, top each serving with cheese, salsa, sour cream, avocado and green onions and serve.

Nutrition: calories 200, fat 8, fiber 5, carbs 7, protein 11

Kale Muffins

Prep time: 10 minutes | Cooking time: 10 minutes | Servings: 2

Ingredients:

- 4 ounces chicken sausage, cooked and chopped
- 3 teaspoons avocado oil
- 4 kale leaves, chopped
- 4 eggs, whisked
- A pinch of salt and black pepper
- ¼ cup coconut milk
- 4 tablespoons cheddar cheese, shredded
- 1 cup water

Directions:

Grease 4 muffin tins with 1 teaspoon oil and leave them aside for now. Set the instant pot on sauté mode, add the rest of the oil, heat it up, add the sausage and brown for 2 minutes. Add kale, salt and pepper, stir and cook for 2 minutes. In a bowl, combine the eggs with coconut milk, salt and pepper and whisk. Add sausage and kale mix, stir and divide evenly into the muffin tins. Clean the pot, add the water, add the trivet inside and arrange the muffin tin in the pot. Put the lid on, and cook on High for 5 minutes. Release the pressure for 10 minutes and serve the muffins for breakfast.

Nutrition: calories 200, fat 12, fiber 5, carbs 6, protein 8

Grains and Beans Porridge

Prep time: 15 minutes | Cooking time: 10 minutes | Servings: 4

Ingredients:

- 6 tablespoons pearl barley
- 6 tablespoons white rice
- 3 tablespoons black eye beans
- 3 tablespoons red beans
- 3 tablespoons Romano beans
- 3 tablespoons brown rice
- 1 purple yam, peeled and chopped
- ¼ teaspoon baking soda
- 7 cups water

Directions:

In your instant pot, combine all the ingredients, toss, put the lid on and cook on High for 10 minutes. Release the pressure naturally for 15 minutes, stir the porridge, divide into bowls and serve.

Nutrition: calories 180, fat 8, fiber 5, carbs 8, protein 6

Cherries Oatmeal

Prep time: 5 minutes | Cooking time: 10 minutes | Servings: 4

Ingredients:

- 2 and ½ tablespoon cocoa powder
- 4 cups almond milk
- 2 cups coconut, unsweetened and shredded
- 1 teaspoon vanilla extract
- 1 teaspoon cinnamon powder
- 1 pound cherries, pitted

Directions:

In your instant pot, combine all the ingredients, put the lid on and cook on High for 10 minutes. Release the pressure fast for 5 minutes, stir the mix, divide it into bowls and serve for breakfast.

Nutrition: calories 173, fat 5, fiber 2, carbs 5, protein 5

Banana and Chia Seeds Mix

Prep time: 10 minutes | Cooking time: 6 minutes | Servings: 2

Ingredients:

- 1 cup coconut milk
- 1/3 cup coconut, unsweetened and flaked
- 1 banana, peeled and sliced
- 1 tablespoon chia seeds
- ½ teaspoon coconut sugar
- ¼ teaspoon vanilla extract
- 1 cup water

Directions:

In a bowl, combine all the ingredients except the water, stir and divide into 2 ramekins. Put the water in your instant pot, add the trivet inside, add the ramekins, put the lid on and cook on High for 6 minutes. Release the pressure naturally for 10 minutes and serve for breakfast.

Nutrition: calories 167, fat 8, fiber 4, carbs 6, protein 10

Pear Rice Bowls

Prep time: 10 minutes | Cooking time: 15 minutes | Servings: 4

Ingredients:

- 1 and ½ cups white rice
- 1 and ½ teaspoons cinnamon powder
- 1/3 cup coconut sugar
- 2 tablespoons avocado oil
- 2 pears, cored and sliced
- 3 cups almond milk

Directions:

Set your instant pot on Sauté mode, add the oil, heat it up, add the rice, stir and toast for 5 minutes. Add the rest of the ingredients, toss, put the lid on and cook on High for 10 minutes. Release the pressure naturally for 10 minutes, divide the mix into bowls and serve for breakfast.

Nutrition: calories 180, fat 11, fiber 2, carbs 4, protein 7

Bread Pudding

Prep time: 10 minutes | Cooking time: 25 minutes | Servings: 8

Ingredients:

- 1 cup water
- Cooking spray
- 4 tablespoons avocado oil
- 1 cup spring onions, sliced
- 1 cup white mushrooms, sliced
- 1 cup ham, diced
- 2 tablespoons coconut sugar
- 3 eggs, whisked
- 2 cups coconut cream
- ½ teaspoon mustard powder
- Salt and black pepper to the taste
- 1 cup cheddar cheese, grated
- ½ teaspoon thyme, dried
- 14 ounces loaf and bread, cubed

Directions:

Set your instant pot on Sauté mode, add the oil, heat it up, add the onions, stir and sauté for 2 minutes. Add the ham, stir, cook for 2 minutes more and transfer to a bowl. In a bowl, mix eggs with sugar, cream, thyme, cheese, salt, pepper, bread, mushrooms, ham and onions mix, whisk and pour into a big ramekin that fits your instant pot. Clean the pot, add the water, add the trivet inside, add the ramekin, put the lid on and cook on High for 25 minutes. Release the pressure naturally for 10 minutes, divide the pudding between plates and serve for breakfast.

Nutrition: calories 201, fat 11, fiber 2, carbs 5, protein 10

Espresso Almond Oatmeal

Prep time: 10 minutes | Cooking time: 10 minutes | Servings: 4

Ingredients:

- 1 cup almond milk
- 1 cup steel cut oats
- 2 cups water
- 2 tablespoons coconut sugar
- 1 teaspoon espresso powder
- 2 teaspoons vanilla extract

Directions:

In your instant pot, combine all the ingredients, toss, put the lid on and cook on High for 10 minutes. Release the pressure naturally for 10 minutes, divide everything into bowls and serve.

Nutrition: calories 200, fat 8, fiber 2, carbs 7, protein 10

Orange Apricot Oatmeal

Prep time: 10 minutes | Cooking time: 10 minutes | Servings: 4

Ingredients:

- 1 and ½ cups almond milk
- 1 cup steel cut oats
- 1 cup orange juice
- 1 cup apricots, chopped
- 2 tablespoons coconut cream
- 2 tablespoons coconut sugar
- 2 tablespoons pecans, chopped
- ¼ teaspoon cinnamon powder

Directions:

In your instant pot, combine all the ingredients, toss, put the lid on and coo on High for 10 minutes. Release the pressure naturally for 10 minutes, divide the mix into bowls and serve for breakfast.

Nutrition: calories 190, fat 4, fiber 2, carbs 8, protein 10

Creamy Bell Pepper Omelet

Prep time: 5 minutes | Cooking time: 30 minutes | Servings: 4

Ingredients:

- 6 eggs, whisked
- A pinch of black pepper
- ½ cup coconut cream
- 1 cup red bell peppers, chopped
- 4 spring onions, chopped
- ¾ cup cheddar cheese, shredded
- 1 and ½ cups water
- Cooking spray

Directions:

In a bowl, mix the eggs with the other ingredients except the cooking spray and the water and whisk well Grease a pan that fits your instant pot with cooking spray and pour the omelet mix inside. Add the water to your instant pot, add the trivet inside, add the pan with the omelet mix, put the lid on and cook on High for 30 minutes. Release the pressure fast for 5 minutes, divide the omelet between plates and serve.

Nutrition: calories 211, fat 12, fiber 5, carbs 6, protein 10

Pears Yogurt

Prep time: 5 minutes | Cooking time: 10 minutes | Servings: 4

Ingredients:

- 4 cups Greek yogurt
- 1 tablespoon vanilla extract
- 1 cup pears, chopped
- 4 tablespoons coconut sugar

Directions:

In your instant pot, mix all the ingredients, stir, put the lid on and cook on Low for 10 minutes. Release the pressure fast for 5 minutes, divide into bowls and serve for breakfast.

Nutrition: calories 152, fat 4, fiber 3, carbs 6, protein 9

Coconut Figs Bowls

Prep time: 10 minutes | Cooking time: 4 minutes | Servings: 4

Ingredients:
- 1 pound figs, halved
- ½ cup coconut sugar
- 3 cups coconut cream

Directions:

In your instant pot, combine all the ingredients, toss, put the lid on and cook on Low for 4 minutes. Release the pressure naturally for 10 minutes, divide into bowls and serve for breakfast.

Nutrition: calories 161, fat 7, fiber 3, carbs 5, protein 5

Apple Millet Oatmeal

Prep time: 10 minutes | Cooking time: 10 minutes | Servings: 4

Ingredients:
- 1 cup millet
- ½ cup steel cut oats
- 2 apples, cored and chopped
- 3 cups almond milk
- ½ teaspoon ginger, grated

Directions:

In your instant pot, combine all the ingredients, toss, put the lid on and cook on High for 10 minutes. Release the pressure naturally for 10 minutes, stir the oatmeal, divide it into bowls and serve for breakfast.

Nutrition: calories 170, fat 6, fiber 4, carbs 8, protein 10

Carrot Chia Oatmeal

Prep time: 10 minutes | Cooking time: 10 minutes | Servings: 6

Ingredients:
- 1 cup steel cut oats
- 4 cups almond milk
- 3 tablespoons coconut sugar
- 2 teaspoons cinnamon powder
- 1 cup carrots, grated
- ¼ cup chia seeds

Directions:

In your instant pot, combine all the ingredients except the chia seeds, toss, put the lid on and cook on High for 10 minutes. Release the pressure naturally for 10 minutes, stir the oatmeal, add chia seeds, toss, divide into bowls and serve for breakfast.

Nutrition: calories 180, fat 5, fiber 5, carbs 7, protein 6

Lime Tapioca Bowls

Prep time: 5 minutes | Cooking time: 10 minutes | Servings: 4

Ingredients:

- 1/3 cup tapioca pearls
- 2 tablespoons coconut sugar
- 2 cups coconut milk
- Zest of 1 lime, grated

Directions:

In your instant pot, combine all the ingredients, put the lid on and cook on High for 10 minutes. Release the pressure fast for 5 minutes, stir the mix, divide it into bowls and serve.

Nutrition: calories 172, fat 5, fiber 4, carbs 7, protein 6

Veggie Medley

Prep time: 10 minutes | Cooking time: 12 minutes | Servings: 6

Ingredients:

- 1 sweet potato, chopped
- 1 broccoli head, florets separated
- 1 red onion, chopped
- 15 ounces canned chickpeas
- 28 ounces canned tomatoes, no-salt-added and chopped
- 14 ounces coconut milk
- 1 tablespoon ginger, grated
- 2 garlic cloves, minced

Directions:

In your instant pot, mix combine all the ingredients, toss, put the lid on and cook on High for 12 minutes. Release the pressure naturally for 10 minutes, toss the mix once mode, divide into bowls and serve for breakfast.

Nutrition: calories 190, fat 7, fiber 2, carbs 5, protein 7

Greek Quinoa Bowls

Prep time: 10 minutes | Cooking time: 4 minutes | Servings: 4

Ingredients:

- 1 cup black quinoa
- 1 and ½ cups water
- Zest of ½ lemon, grated
- Juice of ½ lemon
- 1 tablespoon basil, chopped
- ½ cup black olives, pitted and sliced
- 1 sweet red bell pepper, chopped
- 1 cucumber, chopped
- A pinch of salt and black pepper

Directions:

In your instant pot, combine the quinoa with salt, pepper, lemon juice and lemon zest, toss, put the lid on and cook on High for 4 minutes. Release the pressure naturally for 10 minutes, stir the quinoa, divide it into bowls, add the rest of the ingredients, toss them gently and serve.

Nutrition: calories 193, fat 6, fiber 3, carbs 6, protein 6

Coconut Sweet Potato Mix

Prep time: 10 minutes | Cooking time: 10 minutes | Servings: 4

Ingredients:

- 1 cup coconut cream
- 1 tablespoon lime zest, grated
- ½ cup coconut sugar
- 4 sweet potatoes, peeled and roughly cubed
- 1 cup almonds, chopped

Directions:

In your instant pot, combine all the ingredients, put the lid on and cook on High for 10 minutes. Release the pressure naturally for 10 minutes, divide the mix into bowls and serve for breakfast.

Nutrition: calories 200, fat 12, fiber 4, carbs 7, protein 8

Squash and Apple Salad

Prep time: 10 minutes | Cooking time: 10 minutes | Servings: 6

Ingredients:

- 1 squash, cubed
- 1 tablespoon pumpkin spice
- ½ cup coconut sugar
- 2 apples, peeled and cubed
- 1 cup apple juice

Directions:

In your instant pot, combine all the ingredients, toss, put the lid on and cook on High for 10 minutes. Release the pressure naturally for 10 minutes, divide the mix into bowls and serve.

Nutrition: calories 171, fat 11, fiber 5, carbs 9, protein 5

Chickpeas Salad

Prep time: 10 minutes | Cooking time: 15 minutes | Servings: 4

Ingredients:

- 2 cups chickpeas, soaked and drained
- 3 cups veggie stock
- 1 garlic clove, minced
- 1 and ½ cups red bell pepper, chopped
- 1 teaspoon sweet paprika
- ½ teaspoon chili powder
- 1 carrot, roughly chopped
- 2 celery stalks, chopped
- 1 red onion, chopped
- 1 tablespoon chives, chopped
- 5 tablespoons balsamic vinegar
- 3 tablespoons olive oil
- A pinch of salt and black pepper

Directions:

In your instant pot, combine all the ingredients except the chives, toss, put the lid on and cook on High for 15 minutes. Release the pressure naturally for 10 minutes, toss the mix, divide the salad into bowls and serve for breakfast.

Nutrition: calories 200, fat 12, fiber 2, carbs 5, protein 9

Thyme Potato Salad

Prep time: 10 minutes | Cooking time: 12 minutes | Servings: 4

Ingredients:

- 2 pounds red potatoes, peeled and cut into wedges
- 1 small red onion, chopped
- 1 tablespoon thyme, chopped
- 4 tablespoons olive oil
- 4 tablespoons balsamic vinegar
- A pinch of salt and black pepper
- 1 and ½ cups water

Directions:

Put the water in your instant pot, add steamer basket and the potato wedges inside, put the lid on and cook on High for 12 minutes. Release the pressure naturally for 10 minutes, transfer the potatoes to a bowl, add the rest of the ingredients, toss and serve for breakfast.

Nutrition: calories 221, fat 6, fiber 4, carbs 7, protein 10

Berries and Banana Salad

Prep time: 5 minutes | Cooking time: 8 minutes | Servings: 4

Ingredients:

- 2 cups coconut milk
- 3 tablespoons coconut sugar
- 1 cup blueberries
- 1 cup blackberries
- 1 cup strawberries, sliced
- 1 banana, peeled and sliced
- 1 teaspoon vanilla extract

Directions:

In your instant pot, combine all the ingredients except the banana, toss, put the lid on and cook on High for 8 minutes. Release the pressure fast for 5 minutes, divide the berries mix into bowls and serve with banana slices on top.

Nutrition: calories 190, fat 7, fiber 4, carbs 7, protein 5

Cinnamon Quinoa Pudding

Prep time: 10 minutes | Cooking time: 5 minutes | Servings: 4

Ingredients:

- 1 and ½ cups quinoa
- 2 teaspoons cinnamon
- 1 and ½ cups coconut milk
- 1 and ½ cups coconut cream
- 2 tablespoons walnuts

Directions:

In your instant pot, combine all the ingredients except the walnuts, put the lid on and cook on High for 5 minutes. Release the pressure naturally for 10 minutes, stir the quinoa pudding gently, divide into bowls and serve for breakfast with walnuts sprinkled on top.

Nutrition: calories 192, fat 6, fiber 3, carbs 6, protein 9

Cauliflower Buckwheat Mix

Prep time: 10 minutes | Cooking time: 10 minutes | Servings: 4

Ingredients:

- 1 cup buckwheat
- 3 cups almond milk
- 1 cauliflower head, riced
- ½ teaspoon vanilla extract
- 1 teaspoon cinnamon powder

Directions:

In your instant pot, combine all the ingredients, toss, put the lid on and cook on High for 10 minutes. Release the pressure naturally for 10 minutes, toss, divide the mix into bowls and serve for breakfast.

Nutrition: calories 198, fat 7, fiber 5, carbs 7, protein 8

Cauliflower and Peppers Mix

Prep time: 10 minutes | Cooking time: 12 minutes | Servings: 4

Ingredients:

- 1 cauliflower head, florets separated
- 1 tablespoon avocado oil
- 1 red onion, chopped
- 1 red bell pepper, sliced
- 1 yellow bell pepper, sliced
- 1 green bell pepper, sliced
- 2 eggs, whisked
- A pinch of salt and black pepper
- 1 teaspoon turmeric powder
- 1 teaspoon hot paprika

Directions:

Set your instant pot on sauté mode, add the oil, heat it up, add the onion and the bell pepper, stir and sauté for 3 minutes. Add cauliflower, stir and cook for 2 minutes more. Add the rest of the ingredients, toss, put the lid on and cook on High for 7 minutes. Release the pressure naturally for 10 minutes, divide the mix between plates and serve.

Nutrition: calories 201, fat 9, fiber 4, carbs 7, protein 10

Rosemary Sausage and Cauliflower

Prep time: 10 minutes | Cooking time: 12 minutes | Servings: 4

Ingredients:

- 2 tablespoons olive oil
- 1 yellow onion, chopped
- 2 tablespoons garlic, minced
- 1 pound cauliflower florets
- 1 teaspoon sage, chopped
- 1 tablespoon rosemary
- 8 ounces pork sausage, sliced
- ¼ cup veggie stock

Directions:

Set your instant pot on sauté mode, add the oil, heat it up, add the onion, stir and sauté for 2 minutes. Add the sausage and the garlic, stir and brown for 2 minutes more. Add the rest of the ingredients, toss, put the lid on and cook on High for 8 minutes. Release the pressure naturally for 10 minutes, divide between plates and serve for breakfast.

Nutrition: calories 222, fat 13, fiber 4, carbs 7, protein 10

French Toast

Prep time: 10 minutes | Cooking time: 25 minutes | Servings: 4

Ingredients:

- 2 cups coconut milk
- 3 eggs, whisked
- ½ cup coconut sugar
- Zest of 1 orange, grated
- 1 teaspoon vanilla extract
- 1 loaf bread, cubed
- 1 cup water

Directions:

In a pan that fits the instant pot, combine all the ingredients except the water and the bread and stir. Add the bread and toss gently. Put the water in the instant pot, add the trivet inside, add the pan in the trivet, put the lid on and cook on High for 25 minutes. Release the pressure naturally, divide the mix into bowls and serve.

Nutrition: calories 200, fat 7, fiber 5, carbs 7, protein 10

Coconut Cauliflower Spread

Prep time: 10 minutes | Cooking time: 10 minutes | Servings: 4

Ingredients:

- 1 cup coconut milk
- 2 cups cauliflower florets
- A pinch of salt and black pepper
- 2 teaspoons sweet paprika
- 1 tablespoon lime juice
- 1 tablespoon olive oil
- 1 tablespoon chives, chopped

Directions:

In your instant pot combine the cauliflower with salt, pepper and coconut milk, put the lid on and cook on High for 12 minutes. Release the pressure naturally for 10 minutes, transfer the mix to a blender, add the oil and lime juice and pulse well. Divide into bowls, top each serving with paprika and chives and serve for breakfast.

Nutrition: calories 200, fat 7, fiber 3, carbs 7, protein 10

Mushroom Spread

Prep time: 10 minutes | Cooking time: 15 minutes | Servings: 4

Ingredients:

- 1 yellow onion, chopped
- 3 tablespoons mayonnaise
- 2 garlic cloves, minced
- 2 tablespoons chicken stock
- 3 thyme springs, chopped
- 2 tablespoons olive oil
- 1 pound white mushroom, sliced
- Salt and black pepper to the taste

Directions:

Set your instant pot on sauté mode, add the oil, heat it up, add the onion, stir and sauté for 2 minutes. Add the garlic, stir and cook for another minute. Add the rest of the ingredients except the mayonnaise, put the lid on and cook on High for 8 minutes. Release the pressure fast for 5 minutes, cool the mix down, transfer to a bowl, add the mayonnaise, toss and serve as a morning spread.

Nutrition: calories 221, fat 11, fiber 5, carbs 7, protein 8

Pomegranate and Apple Oatmeal

Prep time: 5 minutes | Cooking time: 5 minutes | Servings: 4

Ingredients:
- 1 cup steel cut oats
- 1 and ½ cups pomegranate juice
- Seeds of 1 pomegranate
- 2 green apples, cored and cubed
- 1 teaspoon cinnamon powder

Directions:
In your instant pot, combine all the ingredients except the pomegranate seeds, toss, put the lid on and cook on High for 5 minutes Release the pressure fast for 5 minutes, stir the oatmeal, divide it into bowls, sprinkle the pomegranate seeds on top and serve.

Nutrition: calories 180, fat 4, fiber 3, carbs 7, protein 10

Grapes and Apples Rice Pudding

Prep time: 10 minutes | Cooking time: 12 minutes | Servings: 4

Ingredients:
- 1 and ½ cups Arborio rice
- 1 and ½ teaspoons cinnamon powder
- 1/3 cup grapes
- 2 apples, cored and sliced
- 3 cups almond milk

Directions:
In your instant pot, combine all the ingredients, toss, put the pressure lid on and cook on High for 12 minutes. Release the pressure naturally for 10 minutes, divide the pudding into bowls and serve for breakfast.

Nutrition: calories 181, fat 11, fiber 4, carbs 7, protein 9

Nuts and Rice Bowls

Prep time: 5 minutes | Cooking time: 8 minutes | Servings: 4

Ingredients:
- 1 cup brown rice
- 2 cups coconut milk
- ¼ cup walnuts, chopped
- ¼ cup pecans, chopped
- 2 tablespoons sunflower seeds
- ¼ cup almonds, chopped
- 1 teaspoon cinnamon powder

Directions:
In your instant pot, combine all the ingredients, toss, put the lid on and cook on High for 8 minutes. Release the pressure fast for 5 minutes, stir the mix, divide into bowls and serve.

Nutrition: calories 200, fat 8, fiber 5, carbs 7, protein 9

Black Rice and Veggies Salad

Prep time: 10 minutes | Cooking time: 20 minutes | Servings: 6

Ingredients:

- 6 and ½ cups water
- 2 cups black rice, washed and rinsed
- A pinch of salt and black pepper
- 1 cup tomato, cubed
- 1 avocado, peeled, pitted and cubed
- 1 cup brown mushrooms, sliced
- ½ cup coconut, grated

Directions:

In your instant pot, combine all the ingredients except the avocado and the coconut, put the lid on and cook on High for 20 minutes. Release the pressure naturally for 10 minutes, stir the mix, divide it into bowls, top each bowl with coconut and avocado pieces and serve.

Nutrition: calories 181, fat 7, fiber 6, carbs 8, protein 11

Turmeric Lentils Spread

Prep time: 10 minutes | Cooking time: 20 minutes | Servings: 4

Ingredients:

- 1 cup red lentils, soaked for 4 hours and drained
- 2 cups veggie stock
- A pinch of salt and black pepper
- 1 teaspoon turmeric powder
- 1 tablespoon olive oil
- 1 tablespoon tahini paste
- 1 tablespoon lemon juice

Directions:

In your instant pot, combine lentils with salt, pepper and the stock, put the lid on and cook on High for 20 minutes. Release the pressure naturally for 10 minutes, transfer the mix to a blender, add the rest of the ingredients and pulse well. Divide into bowls and serve as a morning spread.

Nutrition: calories 171, fat 8, fiber 4, carbs 6, protein 8

Cinnamon Potatoes

Prep time: 10 minutes | Cooking time: 25 minutes | Servings: 4

Ingredients:

- 3 pounds sweet potatoes, peeled and roughly cut into wedges
- 1 cup water
- ¼ cup coconut milk
- 1/3 cup coconut sugar
- ½ teaspoon nutmeg, ground
- 1 teaspoon cinnamon powder
- ¼ teaspoon allspice
- A pinch of cayenne pepper
- ¼ cup coconut, unsweetened and shredded

Directions:

Add the water to your instant pot, add steamer basket, add the potatoes into the basket, put the lid on and cook on High for 20 minutes. Release the pressure fast for 5 minutes, drain the water, transfer the potatoes to a bowl and clean the instant pot. In the clean instant pot, combine the potatoes with the rest of the ingredients except the coconut, put the lid on and cook on High for 5 minutes. Release the pressure fast for 5 minutes, divide the mix between plates and serve as a side dish.

Nutrition: calories 175, fat 4, fiber 2, carbs 6, protein 8

Paprika Hummus

Prep time: 5 minutes | Cooking time: 20 minutes | Servings: 8

Ingredients:

- 1 cup chickpeas, soaked and drained
- 6 cups water
- 4 garlic cloves, minced
- 2 tablespoons tahini paste
- Juice of 1 lime
- ¼ teaspoon cumin, ground
- A pinch of salt and black pepper
- 1 tablespoon avocado oil
- ½ teaspoon sweet paprika
- ¼ cup chives, chopped

Directions:

In your instant pot, combine the chickpeas with the water, salt and pepper, put the lid on and cook on High for 20 minutes. Release the pressure naturally for 10 minutes, drain the chickpeas, transfer them to a blender, add 3 tablespoons of the cooking liquid and pulse. Add the rest of the ingredients except the paprika and the chives, pulse well and divide into bowls. Sprinkle chives and paprika on top and serve for breakfast.

Nutrition: calories 200, fat 12, fiber 3, carbs 5, protein 9

Tomato and Sausage Mix

Prep time: 10 minutes | Cooking time: 15 minutes | Servings: 4

Ingredients:

- 10 ounces canned tomatoes, chopped
- 1 and ¾ cups Italian sausage, casings removed and ground
- 3 tablespoons chicken stock
- A pinch of salt and black pepper
- 1 tablespoon oregano, chopped
- 1 tablespoon chives, chopped
- 4 eggs, whisked

Directions:

In your instant pot, combine all the ingredients except the chives, oregano and the eggs, toss, put the lid on and cook on High for 10 minutes. Release the pressure fast for 5 minutes, add the eggs, toss the mix, put the lid back on and cook on High for 5 minutes. Release the pressure fast again for 5 minutes, divide the mix between plates, sprinkle the chives and oregano on top.

Nutrition: calories 273, fat 13, fiber 3, carbs 6, protein 14

Potato and Eggs Salad

rep time: 10 minutes | Cooking time: 10 minutes | Servings: 4

Ingredients:

- 6 potatoes, peeled and cubed
- 4 eggs, hard boiled, peeled and cubed
- 1 and ½ cups water
- 1 cup homemade mayonnaise
- ¼ cup spring onions, chopped
- 1 tablespoon white vinegar
- 2 tablespoons parsley, chopped
- 1 tablespoon chives, chopped
- 1 tablespoon rosemary, chopped
- 1 tablespoon mustard
- Salt and black pepper to the taste

Directions:

Put the water in your instant pot, add steamer basket, add potatoes inside, put the lid on and cook on High for 10 minutes. Release the pressure naturally for 10 minutes, and transfer the potatoes to a bowl. Add the rest of the ingredients, toss and serve cold for breakfast.

Nutrition: calories 200, fat 11, fiber 4, carbs 7, protein 9

Potato, Bacon and Chives Mix

Prep time: 5 minutes | Cooking time: 10 minutes | Servings: 4

Ingredients:

- 4 gold potatoes, peeled and roughly cubed
- 2 teaspoons Italian seasoning
- 1 teaspoon hot paprika
- 1 teaspoon basil, chopped
- ¼ cup bacon, cooked and crumbled
- 1 cup chives, chopped
- A pinch of salt and black pepper

Directions:

Put potatoes in your instant pot, add water to cover them, put the lid on and cook on High for 10 minutes. Release the pressure fast, drain the potatoes and transfer them to a bowl Add the rest of the ingredients except the bacon, and toss. Divide the mix between plates, sprinkle the bacon on top and serve for breakfast.

Nutrition: calories 161, fat 7, fiber 4, carbs 8, protein 11

Kale, Leeks and Tofu Salad

Prep time: 10 minutes | Cooking time: 10 minutes | Servings: 4

Ingredients:

- 1 bunch kale leaves, roughly chopped
- 2 leeks, sliced
- 1 teaspoon sweet paprika
- 1 tablespoon olive oil
- ½ cup tomato sauce
- A pinch of salt and black pepper
- 2 teaspoons balsamic vinegar
- 3 ounces tofu, pressed and cubed

Directions:

In your instant pot, combine all the ingredients, toss, put the lid on and cook on High for 10 minutes. Release the pressure naturally for 10 minutes, divide the salad into bowls and serve.

Nutrition: calories 200, fat 9, fiber 5, carbs 7, protein 10

Peppers and Tomato Scramble

Prep time: 10 minutes | Cooking time: 13 minutes | Servings: 4

Ingredients:

- 2 spring onions, chopped
- 1 teaspoon avocado oil
- 3 garlic cloves, minced
- ¼ cup veggie stock
- 1 cup carrot, chopped
- 1 pint tomatoes, halved
- 1 red bell pepper, chopped
- 1 tablespoon Italian seasoning
- Salt and black pepper to the taste
- 1 tablespoon cheddar, grated
- 6 eggs, whisked

Directions:

Set your instant pot on Sauté mode, add oil, heat it up, add garlic, onion and carrot, stir and sauté for 3 minutes. Add the rest of the ingredients except the cheese, toss, put the lid on and cook on High for 10 minutes. Release the pressure naturally for 10 minutes, sprinkle the cheese over the mix, divide everything between plates and serve.

Nutrition: calories 188, fat 11, fiber 6, carbs 7, protein 9

Salsa Peppers and Tofu Mix

Prep time: 10 minutes | Cooking time: 10 minutes | Servings: 6

Ingredients:

- 28 ounces firm tofu, cubed
- 1 cup salsa
- 2 tablespoons olive oil
- 4 garlic cloves, minced
- 1 yellow onion, chopped
- 1 red bell pepper, cut into strips
- 1 green bell pepper, cut into strips
- ½ teaspoon curry powder
- A pinch of salt and black pepper

Directions:

Set your instant pot on Sauté mode, add the oil, heat it up, add the onion and salsa, stir and sauté for 3 minutes. Add the rest of the ingredients, toss, put the lid on and cook on High for 7 minutes. Release the pressure naturally for 10 minutes, divide the mix between plates and serve for breakfast.

Nutrition: calories 200, fat 12, fiber 6, carbs 8, protein 7

Potato and Brussels Sprouts Salad

Prep time: 10 minutes | Cooking time: 12 minutes | Servings: 4

Ingredients:

- 3 purple potatoes, peeled and cut into wedges
- 1 red onion, chopped
- 2 garlic cloves, minced
- 1 carrot, chopped
- 3 tablespoons chicken stock
- 3 tablespoons tomato sauce
- 1 tablespoon sweet paprika
- 1 and ½ cups Brussels sprouts, shredded

Directions:

In your instant pot, combine all the ingredients, toss, put the lid on and cook on High for 12 minutes. Release the pressure naturally for 10 minutes, divide the mix into bowls and serve for breakfast.

Nutrition: calories 199, fat 11, fiber 3, carbs 6, protein 8

Wild Rice Mix

Prep time: 10 minutes | Cooking time: 30 minutes | Servings: 6

Ingredients:

- 1 red onion, chopped
- 1 teaspoon garlic, minced
- 1 tablespoon olive oil
- 1 cup wild rice
- 3 cups chicken stock
- Salt and black pepper to the taste
- 1 tablespoon cilantro, chopped
- 1 tablespoon chives, chopped
- ½ cup walnuts, toasted and chopped

Directions: Set your instant pot on Sauté mode, add the oil, heat it up, add the onion and garlic, stir and sauté for 2-3 minutes. Add the rest of the ingredients except the chives and walnuts, toss, put the lid on and cook on High for 25 minutes. Release the pressure naturally for 10 minutes, divide the mix between plates, sprinkle chives and walnuts on top and serve as a side dish.

Nutrition: calories 151, fat 7, fiber 6, carbs 9, protein 6

Chili Rice and Leeks Pilaf

Prep time: 10 minutes | Cooking time: 20 minutes | Servings: 4

Ingredients:

- 1 and ½ cups rice
- 2 garlic cloves, minced
- 2 tablespoons olive oil
- 2 leeks, chopped
- A pinch of salt and black pepper
- 1 teaspoon chili powder
- 3 cups chicken stock
- 2 tablespoons parsley, chopped
- 2 teaspoons cumin, ground

Directions:

Set your instant pot on Sauté mode, add oil, heat it up, add garlic and leeks, stir and cook for 3 minutes. Add the rest of the ingredients except the parsley, toss, put the lid on and cook on High for 18 minutes. Release the pressure naturally for 10 minutes, divide the mix between plates and serve as a side dish.

Nutrition: calories 171, fat 4, fiber 5, carbs 9, protein 6

Quinoa and Chives

Prep time: 10 minutes | Cooking time: 13 minutes | Servings: 4

Ingredients:

- 1 red onion, chopped
- 1 tablespoon olive oil
- 1 tablespoon chives, chopped
- 1 and ½ cups quinoa, rinsed
- 14 ounces chicken stock
- A pinch of salt and black pepper
- 2 tablespoons parsley, chopped

Directions:

Set your instant pot on Sauté mode, add the oil, heat it up, add the onion, stir and sauté for 5 minutes. Add the rest of the ingredients except the parsley, put the lid on and cook on High for 8 minutes. Release the pressure naturally for 10 minutes, divide the mix between plates, sprinkle the parsley on top and serve as a side dish.

Nutrition: calories 182, fat 6, fiber 3, carbs 6, protein 7

Rice and Beets Mix

Prep time: 10 minutes | Cooking time: 20 minutes | Servings: 4

Ingredients:

- A pinch of salt and black pepper
- ½ teaspoon cayenne pepper
- 1 red onion, chopped
- 1 tablespoon olive oil
- 2 and ½ cups water
- 2 cups white rice
- 1 beet, peeled and cubed

Directions:

Set the instant pot on Sauté mode, add the oil, heat it up, add the onion and sauté for 3 minutes. Add the rest of the ingredients, put the lid on and cook on High for 15 minutes. Release the pressure naturally for 10 minutes, stir the mix, divide it between plates and serve as a side dish.

Nutrition: calories 162, fat 6, fiber 4, carbs 6, protein 8

Creamy Herbed Risotto

Prep time: 10 minutes | Cooking time: 15 minutes | Servings: 4

Ingredients:

- 2 cups white rice
- 4 cups chicken stock
- 2 garlic cloves, minced
- 2 tablespoon olive oil
- 1 yellow onion, chopped
- 1 tablespoon sage, chopped
- 1 tablespoon basil, chopped
- 1 tablespoon oregano, chopped
- 4 ounces heavy cream
- 2 tablespoons parmesan, grated

Directions:

Set your instant pot on Sauté mode, add the oil, heat it up, add onions and garlic, stir and cook for 3 minutes. Add rest of the ingredients except the cream and parmesan, put the lid on and cook on High for 12 minutes. Release the pressure naturally for 10 minutes, add the cream and parmesan, toss, divide between plates and serve.

Nutrition: calories 200, fat 8, fiber 4, carbs 6, protein 7

Zucchini Rice

Prep time: 5 minutes | Cooking time: 15 minutes | Servings: 4

Ingredients:

- 2 tablespoons olive oil
- 1 yellow onion, chopped
- 2 garlic cloves, minced
- 12 ounces risotto rice
- 4 cups chicken stock
- 1 big zucchini, grated
- ½ teaspoon nutmeg, ground
- 1 teaspoon thyme, chopped
- ½ teaspoon ginger, grated
- ½ teaspoon allspice, ground

Directions:

Set your instant pot on Sauté mode, add the oil, heat it up, add onion and garlic, stir and cook for 1-2 minutes. Add the rest of the ingredients, toss, put the lid on and cook on High for 12 minutes. Release the pressure fast for 5 minutes, divide the mix between plates and serve as a side dish.

Nutrition: calories 200, fat 7, fiber 4, carbs 7, protein 6

Spiced Carrot Rice

Prep time: 5 minutes | Cooking time: 15 minutes | Servings: 4

Ingredients:

- 2 cups basmati rice
- 1 cup carrots, grated
- 2 cups chicken stock
- ½ teaspoon ginger, grated
- 3 garlic cloves, minced
- 2 tablespoons olive oil
- 1 yellow onion, chopped
- 1 tablespoon cumin, ground
- 1 teaspoon cloves, ground
- 1 teaspoon cardamom, ground
- 1 teaspoon sweet paprika
- A pinch of salt and black pepper

Directions:

Set the instant pot on sauté mode, add the oil, heat it up, add onion, carrots, garlic and ginger, stir and sauté for 3 minutes. Add cumin, cloves, cardamom, paprika, salt and pepper, stir and cook for 2 minutes more. Add the remaining ingredients, put the lid on and cook on High for 10 minutes. Release the pressure fast for 5 minutes, stir the mix, divide between plates and serve as a side dish.

Nutrition: calories 200, fat 8, fiber 4, carbs 6, protein 8

Herbed Mash

Prep time: 10 minutes | Cooking time: 10 minutes | Servings: 8

Ingredients:

- 2 garlic cloves, minced
- 3 pounds potatoes, peeled and cubed
- A pinch of salt and black pepper
- ¼ teaspoon sage, dried
- ½ teaspoon rosemary, dried
- ½ teaspoon thyme dried
- 1 and ½ cups water
- ¼ cup almond milk
- ½ cup parmesan, grated

Directions:

Add the water to the instant pot, add the steamer basket inside and put the potatoes in it. Put the lid on and cook on High for 10 minutes. Release the pressure naturally for 10 minutes, transfer the potatoes to a bowl and mash them with a potato masher. Add the rest of the ingredients gradually, whisk well, divide between plates and serve as a side dish.

Nutrition: calories 181, fat 7, fiber 3, carbs 6, protein 7

Currant Rice

Prep time: 10 minutes | Cooking time: 15 minutes | Servings: 6

Ingredients:

- 2 tablespoons olive oil
- ½ teaspoon chili powder
- ½ cup yellow onion, chopped
- 2 tablespoons coconut milk
- 1 and ½ cups Arborio rice
- 3 and ½ cups veggie stock
- A pinch of salt and black pepper
- ½ cup currants, chopped

Directions:

Set your instant pot on Sauté mode, add the oil, heat it up, add onion, stir and sauté for 5 minutes. Add the rest of the ingredients, stir, put the lid on and cook on High for 10 minutes. Release the pressure naturally for 10 minutes, divide between plates and serve as a side dish.

Nutrition: calories 184, fat 6, fiber 3, carbs 6, protein 6

Mint Farro Side Salad

Prep time: 10 minutes | Cooking time: 30 minutes | Servings: 6

Ingredients:

- 1 tablespoon balsamic vinegar
- 1 cup whole grain farro
- 1 teaspoon lime juice
- A pinch of salt and black pepper
- 3 cups veggie stock
- 1 tablespoon olive oil
- ½ cup green onions, chopped
- 2 tablespoons mint leaves, chopped

Directions:

In your instant pot, combine the farro with salt, pepper and the stock, put the lid on and cook on High for 30 minutes. Release the pressure naturally for 10 minutes, transfer the farro to a bowl, add the rest of the ingredients, toss, divide between plates and serve as a side dish.

Nutrition: calories 200, fat 8, fiber 3, carbs 7, protein 8

Lemon Spinach Rice

Prep time: 10 minutes | Cooking time: 20 minutes | Servings: 4

Ingredients:

- 2 garlic cloves, minced
- 2 tablespoons olive oil
- ¾ cup yellow onion, chopped
- 1 and ½ cups white rice
- 12 ounces spinach, chopped
- 3 and ½ cups hot veggie stock
- A pinch of salt and black pepper
- 2 tablespoons lemon juice

Directions:

Set your instant pot on sauté mode, add the oil, heat it up, add garlic and onions, stir and sauté for 5 minutes. Add the rest of the ingredients except the spinach, put the lid on and cook on High for 8 minutes. Release the pressure fast for 5 minutes, add the spinach, toss, put the lid back on and cook on High for 3 minutes more. Release the pressure fast again for 5 minutes, divide the mix between plates and serve as a side dish.

Nutrition: calories 200, fat 7, fiber 4, carbs 6, protein 5

Cheesy Thyme Rice

Prep time: 10 minutes | Cooking time: 20 minutes | Servings: 4

Ingredients:

- 1 tablespoon olive oil
- 1 cup Arborio rice
- 2 garlic cloves, minced
- 2 cups chicken stock
- 16 ounces cream cheese
- 1 tablespoon parmesan, grated
- 1 and ½ tablespoons thyme, chopped
- A pinch of salt and black pepper

Directions:

Set your instant pot on Sauté mode, add the oil, heat up, add the garlic, stir and cook for 1 minute. Add the rest of the ingredients, toss, put the lid on and cook on High for 20 minutes. Release the pressure naturally for 10 minutes, divide the mix between plates and serve as a side dish.

Nutrition: calories 185, fat 6, fiber 4, carbs 6, protein 8

Greek Potato Mix

Prep time: 10 minutes | Cooking time: 15 minutes | Servings: 6

Ingredients:

- ¼ cup chicken stock
- ½ cup yellow onion, chopped
- 2 tablespoons avocado oil
- 6 potatoes, peeled and cut into wedges

- A pinch of salt and black pepper
- ½ cup sour cream
- 1 tablespoon basil, chopped
- 1 cup mozzarella cheese, shredded

Directions:

Set your instant pot on Sauté mode, add the oil, heat it up, add the onion, stir and sauté for 3 minutes. Add the potatoes, stock, salt and pepper, put the lid on and cook on High for 12 minutes. Release the pressure naturally for 10 minutes, transfer the potato mix to a bowl, add the rest of the ingredients, toss and serve as side dish.

Nutrition: calories 200, fat 7, fiber 2, carbs 5, protein 6

Squash and Potato Mash

Prep time: 10 minutes | Cooking time: 20 minutes | Servings: 4

Ingredients:

- ½ cup water
- 1 butternut squash, peeled and cubed
- 2 sweet potatoes, peeled and cubed

- A pinch of salt and black pepper
- 2 tablespoons butter
- ½ teaspoon nutmeg, grated

Directions: Add the water to your instant pot, add steamer basket, add squash and sweet potatoes inside, put the lid on and cook on High for 20 minutes. Release the pressure naturally for 10 minutes, transfer the mix to a bowl and mash well with a potato masher. Add the rest of the ingredients, whisk well, divide between plates and serve as a side dish.

Nutrition: calories 126, fat 4, fiber 5, carbs 8, protein 5

Potato and Parsnip Wedges

Prep time: 10 minutes | Cooking time: 12 minutes | Servings: 4

Ingredients:

- 4 potatoes, peeled and cut into wedges
- 2 parsnips, cut into wedges
- 1 cup water

- A pinch of salt and black pepper
- 1 tablespoon olive oil
- ¼ teaspoon sweet paprika
- ¼ teaspoon oregano, dried

Directions:

In a bowl, combine all the ingredients except the water and toss. Put the water in the instant pot, add the steamer basket inside, put the vegetable wedges in the basket, put the lid on and cook on High for 12 minutes. Release the pressure naturally for 10 minutes, divide the veggie wedges between plates and serve as a side dish.

Nutrition: calories 200, fat 5, fiber 3, carbs 6, protein 7

Balsamic Green Beans

Prep time: 10 minutes | Cooking time: 12 minutes | Servings: 4

Ingredients:

- 1 pound fresh green beans, trimmed
- 2 spring onions, chopped
- 1 garlic clove, minced
- 2 cups tomatoes, cubed
- A pinch of salt and black pepper
- 1 tablespoon cilantro, chopped
- 1 tablespoon olive oil
- 2 teaspoons balsamic vinegar

Directions:

Set the pot on sauté mode, add the oil, heat it up, add the onions and garlic and sauté for 2 minutes. Add the rest of the ingredients except the cilantro, toss, put the lid on and cook on High for 10 minutes. Release the pressure naturally for 10 minutes, divide the mix between plates and serve as a side dish with the cilantro sprinkled on top.

Nutrition: calories 162, fat 6, fiber 2, carbs 6, protein 4

Red Beans Side Salad

Prep time: 10 minutes | Cooking time: 15 minutes | Servings: 4

Ingredients:

- 1 pound red kidney beans, soaked over night and drained
- A pinch of salt and black pepper
- 1 teaspoon avocado oil
- 1 yellow onion, chopped
- 4 garlic cloves, chopped
- 1 red bell pepper, chopped
- 1 teaspoon thyme, dried
- 1 and ½ cups veggie stock
- 2 green onions, minced
- 2 tablespoons cilantro, chopped

Directions:

Set your instant pot on Sauté mode, add the oil, heat it up, add the onion and garlic, stir and sauté for 2 minutes. Add the rest of the ingredients except the cilantro, put the lid on and cook on High for 15 minutes. Release the pressure naturally for 10 minutes, divide the salad between plates and serve as a side dish with the cilantro sprinkled on top.

Nutrition: calories 152, fat 4, fiber 2, carbs 6, protein 8

Eggplant Salad

Prep time: 5 minutes | Cooking time: 14 minutes | Servings: 4

Ingredients:

- ½ cup veggie stock
- 2 eggplants, roughly cubed
- 1 cup celery, chopped
- 1 red onion, chopped
- A pinch of salt and black pepper
- 1 teaspoon sage,
- 1 teaspoon thyme, dried

Directions:

In your instant pot, combine all the ingredients, put the lid on and cook on High for 14 minutes. Release the pressure fast for 5 minutes, divide the mix between plates and serve as a side salad.

Nutrition: calories 200, fat 8, fiber 4, carbs 7, protein 9

Spiced Carrots

Prep time: 10 minutes | Cooking time: 15 minutes | Servings: 4

Ingredients:

- 2 and ½ pounds carrots, sliced
- 3 tablespoons avocado oil
- Salt and black pepper to the taste
- 1 cup veggie stock
- 1 teaspoon garam masala
- ½ teaspoon sweet chili powder
- 1 teaspoon rosemary, dried

Directions:

Set your instant pot on Sauté mode, add the oil, heat it up, add the carrots and brown for 5 minutes. Add the rest of the ingredients, put the lid on and cook on High for 10 minutes. Release the pressure naturally for 10 minutes, divide the mix between plates and serve as a side dish.

Nutrition: calories 162, fat 4, fiber 4, carbs 9, protein 7

Parsnips and Beets Mix

Prep time: 10 minutes | Cooking time: 10 minutes | Servings: 4

Ingredients:

- 1 pound parsnips, peeled and roughly cubed
- 2 beets, peeled and roughly cubed
- A pinch of salt and black pepper
- 1 cup veggie stock
- ½ teaspoon turmeric powder
- 1 tablespoon chives, chopped

Directions:

In your instant pot, combine all the ingredients except the chives, put the lid on and cook on High for 10 minutes. Release the pressure naturally for 10 minutes, divide the mix between plates and serve with the chives sprinkled on top.

Nutrition: calories 142, fat 2, fiber 4, carbs 9, protein 4

Coconut Cauliflower Mash

Prep time: 10 minutes | Cooking time: 8 minutes | Servings: 4

Ingredients:

- 1 pound cauliflower florets
- 1 teaspoon Italian seasoning
- 1 teaspoon sage, dried
- Salt and black pepper to the taste
- 2 spring onions, chopped
- ¼ cup coconut cream
- ½ cup chicken stock

Directions:

In your instant pot, mix the cauliflower with the stock, salt, pepper, Italian seasoning and the sage, put the lid on and cook on High for 8 minutes. Release the pressure naturally for 10 minutes, mash the mix with a potato masher, add the rest of the ingredients, whisk well, divide between plates and serve as a side dish.

Nutrition: calories 142, fat 4, fiber 3, carbs 6, protein 10

Sweet Carrot and Potato Mix

Prep time: 5 minutes | Cooking time: 12 minutes | Servings: 4

Ingredients:

- 1 and ½ pounds carrots, peeled and sliced
- ½ teaspoon allspice, ground
- ½ teaspoon cumin, ground
- 2 sweet potatoes, cubed
- 1 tablespoon avocado oil
- A pinch of salt and black pepper
- 1 cup water
- 1 tablespoon coconut sugar

Directions:

In your instant pot, combine the carrots with the potatoes, allspice, cumin, salt, pepper and the water, put the lid on and cook on High for 12 minutes. Release the pressure fast for 5 minutes, transfer the veggies to a bowl, add the rest of the ingredients, toss, divide between plates and serve as a side dish.

Nutrition: calories 132, fat 4, fiber 3, carbs 6, protein 9

Zucchini, Carrots and Eggplant Hash

Prep time: 5 minutes | Cooking time: 15 minutes | Servings: 4

Ingredients:

- ½ cup veggie stock
- 1 zucchini, roughly cubed
- 1 eggplant, roughly cubed
- 2 carrots, sliced
- 2 tablespoons avocado oil
- 1 red onion, chopped
- ½ teaspoon oregano, dried

Directions:

Set the instant pot on Sauté mode, add the oil, heat it up, add the onion, salt, pepper and oregano, stir and cook for 3-4 minutes. Add the rest of the ingredients, put the lid on and cook on High for 10 minutes. Release the pressure fast for 5 minutes, divide the mix between plates and serve.

Nutrition: calories 142, fat 7, fiber 4, carbs 6, protein 8

Balsamic Carrots

Prep time: 10 minutes | Cooking time: 7 minutes | Servings: 4

Ingredients:

- ½ cup veggie stock
- 1 pound baby carrots
- 1 teaspoon thyme, dried
- 1 teaspoon dill, dried
- A pinch of salt and black pepper
- 2 tablespoons balsamic vinegar

Directions:

In your instant pot, combine all the ingredients, put the lid on and cook on High for 7 minutes. Release the pressure naturally for 10 minutes, divide the mix between plates and serve as a side dish.

Nutrition: calories 152, fat 7, fiber 2, carbs 7, protein 5

Citrus Brussels Sprouts

Prep time: 10 minutes | Cooking time: 8 minutes | Servings: 6

Ingredients:

- 1 and ½ pounds Brussels sprouts, halved
- A pinch of salt and black pepper
- ¼ cup orange juice
- 1 teaspoon orange zest, grated
- 1 teaspoon lime zest, grated
- 1 tablespoon olive oil

Directions:

In your instant pot, combine all the ingredients, toss, put the lid on and cook on High for 8 minutes. Release the pressure naturally for 10 minutes, divide the mix between plates and serve.

Nutrition: calories 152, fat 4, fiber 3, carbs 4, protein 3

Simple Broccoli Salad

Prep time: 10 minutes | Cooking time: 15 minutes | Servings: 4

Ingredients:

- 1 pound broccoli florets
- Salt and black pepper to the taste
- 2 tablespoons olive oil
- ½ cup chicken stock
- 1 teaspoon thyme, dried
- 1 teaspoon sweet paprika

Directions:

In your instant pot, combine all the ingredients, put the lid on and cook on High for 15 minutes. Release the pressure naturally for 10 minutes, divide the mix between plates and serve as a side dish.

Nutrition: calories 187, fat 7, fiber 3, carbs 5, protein 5

Rosemary Beet Salad

Prep time: 10 minutes | Cooking time: 20 minutes | Servings: 4

Ingredients:

- 4 beets
- 1 cup water
- 2 tablespoon balsamic vinegar
- 2 tablespoons rosemary, chopped
- 2 tablespoons capers, drained
- A pinch of salt and black pepper
- 1 garlic clove, minced
- 1 tablespoon avocado oil

Directions:

Put the water in your instant pot, add the steamer basket, add the beets inside, put the lid on and cook on High for 20 minutes. Release the pressure naturally for 10 minutes, drain the beets, cool them down, peel and cut into cubes. In a salad bowl, combine the beets with the remaining ingredients, toss and serve as a side salad.

Nutrition: calories 120, fat 4, fiber 3, carbs 8, protein 4

Baby Spinach and Beets

Prep time: 5 minutes | Cooking time: 20 minutes | Servings: 4

Ingredients:

- 2 cups baby spinach
- 2 tablespoons olive oil
- Juice of 1 lime
- 2 cups water
- 4 beets
- A pinch of salt and black pepper
- ½ cup pecorino cheese, grated
- 2 spring onions, chopped
- 1 tablespoon balsamic vinegar

Directions:

Put the water in your instant pot, add the steamer basket, add the beet inside, put the lid on and cook on High for 20 minutes. Release the pressure fast for 5 minutes, drain the beets, cool them down, peel and cut into chunks. In a salad bowl, combine the beets with the remaining ingredients, toss and serve as a side salad.

Nutrition: calories 165, fat 4, fiber 3, carbs 7, protein 6

Green Bean and Mushroom Salad

Prep time: 10 minutes | Cooking time: 10 minutes | Servings: 4

Ingredients:

- 1 cup cremini mushrooms, sliced
- ½ cup chicken stock
- 2 pounds green beans, trimmed and halved
- 1 tablespoon balsamic vinegar

Directions:

In your instant pot, combine all the ingredients, put the lid on and cook on High for 10 minutes. Release the pressure naturally for 10 minutes, divide the mix between plates and serve.

Nutrition: calories 173, fat 5, fiber 2, carbs 5, protein 6

Pesto Potato Salad

Prep time: 10 minutes | Cooking time: 8 minutes | Servings: 4

Ingredients:

- 1 and ½ cups water
- 2 pounds red potatoes, roughly cubed
- 1 red onion, chopped
- 2 tablespoons olive oil
- 3 tablespoons balsamic vinegar
- 2 tablespoons basil pesto

Directions:

Put the water in your instant pot, add the steamer basket, add the potatoes inside, put the lid on and cook on High for 8 minutes. Release the pressure naturally for 10 minutes, drain the potatoes and transfer them to a bowl. Add the rest of the ingredients, toss, and serve as a side dish.

Nutrition: calories 173, fat 8, fiber 2, carbs 6, protein 6

Broccoli and Brussels Sprouts Mix

Prep time: 10 minutes | Cooking time: 12 minutes | Servings: 4

Ingredients:

- 1 cup water
- 1 pound Brussels sprouts, trimmed and halved
- 1 broccoli head, florets separated
- A pinch of salt and black pepper
- ¼ cup pine nuts, toasted
- Seeds of 1 pomegranate
- A drizzle of olive oil

Directions:

Put the water in your instant pot, add the steamer basket, add Brussels sprouts and broccoli inside, put the lid on and cook on High for 12 minutes. Drain the sprouts and the broccoli and transfer them to a bowl. Add the rest of the ingredients, toss and serve as a side dish.

Nutrition: calories 130, fat 5, fiber 3, carbs 6, protein 7

Broccoli and Orange Salad

Prep time: 10 minutes | Cooking time: 7 minutes | Servings: 4

Ingredients:

- 1 pound broccoli, florets separated
- 2 oranges, peeled and cut into segments
- Zest of 1 orange, grated
- Juice of 1 orange
- 1 cup water
- 1 red chili pepper, chopped
- 3 tablespoons avocado oil

Directions:

Put the water in your instant pot, add steamer basket, add the broccoli inside, put the lid on and cook on High for 7 minutes. Release the pressure naturally for 10 minutes, drain the broccoli, transfer it to a bowl, add the rest of the ingredients, toss and serve as a side salad.

Nutrition: calories 142, fat 4, fiber 2, carbs 4, protein 5

Green Beans Rice

Prep time: 10 minutes | Cooking time: 20 minutes | Servings: 4

Ingredients:

- 4 cups water
- 2 cups green beans, trimmed and halved
- 2 cups brown rice
- 4 garlic cloves, minced
- 1 teaspoon nutmeg, ground
- Salt and black pepper to the taste

Directions:

In your instant pot, combine the rice with the rest of the ingredients except the green beans, put the lid on and cook on High for 15 minutes Release the pressure fast for 5 minutes, add the green beans, put the lid back on and cook on High for 5 minutes more. Release the pressure fast again for 5 minutes, divide the mix between plates and serve.

Nutrition: calories 190, fat 6, fiber 2, carbs 6, protein 7

Garlic Kale

Prep time: 5 minutes | Cooking time: 5 minutes | Servings: 4

Ingredients:

- 1 pound kale, roughly torn
- ¼ cup chicken stock
- 1 tablespoons spring onions, chopped
- 4 garlic cloves, minced

Directions:

In your instant pot, combine all the ingredients, put the lid on and cook on High for 5 minutes. Release the pressure fast for 5 minutes, divide the mix between plates and serve.

Nutrition: calories 141, fat 5, fiber 4, carbs 6, protein 6

Thyme Beans

Prep time: 10 minutes | Cooking time: 15 minutes | Servings: 4

Ingredients:

- 3 cups pinto beans, soaked overnight
- 6 cups chicken stock
- 1 yellow onion, minced
- 1 tablespoon olive oil
- 1 red chili pepper, chopped
- ¼ teaspoon cumin, ground
- 1 tablespoon thyme, chopped
- 2 tablespoons garlic, minced
- A pinch of salt and black pepper

Directions:

Set the instant pot on Sauté mode, add the oil, heat it up, add the onion and garlic, stir and cook for 5 minutes. Add the rest of the ingredients except the thyme, put the lid on and cook on High for 20 minutes. Release the pressure naturally for 10 minutes, add the thyme, toss, divide the mix between plates and serve.

Nutrition: calories 161, fat 6, fiber 5, carbs 7, protein 7

Celery and Green Beans Mix

Prep time: 10 minutes | Cooking time: 12 minutes | Servings: 4

Ingredients:

- 1 pound green beans, trimmed and halved
- 1 celery stalk, chopped
- 2 tablespoons olive oil
- 1 red onion, chopped
- 1 cup chicken stock
- 1 tablespoon rosemary, chopped
- Salt and black pepper to the taste

Directions:

Set your instant pot on Sauté mode, add the oil, heat it up, add the onion, stir and sauté for 5 minutes. Add the rest of the ingredients, put the lid on and cook on High for 7 minutes Release the pressure fast for 10 minutes, divide between plates and serve.

Nutrition: calories 162, fat 4, fiber 3, carbs 7, protein 4

Parmesan Asparagus

Prep time: 5 minutes | Cooking time: 8 minutes | Servings: 4

Ingredients:

- 3 garlic cloves, minced
- 1 bunch asparagus, trimmed
- 1 cup water
- 3 tablespoons olive oil
- 3 tablespoons parmesan, grated

Directions:

Put the water in your instant pot, add the steamer basket, add the asparagus inside, put the lid on and cook on High for 8 minutes. Release the pressure fast for 5 minutes, transfer the asparagus to a bowl, add the rest of the ingredients, toss and serve as a side dish.

Nutrition: calories 130, fat 4, fiber 4, carbs 5, protein 8

Spicy Eggplant

Prep time: 10 minutes | Cooking time: 12 minutes | Servings: 4

Ingredients:

- 2 eggplants, roughly cubed
- ½ cup veggie stock
- A pinch of salt and black pepper
- 2 tablespoons olive oil
- 2 garlic cloves, minced
- 1 teaspoon hot pepper flakes
- 1 bunch oregano, chopped

Directions:

Set your instant pot on Sauté mode, add the oil, heat it up, add the garlic and pepper flakes, stir and cook for 5 minutes. Add the rest of the ingredients, put the lid on and cook on High for 7 minutes. Release the pressure naturally for 10 minutes, divide between plates and serve.

Nutrition: calories 183, fat 4, fiber 4, carbs 7, protein 9

Ginger Kale

Prep time: 4 minutes | Cooking time: 6 minutes | Servings: 4

Ingredients:

- 1 pound kale, torn
- ¼ cup veggie stock
- 2 teaspoons ginger, grated
- 2 garlic cloves, minced
- 1 tablespoon balsamic vinegar
- Salt and white pepper to the taste

Directions:

In your instant pot, combine all the ingredients, put the lid on and cook on High for 6 minutes. Release the pressure fast for 4 minutes, divide the mix between plates and serve.

Nutrition: calories 120, fat 4, fiber 3, carbs 7, protein 4

Spicy Red Cabbage

Prep time: 10 minutes | Cooking time: 15 minutes | Servings: 4

Ingredients:

- 6 cups red cabbage, shredded
- ½ cup yellow onion, chopped
- 1 tablespoon olive oil
- 1 teaspoon hot paprika
- Salt and black pepper to the taste
- 1 tablespoon apple cider vinegar

Directions:

Set your instant pot on Sauté mode, add the oil, heat it up, add the onion, stir and sauté for 5 minutes Add the rest of the ingredients, toss, put the lid on and cook on High for 10 minutes. Release the pressure naturally for 10 minutes, divide the mix between plates and serve as a side dish.

Nutrition: calories 132, fat 7, fiber 3, carbs 6, protein 8

Balsamic Cabbage

Prep time: 10 minutes | Cooking time: 15 minutes | Servings: 4

Ingredients:

- 1 green cabbage head, shredded
- 2 tablespoons lime juice
- 1 red onion, chopped
- ½ cup veggie stock
- A pinch of salt and black pepper
- 2 tablespoons olive oil
- 2 teaspoons balsamic vinegar
- 1 teaspoon dill, chopped

Directions:

Set the instant pot on Sauté mode, add the oil, heat it up, add the onion and sauté for 5 minutes. Add the rest of the ingredients, put the lid on and cook on High for 10 minutes. Release the pressure naturally for 10 minutes, divide the mix between plates and serve.

Nutrition: calories 163, fat 4, fiber 4, carbs 8, protein 6

Creamy Green Beans

Prep time: 10 minutes | Cooking time: 15 minutes | Servings: 4

Ingredients:

- 1 pound green beans, trimmed
- 1 cup coconut cream
- 5 garlic cloves, minced
- A pinch of salt and black pepper
- 1 teaspoon sweet paprika

Directions:

In your instant pot, combine all the ingredients, put the lid on and cook on High for 15 minutes. Release the pressure naturally for 10 minutes, divide the mix between plates and serve as a side dish.

Nutrition: calories 191, fat 7, fiber 4, carbs 9, protein 11

Cheesy Tomatoes

Prep time: 10 minutes | Cooking time: 10 minutes | Servings: 4

Ingredients:

1. 1 pound cherry tomatoes, halved
2. ¼ cup veggie stock
3. A pinch of cayenne pepper
4. A pinch of salt and black pepper
5. 1 tablespoon olive oil
6. ¼ cup mozzarella, shredded

Directions:

In your instant pot, combine all the ingredients except the mozzarella, put the lid on and cook on High for 10 minutes. Release the pressure naturally for 10 minutes, divide the mix between plates, sprinkle the mozzarella all over and serve.

Nutrition: calories 172, fat 4, fiber 4, carbs 9, protein 8

Beets and Pecans Mix

Prep time: 10 minutes | Cooking time: 20 minutes | Servings: 4

Ingredients:

- 2 cups water
- 1 red onion, sliced
- 4 beets
- 2 tablespoons olive oil
- 2 tablespoons balsamic vinegar
- A pinch of salt and black pepper
- 2 tablespoons pecans, chopped

Directions:

Add the water to your instant pot, add the steamer basket, add the beets inside, put the lid on and cook on High for 20 minutes. Release the pressure naturally for 10 minutes, drain the beets, cool them down, peel and cut into cubes. In a salad bowl, combine the beets with the rest of the ingredients, toss and serve as a side dish.

Nutrition: calories 142, fat 5, fiber 3, carbs 8, protein 6

Spicy Artichokes

Prep time: 10 minutes | Cooking time: 8 minutes | Servings: 4

Ingredients:

- 4 artichokes, trimmed and halved
- 1 tablespoon olive oil
- 2 tablespoons lemon juice
- ¼ cup veggie stock
- A pinch of cayenne pepper
- ½ teaspoon red pepper flakes

Directions:

In your instant pot, combine all the ingredients, put the lid on and cook on High for 8 minutes. Release the pressure naturally for 10 minutes, divide the artichokes between plates and serve.

Nutrition: calories 152, fat 4, fiber 4, carbs 8, protein 6

Mustard Greens Sauté

Prep time: 5 minutes | Cooking time: 8 minutes | Servings: 4

Ingredients:

- 1 bunch mustard greens
- 2 tablespoons olive oil
- A pinch of salt and black pepper
- ¼ cup veggie stock
- 2 tablespoons tomato puree
- 3 garlic cloves, minced
- 1 tablespoon balsamic vinegar

Directions:

In your instant pot, combine all the ingredients, put the lid on and cook on High for 8 minutes. Release the pressure fast for 5 minutes, divide the mix between plates and serve.

Nutrition: calories 140, fat 4, fiber 4, carbs 8, protein 4

Lime Endives

Prep time: 5 minutes | Cooking time: 15 minutes | Servings: 4

Ingredients:

- 8 endives, trimmed and sliced
- 2 tablespoons olive oil
- Salt and black pepper to the taste
- Juice of 1 lime
- ¼ cup veggie stock
- 2 tablespoons parsley, chopped

Directions:

In your instant pot, combine all the ingredients except the parsley, put the lid on and cook on High for 15 minutes. Release the pressure fast for 5 minutes, divide the mix between plates and serve with the parsley on top.

Nutrition: calories 140, fat 4, fiber 4, carbs 8, protein 5

Kale and Onion Mix

Prep time: 10 minutes | Cooking time: 10 minutes | Servings: 4

Ingredients:

- 1 pound kale, chopped
- 1 cup pearl onions
- 1 tablespoon olive oil
- 1 teaspoon balsamic vinegar
- ¼ cup chicken stock
- ¼ teaspoon red pepper flakes

Directions:

Set your instant pot on Sauté mode, add the oil, heat it up, add the onions, and sauté for 3 minutes. Add the rest of the ingredients, put the lid on and cook on High for 7 minutes. Release the pressure naturally for 10 minutes, divide the mix between plates and serve as a side dish.

Nutrition: calories 180, fat 4, fiber 5, carbs 9, protein 6

Bacon Brussels Sprouts

Prep time: 10 minutes | Cooking time: 10 minutes | Servings: 4

Ingredients:

- 6 bacon slices, chopped
- 1 pound Brussels sprouts, halved
- 1 tablespoon olive oil
- 1 yellow onion, chopped
- 1 and ½ cups chicken stock
- 6 garlic cloves, chopped
- Salt and black pepper to the taste
- 2 tablespoons apple cider vinegar

Directions:

Set your instant pot on Sauté mode, add the oil, heat up, add bacon and the onions, stir and cook for 4 minutes. Add the rest of the ingredients, put the lid on and cook on High for 6 minutes. Release the pressure naturally for 10 minutes, divide the mix between plates and serve.

Nutrition: calories 183, fat 4, fiber 4, carbs 8, protein 6

Zucchinis and Tomato Mix

Prep time: 10 minutes | Cooking time: 12 minutes | Servings: 4

Ingredients:

- 8 zucchinis, roughly sliced
- 1 yellow onion, chopped
- 1 tablespoon olive oil
- 1 cup tomato paste
- 2 garlic cloves, minced
- 1 bunch basil, chopped

Directions:

Set your instant pot on Sauté mode, add the oil, heat it up, add the onion, stir and sauté for 5 minutes. Add the rest of the ingredients, toss, put the lid on and cook on High for 7 minutes. Release the pressure naturally for 10 minutes, divide the mix between plates and serve.

Nutrition: calories 169, fat 4, fiber 4, carbs 8, protein 6

Creamy Turmeric Fennel

Prep time: 5 minutes | Cooking time: 6 minutes | Servings: 4

Ingredients:

- 2 fennel bulbs, sliced
- 2 tablespoons turmeric powder
- 2 cups coconut cream
- A pinch of salt and black pepper

Directions:

In your instant pot, combine all the ingredients, put the lid on and cook on High for 6 minutes. Release the pressure fast for 5 minutes, divide the mix between plates and serve as a side dish.

Nutrition: calories 152, fat 5, fiber 4, carbs 8, protein 7

Kale and Peas Mix

Prep time: 5 minutes | Cooking time: 15 minutes | Servings: 4

Ingredients:

- 1 pound fresh peas
- 1 pound kale, torn
- 1 spring onion, chopped
- 1 tablespoon mint, chopped
- ½ cup veggie stock
- A pinch of salt and black pepper

Directions:

In your instant pot, combine all the ingredients, put the lid on and cook on High for 15 minutes. Release the pressure fast for 5 minutes, divide the mix between plates and serve.

Nutrition: calories 162, fat 5, fiber 5, carbs 9, protein 7

Garlic Tomato and Brussels Sprouts

Prep time: 10 minutes | Cooking time: 15 minutes | Servings: 4

Ingredients:

- 1 and ½ pounds Brussels sprouts, trimmed and halved
- A pinch of salt and black pepper
- 14 ounces canned tomatoes, chopped
- 1 bunch parsley, chopped
- 2 garlic clove, crushed

Directions:

In your instant pot, combine all the ingredients, put the lid on and cook on High for 15 minutes. Release the pressure naturally for 10 minutes, divide the mix between plates and serve.

Nutrition: calories 171, fat 6, fiber 6, carbs 9, protein 6

Cauliflower and Arugula Salad

Prep time: 5 minutes | Cooking time: 10 minutes | Servings: 4

Ingredients:

- 1 cauliflower, florets separated
- ¼ cup veggie stock
- 1 cup cherry tomatoes, halved
- A pinch of salt and black pepper
- 1 tablespoon olive oil
- 2 cups baby arugula
- Juice of 1 lime

Directions:

In your instant pot, combine the cauliflower with the stock, salt and pepper, put the lid on and cook on High for 10 minutes. Release the pressure fast for 5 minutes, transfer the cauliflower to a bowl, add the rest of the ingredients, toss and serve as a side dish.

Nutrition: calories 172, fat 3, fiber 6, carbs 8, protein 5

Cilantro Couscous

Prep time: 10 minutes | Cooking time: 5 minutes | Servings: 4

Ingredients:

- 2 cups couscous
- Salt and black pepper to the taste
- 2 and ½ cups chicken stock
- 2 tablespoons cilantro, chopped

Directions:

In your instant pot, combine the couscous with the stock, put the lid on and cook on High for 5 minutes. Release the pressure naturally for 10 minutes, fluff the couscous with a fork, add the rest of the ingredients, toss, divide between plates and serve.

Nutrition: calories 172, fat 3, fiber 4, carbs 9, protein 6

Paprika Green Cabbage

Prep time: 10 minutes | Cooking time: 10 minutes | Servings: 4

Ingredients:

- ½ cup yellow onion, chopped
- 1 tablespoon avocado oil
- 1 red cabbage, shredded
- ¼ cup veggie stock
- 1 tablespoon sweet paprika
- A pinch of salt and black pepper

Directions:

Set your instant pot on Sauté mode, add the oil, heat it up, add the onion, stir and cook for 3 minutes. Add the rest of the ingredients, put the lid on and cook on High for 7 minutes. Release the pressure naturally for 10 minutes, divide everything between plates and serve as a side dish.

Nutrition: calories 172, fat 4, fiber 5, carbs 8, protein 7

Coriander Lentils

Prep time: 10 minutes | Cooking time: 20 minutes | Servings: 4

Ingredients:

- 1 tablespoon olive oil
- 1 cup red lentils, rinsed and drained
- 1 yellow onion, chopped
- 1 teaspoon coriander, ground
- ¼ teaspoon red pepper flakes
- Salt and black pepper to the taste
- 3 cups chicken stock

Directions:

Set your instant pot on Sauté mode, add the oil, heat it up, add the onion, stir and cook for 4 minutes. Add the rest of the ingredients, put the lid on and cook on High for 15 minutes. Release the pressure naturally for 10 minutes, divide the mix between plates and serve as a side dish.

Nutrition: calories 162, fat 7, fiber 5, carbs 9, protein 7

Lentils and Chickpeas Salad

Prep time: 10 minutes | Cooking time: 20 minutes | Servings: 4

Ingredients:

- 4 cups chicken stock
- 1 cup lentils, rinsed and drained
- 1 cup chickpeas, rinsed and drained
- ½ teaspoon thyme, dried
- ¼ cup red onion, chopped
- 2 tablespoons olive oil
- 1 tablespoon garlic, minced
- ½ teaspoon oregano, dried
- Juice of 1 lemon
- 2 tablespoons cilantro, chopped
- Salt and black pepper to the taste

Directions:

Set the instant pot on Sauté mode, add the oil, heat it up, add the onion and garlic, stir and cook for 3 minutes. Add the rest of the ingredients, put the lid on and cook on High for 16 minutes. Release the pressure naturally for 10 minutes, toss the mix again, divide between plates and serve as a side dish.

Nutrition: calories 172, fat 4, fiber 7, carbs 11, protein 7

Curry Green Beans

Prep time: 10 minutes | Cooking time: 12 minutes | Servings: 4

Ingredients:

- 2 tablespoons olive oil
- 2 teaspoons garlic, minced
- 1 yellow onion, chopped
- 2 teaspoons sweet paprika
- 2 teaspoons turmeric powder
- 1 pound green beans, trimmed
- 10 ounces canned tomatoes, chopped
- A pinch of salt and black pepper
- 1 tablespoon green curry paste

Directions:

Set your instant pot on Sauté mode, add the oil, heat it up, add the onion and garlic, stir and sauté for 2 minutes. Add paprika, turmeric, curry paste, salt and pepper, stir well and cook for 2 minutes more. Add the green beans and tomatoes, toss, put the lid on and cook on High for 8 minutes. Release the pressure naturally for 10 minutes, divide the mix between plates and serve as a side dish.

Nutrition: calories 182, fat 5, fiber 5, carbs 9, protein 7

Chicken and Corn Soup

Prep time: 10 minutes | Cooking time: 15 minutes | Servings: 4

Ingredients:

- 2 tablespoons avocado oil
- ¼ cup yellow onion, chopped
- 1 teaspoon garlic, minced
- ½ cup red bell pepper, chopped
- 30 ounces chicken stock, low-sodium
- 1 and ½ pounds chicken breasts, skinless, boneless and cubed
- 20 ounces canned corn, drained
- 1 cup tomatoes, chopped
- 1 tablespoon chili powder
- 1 cup coconut cream

Directions:

Set your instant pot on sauté mode, add the oil, heat it up, add the meat, onion, bell pepper and garlic, stir and cook for 3 minutes. Add the rest of the ingredients except the cream, toss, put the lid on and cook on High for 10 minutes. Release the pressure naturally for 10 minutes, set the pot on sauté mode again, add the cream, stir well, cook for 2 minutes more, divide into bowls and serve.

Nutrition: calories 273, fat 14, fiber 4, carbs 6, protein 18

Broccoli and Squash Soup

Prep time: 10 minutes | Cooking time: 15 minutes | Servings: 4

Ingredients:

- 1 yellow onion, chopped
- 2 teaspoons olive oil
- 3 garlic cloves, minced
- 1 pound broccoli florets
- 1 pound butternut squash, peeled and cubed
- 2 cups veggie stock
- 1 teaspoon sweet paprika
- 1 teaspoon basil, dried
- ½ cup coconut milk

Directions:

Set your instant pot on sauté mode, add the oil, heat it up, add the onion and garlic, stir and cook for 1-2 minutes. Add the rest of the ingredients except the coconut milk, put the lid on and cook on High for 12 minutes. Release the pressure naturally for 10 minutes, add the coconut milk, blend the soup using an immersion blender, divide into bowls and serve.

Nutrition: calories 271, fat 12, fiber 5, carbs 7, protein 9

Mushroom and Pork Soup

Prep time: 10 minutes | Cooking time: 30 minutes | Servings: 4

Ingredients:

- 1 and ½ pound pork stew meat, cubed
- 2 tablespoons avocado oil
- A pinch of salt and black pepper
- ½ pound white mushrooms, sliced
- 1 cup yellow onion, chopped
- 6 garlic cloves, minced
- 6 cups veggie stock
- 1 tablespoon parsley,

Directions:

Set your instant pot on sauté mode, add the oil, heat it up, add the meat and brown for 3-4 minutes. Add mushrooms, onions, garlic, salt and pepper, stir and cook for 2 minutes more. Add the rest of the ingredients except the parsley, put the lid on and cook on High for 20 minutes. Release the pressure naturally for 10 minutes, divide the soup into bowls, sprinkle the parsley on top and serve.

Nutrition: calories 283, fat 12, fiber 4, carbs 7, protein 10

Curry Cauliflower Soup

Prep time: 10 minutes | Cooking time: 20 minutes | Servings: 4

Ingredients:

- 1 pound cauliflower florets
- 3 garlic cloves, minced
- 1 yellow onion, chopped
- 14 ounces coconut cream
- 2 cups chicken stock
- 1 tablespoon red curry paste
- 2 tablespoons chives, chopped

Directions:

In your instant pot, combine all the ingredients, toss, put the lid on and cook on High for 20 minutes. Release the pressure naturally for 10 minutes, blend using an immersion blender, ladle into bowls and serve.

Nutrition: calories 201, fat 6, fiber 4, carbs 7, protein 10

Ginger Cod Soup

Prep time: 6 minutes | Cooking time: 15 minutes | Servings: 4

Ingredients:

- 1 yellow onion, chopped
- 1 pound cod fillets, boneless, skinless and cubed
- 12 cups chicken stock
- 1 carrot, sliced
- 1 celery stalk, chopped
- 1 tablespoon olive oil
- A pinch of salt and black pepper
- 2 tablespoons ginger, grated

Directions:

Set your instant pot on sauté mode, add oil, heat it up, add the onion, carrot, celery and ginger, stir and sauté for 4 minutes. Add the rest of the ingredients, put the lid on and cook on High for 10 minutes. Release the pressure fast for 6 minutes, ladle into bowls and serve.

Nutrition: calories 201, fat 8, fiber 2, carbs 5, protein 9

Turmeric Lentils and Spinach Soup

Prep time: 10 minutes | Cooking time: 20 minutes | Servings: 4

Ingredients:

- 2 teaspoons avocado oil
- 1 yellow onion, chopped
- 1 celery stalk, chopped
- 1 cup brown lentils, rinsed and drained
- 2 cups baby spinach
- 4 garlic cloves, minced
- 2 teaspoons cumin, ground
- 1 teaspoon turmeric powder
- 4 cups veggie stock
- 1 teaspoon basil, dried

Directions:

Set your instant pot on sauté mode, add the oil, heat it up, add onions, celery and garlic, stir and cook for about 5 minutes. Add the rest of the ingredients except the spinach, put the lid on and cook on High or 12 minutes. Release the pressure naturally for 10 minutes, set the pot on Sauté mode again, add the spinach, cook for 3 minutes more, ladle the soup into bowls and serve.

Nutrition: calories 199, fat 5, fiber 4, carbs 6, protein 11

Potato and Parsley Cream

Prep time: 5 minutes | Cooking time: 20 minutes | Servings: 4

Ingredients:

- 6 cups gold potatoes, cubed
- 2 tablespoons olive oil
- ½ cup yellow onion, chopped
- 6 cups chicken stock
- A pinch of salt and black pepper
- 2 tablespoons parsley, chopped
- 2 cups coconut cream
- 1 cup cheddar cheese, grated

Directions:

Set your instant pot on Sauté mode, add the oil, heat it up, add the onion, stir and sauté 5 minutes Add the potatoes, stock, salt and pepper, put the lid on and cook on High for 10 minutes. Release the pressure fast for 5 minutes, add the cream, and blend the soup using an immersion blender. Set the pot on Sauté mode, add the cheese and parsley, cook the soup for 3 minutes more, divide into bowls and serve.

Nutrition: calories 210, fat 7, fiber 4, carbs 6, protein 11

Corn and Zucchini Soup

Prep time: 10 minutes | Cooking time: 15 minutes | Servings: 4

Ingredients:

- 1 tablespoon olive oil
- 1 celery stalk, chopped
- 1 yellow onion, chopped
- 2 cups corn
- 2 zucchinis, cubed
- 2 cups tomatoes, chopped
- 4 garlic cloves, minced
- 30 ounces chicken stock, low-sodium
- A pinch of salt and black pepper
- 2 tablespoons basil, chopped

Directions:

Set your instant pot on Sauté mode, add the oil, heat it up, add the onion, stir and sauté for 5 minutes. Add the rest of the ingredients except the basil, stir, put the lid on and cook on High for 10 minutes. Release the pressure naturally for 10 minutes, add the basil, divide the soup into bowls.

Nutrition: calories 185, fat 6, fiber 4, carbs 8, protein 10

Bell Pepper and Tomato Soup

Prep time: 10 minutes | Cooking time: 20 minutes | Servings: 4

Ingredients:

- 1 yellow onion, chopped
- 2 tablespoons olive oil
- 2 red bell peppers, roughly chopped
- 1 pound tomatoes, cubed
- 3 tablespoons tomato paste
- 2 celery ribs, chopped
- 6 cups chicken stock
- 1 teaspoon garlic powder
- ½ tablespoon basil, dried
- ½ teaspoon red pepper flakes

Directions:

Set the instant pot on Sauté mode, add the oil, heat it up, add the onion, garlic powder, basil and the pepper flakes, stir and sauté for 5 minutes. Add the rest of the ingredients, put the lid on and cook on High for 15 minutes. Release the pressure naturally for 10 minutes, divide the soup into bowls and serve.

Nutrition: calories 180, fat 5, fiber 3, carbs 6, protein 10

Carrots and Cabbage Soup

Prep time: 10 minutes | Cooking time: 10 minutes | Servings: 4

Ingredients:

- 1 green cabbage head, shredded
- A pinch of salt and black pepper
- ½ pound carrots, sliced
- 1 yellow onion, chopped
- 2 tablespoons olive oil
- 3 garlic cloves, minced
- ¼ cup cilantro, chopped
- 4 cups chicken stock

Directions:

In your instant pot, combine all the ingredients, put the lid on and cook on High for 10 minutes. Release the pressure naturally for 10 minutes, ladle the soup into bowls and serve.

Nutrition: calories 172, fat 4, fiber 4, carbs 6, protein 9

Salsa Turkey Soup

Prep time: 10 minutes | Cooking time: 20 minutes | Servings: 4

Ingredients:

- 1 turkey breast, skinless, boneless and cubed
- 2 tablespoons olive oil
- 1 yellow onion, chopped
- 3 garlic cloves, minced
- 16 ounces chunky salsa
- 30 ounces chicken stock
- A pinch of salt and black pepper
- 1 tablespoon parsley, chopped
- 1 tablespoon chili powder

Directions:

Set your instant pot on Sauté mode, add the oil, heat it up, add the onion and garlic, stir and cook 5 minutes. Add the meat and brown for 2 minutes more. Add the rest of the ingredients, put the lid on and cook on High for 13 minutes. Release the pressure naturally for 10 minutes, divide the soup into bowls and serve.

Nutrition: calories 200, fat 4, fiber 4, carbs 7, protein 17

Tarragon Corn Soup

Prep time: 10 minutes | Cooking time: 15 minutes | Servings: 4

Ingredients:

- 2 tablespoons olive oil
- 1 yellow onion, chopped
- 2 garlic cloves, minced
- 3 cups corn
- 4 tarragon springs, chopped
- 1 quart chicken stock
- A pinch of salt and black pepper
- 1 tablespoon chives, chopped

Directions:

Set your instant pot on Sauté mode, add the oil, heat it up, add the onion and the garlic, stir and sauté for 5 minutes. Add the rest of the ingredients except the chives, put the lid on and cook on High for 10 minutes Release the pressure naturally for 10 minutes, ladle the soup into bowls, sprinkle the chives on top and serve.

Nutrition: calories 200, fat 5, fiber 4, carbs 8, protein 11

Zucchini and Chicken Soup

Prep time: 10 minutes | Cooking time: 15 minutes | Servings: 4

Ingredients:

- 2 zucchinis, cubed
- ½ cup green onions, chopped
- ½ cup celery, chopped
- 29 ounces canned chicken stock
- 1 garlic clove, minced
- 2 cups tomatoes, cubed
- 2 chicken breasts, skinless, boneless and cubed
- 1 tablespoon parsley, chopped

Directions:

Set your instant pot on Sauté mode, add the green onions, garlic, celery and tomatoes, toss and cook for 3 minutes. Add the rest of the ingredients except the parsley, put the lid on and cook on High for 12 minutes. Release the pressure naturally for 10 minutes, ladle the soup into bowls, sprinkle the parsley on top and serve.

Nutrition: calories 192, fat 8, fiber 4, carbs 9, protein 12

Bacon Corn Soup

Prep time: 10 minutes | Cooking time: 12 minutes | Servings: 4

Ingredients:

- 6 cups corn
- 2 tablespoons avocado oil
- ½ cup yellow onion, chopped
- 28 ounces canned chicken stock
- A pinch of salt and black pepper
- 3 ounces cream cheese, cubed
- 2 cups coconut cream
- 1 cup cheddar cheese, shredded
- 6 bacon slices, cooked and crumbled

Directions:

Set your instant pot on Sauté mode, add the oil, heat it up, add the onion, stir and cook 5 minutes Add the rest of the ingredients except the cheddar, cream cheese and bacon, put the lid on and cook on High for 10 minutes. Release the pressure naturally for 10 minutes, add the cheddar and cream cheese and blend the soup using an immersion blender. Divide the soup into bowls, sprinkle the bacon on top and serve.

Nutrition: calories 182, fat 3, fiber 4, carbs 6, protein 12

Chicken and Pea Soup

Prep time: 10 minutes | Cooking time: 20 minutes | Servings: 4

Ingredients:

- 2 tablespoons olive oil
- 1 pound chicken breasts, skinless, boneless and cubed
- 1 yellow onion, chopped
- ½ cup carrots, chopped
- 2 garlic cloves, minced
- 28 ounces chicken stock
- A pinch of salt and black pepper
- 1 pound fresh peas
- ½ cup coconut cream
- 1 tablespoon dill, chopped

Directions:

Set the instant pot on Sauté mode, add the oil, heat it up, add the chicken, onion and garlic and brown for 4 minutes. Add the rest of the ingredients except the cream and dill, put the lid on and cook on High for 12 minutes. Release the pressure naturally for 10 minutes, set the pot on Sauté mode again, add the cream and dill, cook for 4 minutes more, ladle into bowls and serve.

Nutrition: calories 192, fat 5, fiber 3, carbs 7, protein 16

Beef and Tomato Soup

Prep time: 10 minutes | Cooking time: 20 minutes | Servings: 4

Ingredients:

- 1 pound beef stew meat, cubed
- 3 garlic cloves, minced
- 1 yellow onion, chopped
- 1 tablespoon olive oil
- 28 ounces beef stock
- 1 pound tomatoes, peeled and chopped
- 1 cup tomato sauce
- A pinch of salt and black pepper
- 1 tablespoon parsley, chopped

Directions:

Set your instant pot on Sauté mode, add the oil, heat it up, add the meat and brown for 3 minutes. Add garlic and onion, stir and cook for 2 minutes more. Add the rest of the ingredients except the parsley, put the lid on and cook on High for 15 minutes. Release the pressure naturally for 10 minutes, add the parsley, ladle the soup into bowls and serve.

Nutrition: calories 261, fat 6, fiber 4, carbs 6, protein 15

Creamy Broccoli and Leeks Soup

Prep time: 10 minutes | Cooking time: 15 minutes | Servings: 6

Ingredients:

- 2 leeks, chopped
- 1 yellow onion, chopped
- 6 cups veggie stock
- 1 pound broccoli florets
- 1 tablespoon mint, chopped
- 1 teaspoon chili powder
- 1 tablespoon olive oil

Directions:

Set your instant pot on sauté mode, add the oil, heat it up, add leeks, onion, chili powder, salt and pepper, stir and cook for 5 minutes. Add the broccoli and stock, put the lid on and cook on High for 10 minutes. Release the pressure naturally for 10 minutes, transfer the soup to a blender, pulse well, ladle into bowls, sprinkle the mint on top and serve.

Nutrition: calories 150, fat 8, fiber 4, carbs 7, protein 5

Chicken and Eggplant Soup

Prep time: 10 minutes | Cooking time: 15 minutes | Servings: 4

Ingredients:

- 1 yellow onion, chopped
- 1 tablespoon olive oil
- 1 celery rib, chopped
- 1 eggplant, cubed
- A pinch of salt and black pepper
- 6 cups chicken stock
- 2 chicken breasts, skinless, boneless and cubed
- 1 tablespoon parsley, chopped

Directions:

Set your instant pot on Sauté mode, add the oil, heat it up, add the onion and celery, stir and cook for 3 minutes. Add the rest of the ingredients except the parsley, put the lid on and cook on High for 12 minutes. Release the pressure naturally for 10 minutes, add the parsley, ladle into bowls and serve.

Nutrition: calories 200, fat 4, fiber 3, carbs 6, protein 12

Chicken and Rice Soup

Prep time: 10 minutes | Cooking time: 15 minutes | Servings: 4

Ingredients:

- 1 yellow onion, chopped
- 2 tablespoons olive oil
- 1 cup carrots, chopped
- 28 ounces chicken stock
- 2 chicken breasts, skinless, boneless and cubed
- 6 ounces wild rice
- A pinch of salt and black pepper
- 1 tablespoon parsley, chopped

Directions:

Set your instant pot on Sauté mode, add the oil, heat it up, add the chicken, onion and carrots, stir and sauté for 3 minutes . Add the rest of the ingredients except the parsley, put the lid on and cook on High for 12 minutes. Release the pressure naturally for 10 minutes, add the parsley, stir, ladle the soup into bowls and serve.

Nutrition: calories 200, fat 8, fiber 4, carbs 6, protein 12

Basil Tomato Soup

Prep time: 5 minutes | Cooking time:10 minutes | Servings: 4

Ingredients:

- 1 yellow onion, chopped
- 2 tablespoons olive oil
- 2 celery stalks, chopped
- 2 garlic cloves, minced
- 30 ounces chicken stock
- A pinch of salt and black pepper
- ¼ cup basil, chopped
- 3 pounds tomatoes, peeled, and roughly cubed
- 1 cup coconut cream

Directions:

Set your instant pot on Sauté mode, add the oil, heat it up, add the onion, garlic and celery, stir and cook for 3 minutes. Add the rest of the ingredients except the cream, put the lid on and cook on High for 7 minutes. Release the pressure fast for 5 minutes, add the cream, blend the soup using and immersion blender, divide into soup bowls and serve.

Nutrition: calories 200, fat 5, fiber 3, carbs 7, protein 12

Turkey and Potato Soup

*Prep time: 10 minutes | **Cooking time:** 20 minutes | Servings: 6*

Ingredients:

- 1 pound turkey breast, skinless, boneless and cubed
- 3 garlic cloves, minced
- 1 cup yellow onion, chopped
- 1 tablespoon olive oil
- 30 ounces chicken stock
- A pinch of salt and black pepper
- 3 gold potatoes, peeled and cubed
- 1 cup coconut cream

Directions:

Set your instant pot on Sauté mode, add the oil, heat it up, add the meat and brown for 3 minutes. Add the onion and garlic, stir and sauté for 2 minutes more.Add the rest of the ingredients, put the lid on and cook on High for 15 minutes. Release the pressure naturally for 10 minutes, ladle the soup into bowls and serve.

Nutrition: calories 200, fat 8, fiber 4, carbs 7, protein 14

Green Beans Soup

*Prep time: 10 minutes | **Cooking time:** 15 minutes | Servings: 6*

Ingredients:

- 1 tablespoon olive oil
- 2 carrots, chopped
- 1 yellow onion, chopped
- 1 cup tomatoes, cubed
- 4 garlic cloves, minced
- 30 ounces chicken stock
- A pinch of salt and black pepper
- 1 pound green beans, trimmed
- 2 tablespoons parsley, chopped

Directions:

Set your instant pot on Sauté mode, add the oil, heat it up, add the onion and garlic stir and cook for 5 minutes. Add the rest of the ingredients except the parsley, put the lid on and cook on High for 10 minutes. Release the pressure naturally for 10 minutes, ladle the soup into bowls, sprinkle the parsley on top and serve.

Nutrition: calories 162, fat 4, fiber 4, carbs 6, protein 9

Spinach Cream Soup

*Prep time: 5 minutes | **Cooking time:** 15 minutes | Servings: 6*

Ingredients:

- 1 yellow onion, chopped
- 2 tablespoons olive oil
- 1 red bell pepper, chopped
- 2 celery ribs, chopped
- 6 cups chicken stock
- 1 pound spinach, torn
- ½ teaspoon red pepper flakes
- A pinch of salt and black pepper
- 1 cup coconut cream

Directions:

Set the instant pot on sauté mode, add the oil, heat it up, add onion, bell pepper and celery, stir and sauté for 5 minutes. Add the rest of the ingredients except the cream, put the lid on and cook on High for 10 minutes. Release the pressure fast for 5 minutes, add the cream, blend using an immersion blender, divide into bowls and serve.

Nutrition: calories 162, fat 3, fiber 4, carbs 7, protein 5

Spicy Carrot Cream

Prep time: 5 minutes | Cooking time: 15 minutes | Servings: 4

Ingredients:

- 1 tablespoon olive oil
- 1 yellow onion, chopped
- 1 garlic clove, minced
- 1 pound carrots, chopped
- 1 tablespoon ginger, grated

- A pinch of salt and black pepper
- 4 cups chicken stock
- 1 tablespoon hot paprika
- 14 ounces canned coconut milk

Directions:

Set your instant pot on Sauté mode, add the oil, heat it up, add the onion, garlic and ginger, stir and sauté for 5 minutes. Add the rest of the ingredients, put the lid on and cook on High for 10 minutes. Release the pressure naturally for 10 minutes, blend the soup using an immersion blender, divide into bowls and serve.

Nutrition: calories 152, fat 4, fiber 3, carbs 8, protein 5

Red Beans Soup

Prep time: 10 minutes | Cooking time: 15 minutes | Servings: 6

Ingredients:

- 1 pound white beans, soaked overnight and drained
- 1 tablespoon olive oil
- 1 yellow onion, chopped
- 3 garlic cloves, minced

- 1 tomato, peeled and chopped
- Salt and black pepper to the taste
- 7 cups veggie stock
- 1 teaspoon sweet paprika

Directions:

Set your instant pot on Sauté mode, add the oil, heat it up, add the onion and garlic, stir and cook for 3 minutes. Add the rest of the ingredients, put the lid on and cook on High for 12 minutes. Release the pressure naturally for 10 minutes, ladle the soup into bowls and serve.

Nutrition: calories 172, fat 5, fiber 3, carbs 9, protein 12

Chickpeas and Tomato Soup

Prep time: 10 minutes | Cooking time: 30 minutes | Servings: 4

Ingredients:

- 2 celery stalks, chopped
- 1 tablespoon olive oil
- 1 yellow onion, chopped
- 4 cups chicken stock

- 2 garlic cloves, minced
- 1 cup chickpeas
- 15 ounces tomatoes, cubed
- A pinch of salt and black pepper

Directions:

Set your instant pot on Sauté mode, add the oil, heat it up, add the celery, onion and the garlic, stir and cook for 4 minutes. Add the rest of the ingredients, put the lid on and cook on High for 25 minutes. Release the pressure naturally for 10 minutes ladle the soup into bowls and serve.

Nutrition: calories 162, fat 3, fiber 4, carbs 5, protein 4

Squash Cream Soup

Prep time: 10 minutes | Cooking time: 15 minutes | Servings: 4

Ingredients:

- 1 butternut squash, peeled and roughly chopped
- 1 cup baby carrots
- 1 yellow onion, chopped
- 2 tablespoons olive oil
- 3 teaspoons garlic, minced
- ¼ cup cilantro, chopped
- 4 cups chicken stock
- A pinch of salt and black pepper
- A pinch of nutmeg, ground

Directions:

In your instant pot, combine all the ingredients, put the lid on and cook on High for 15 minutes. Release the pressure naturally for 10 minutes, blend the soup using an immersion blender, ladle into bowls and serve.

Nutrition: calories 172, fat 4, fiber 2, carbs 7, protein 10

Mint Zucchini Cream

Prep time: 10 minutes | Cooking time: 15 minutes | Servings: 4

Ingredients:

- 2 pounds zucchinis, chopped
- 2 tablespoons avocado oil
- 1 yellow onion, chopped
- 6 cups chicken stock
- ¼ teaspoon lemon juice
- ½ cup coconut cream
- 1 tablespoon mint, chopped
- A pinch of salt and black pepper

Directions:

Set your instant pot on Sauté mode, add the oil, heat it up, add the onion and sauté for 5 minutes. Add the rest of the ingredients except the cream and the mint, put the lid on and cook on High for 10 minutes. Release the pressure naturally for 10 minutes, add the cream, blend the soup using an immersion blender, ladle into bowls, sprinkle the mint on top and serve.

Nutrition: calories 130, fat 3, fiber 4, carbs 7, protein 6

Asparagus Soup

Prep time: 5 minutes | Cooking time: 12 minutes | Servings: 4

Ingredients:

- 1 pound asparagus, trimmed and halved
- 1 leek, sliced
- 2 tablespoons avocado oil
- 2 garlic cloves, minced
- 2 shallots, chopped
- 7 cups chicken stock
- ¼ teaspoon black peppercorns, crushed
- 1 tablespoon parsley, chopped
- 1 tablespoon oregano, chopped
- A pinch of salt and black pepper
- ¼ cup coconut cream

Directions:

Set your instant pot on Sauté mode, add the oil, heat it up, add the leek, garlic and shallots, stir and cook for 3 minutes. Add the rest of the ingredients, put the lid on and cook on High for 10 minutes. Release the pressure fast for 5 minutes, ladle the soup into bowls and serve.

Nutrition: calories 162, fat 5, fiber 4, carbs 7, protein 5

Carrots and Beet Soup

Prep time: 10 minutes | Cooking time: 15 minutes | Servings: 4

Ingredients:

- 1 tablespoon olive oil
- 1 red onion, chopped
- 2 carrots, chopped
- 3 beets, peeled and cubed
- 6 cups chicken stock
- 1 and ½ tablespoons parsley, chopped
- A pinch of salt and black pepper

Directions:

Set your instant pot on Sauté mode, add the oil, heat it up, add the onion, stir and cook for 5 minutes. Add the rest of the ingredients, put the lid on and cook on High for 10 minutes. Release the pressure naturally for 10 minutes, ladle the soup into bowls and serve.

Nutrition: calories 142, fat 4, fiber 3, carbs 6, protein 6

Chives Bell Peppers Soup

Prep time: 10 minutes | Cooking time: 10 minutes | Servings: 4

Ingredients:

- 1 yellow onion, chopped
- 1 pound mixed bell peppers, cut into chunks
- 1 tablespoons olive oil
- 4 cups chicken stock
- 2 garlic cloves, minced
- ¼ cup tomato puree
- A pinch of salt and black pepper
- 1 tablespoon chives, chopped

Directions:

Set your instant pot on Sauté mode, add the oil, heat it up, add onion and garlic, stir and cook for 2 minutes. Add the rest of the ingredients except the chives, put the lid on and cook on High for 8 minutes. Release the pressure naturally for 10 minutes, ladle the soup into bowls, sprinkle the chives on top and serve.

Nutrition: calories 172, fat 3, fiber 4, carbs 6, protein 5

Leeks Soup

Prep time: 10 minutes | Cooking time: 15 minutes | Servings: 4

Ingredients:

- 4 leeks, sliced
- 2 tablespoons avocado oil
- 1 yellow onion, chopped
- 1 tablespoon sage, chopped
- 6 cups chicken stock
- ¼ teaspoon chili powder
- A pinch of salt and black pepper

Directions:

Set your instant pot on Sauté mode, add the oil, heat it up, add the onion and sauté for 2 minutes. Add the rest of the ingredients, put the lid on and cook on High for 10 minutes. Release the pressure naturally for 10 minutes, ladle the soup into bowls and serve.

Nutrition: calories 162, fat 4, fiber 4, carbs 7, protein 3

Potato and Green Beans Soup
Prep time: 10 minutes | Cooking time: 15 minutes | Servings: 4

Ingredients:

- 1 yellow onion, chopped
- 4 gold potatoes, cubed
- 1 pound green beans, trimmed and halved
- 1 tablespoon olive oil
- A pinch of salt and black pepper
- 6 cups veggie stock
- 1 tablespoon sweet paprika
- A handful parsley, chopped

Directions:

Set your instant pot on Sauté mode, add the oil, heat it up, add the onion, stir and cook for 3 minutes. Add the rest of the ingredients except the parsley, put the lid on and cook on High for 12 minutes. Release the pressure naturally for 10 minutes, divide the soup into bowls, sprinkle the parsley on top and serve.

Nutrition: calories 120, fat 3, fiber 3, carbs 6, protein 8

Pork and Fennel Soup
Prep time: 10 minutes | Cooking time: 20 minutes | Servings: 4

Ingredients:

- 1 fennel bulb, shredded
- 4 cups chicken stock
- 1 yellow onion, chopped
- 1 pound pork meat, cubed
- 1 tablespoon olive oil
- A pinch of salt and black pepper
- 2 tablespoons tomato sauce
- 1 tablespoon parsley, chopped

Directions:

Set the instant pot on Sauté mode, add the oil, heat it up, add the onion and the meat and brown for 5 minutes. Add the rest of the ingredients, put the lid on and cook on High for 15 minutes. Release the pressure naturally for 10 minutes, ladle the soup into bowls and serve.

Nutrition: calories 162, fat 10, fiber 3, carbs 8, protein 14

Artichokes and Cauliflower Soup
Prep time: 10 minutes | Cooking time: 11 minutes | Servings: 4

Ingredients:

- 1 yellow onion, chopped
- 12 ounces canned artichokes, drained and chopped
- 1 cauliflower head, florets separated and chopped
- 2 tablespoons olive oil
- 4 cups chicken stock
- A pinch of salt and black pepper
- 1 tablespoon cilantro, chopped

Directions:

Set your instant pot on Sauté mode, add the oil, heat it up, add the onion, stir and cook for 3 minutes. Add the rest of the ingredients, put the lid on and cook on High for 8 minutes. Release the pressure naturally for 10 minutes, divide the soup into bowls and serve.

Nutrition: calories 143, fat 3, fiber 4, carbs 7, protein 6

Herbed Beef Soup

Prep time: 10 minutes | Cooking time: 25 minutes | Servings: 4

Ingredients:

- 1 pound beef meat, cubed
- 1 yellow onion, chopped
- 2 celery stalks, chopped
- 1 tablespoon olive oil
- 5 cups beef stock
- 2 garlic cloves, minced
- 1 teaspoon basil, dried
- 1 teaspoon oregano, dried
- 1 teaspoon thyme, dried
- A pinch of salt and black pepper

Directions:

Set your instant pot on Sauté mode, add the oil, heat it up, add the meat and brown for 5 minutes. Add the rest of the ingredients, put the lid on and cook on High for 20 minutes. Release the pressure naturally for 10 minutes, ladle the soup into bowls and serve.

Nutrition: calories 174, fat 12, fiber 3, carbs 6, protein 15

Turkey Meatballs Soup

Prep time: 10 minutes | Cooking time: 20 minutes | Servings: 6

Ingredients:

- 1 and ½ pounds turkey meat, ground
- A pinch of salt and black pepper
- 1 teaspoon garlic powder
- ½ tablespoon basil, dried
- ½ tablespoon oregano, dried
- 2 eggs, whisked
- 6 cups chicken stock
- 4 celery stalks, chopped
- 2 yellow onions, chopped
- 2 teaspoons thyme, dried
- 2 tablespoons olive oil
- 1 tablespoon parsley, chopped

Directions:

In a bowl, combine the meat with salt, pepper, garlic powder, basil, oregano and the eggs, stir well and shape medium meatballs out of this mix. Set the instant pot on Sauté mode, add the oil, heat it up, add the meatballs and cook for 3 minutes. Add the onion and the rest of the ingredients except the parsley, put the lid on and cook on High for 15 minutes. Release the pressure naturally for 10 minutes, ladle the soup into bowls and serve with parsley sprinkled on top.

Nutrition: calories 173, fat 4, fiber 5, carbs 9, protein 12

Kale and Mushrooms Soup

Prep time: 10 minutes | Cooking time: 15 minutes | Servings: 4

Ingredients:

- 1 yellow onion, chopped
- 1 tablespoon avocado oil
- A pinch of salt and black pepper
- 2 celery sticks, chopped
- ½ pound white mushrooms, sliced
- 2 garlic cloves, minced
- 6 ounces kale leaves, roughly chopped
- 1 cup tomatoes, chopped
- 5 cups veggie stock
- A handful parsley, chopped

Directions:

Set your instant pot on Sauté mode, add the oil, heat it up, add the onion, celery and the garlic, stir and cook for 2 minutes. Add the rest of the ingredients except the parsley, put the lid on and cook on High for 13 minutes. Release the pressure naturally for 10 minutes, add the parsley, divide the soup into bowls and serve.

Nutrition: calories 130, fat 3, fiber 4, carbs 7, protein 6

Chili Pork Soup

Prep time: 10 minutes | Cooking time: 25 minutes | Servings: 4

Ingredients:

- 1 yellow onion, chopped
- 2 tablespoons olive oil
- 2 jalapeno peppers, minced
- 4 garlic cloves, minced
- 2 teaspoons oregano, dried
- ½ teaspoon red pepper flakes, crushed
- 5 cups beef stock
- 1 pound pork meat, cubed
- A pinch of salt and black pepper
- 1 tablespoon cilantro, chopped

Directions:

Set your instant pot on Sauté mode, add the oil, heat it up, add the onion, garlic and jalapenos, stir and sauté for 2 minutes. Add the meat, stir and brown for 3 minutes more. Add the rest of the ingredients except the cilantro, put the lid on and cook on High for 20 minutes. Release the pressure naturally for 10 minutes, ladle the soup into bowls, sprinkle the cilantro on top and serve.

Nutrition: calories 172, fat 4, fiber 3, carbs 9, protein 13

Cauliflower and Spinach Soup

Prep time: 10 minutes | Cooking time: 12 minutes | Servings: 4

Ingredients:

- 1 cauliflower head, florets separated
- 1 teaspoon olive oil
- 1 yellow onion, chopped
- 2 cups spinach, roughly chopped
- 5 cups veggie stock
- A pinch of salt and black pepper
- 1 tablespoon cilantro, chopped

Directions:

Set your instant pot on Sauté mode, add the oil, heat it up, add the onion and sauté for 2 minutes. Add the rest of the ingredients except the cilantro, put the lid on and cook on High for 10 minutes. Release the pressure naturally for 10 minutes, ladle the soup into bowls and serve with cilantro sprinkled on top.

Nutrition: calories 172, fat 4, fiber 3, carbs 6, protein 7

Beef and Kale Soup

Prep time: 10 minutes | Cooking time: 20 minutes | Servings: 4

Ingredients:

- 1 pound beef meat, cubed
- 2 tablespoons olive oil
- A pinch of salt and black pepper
- 4 garlic cloves, minced
- 1 yellow onion, chopped
- 6 cups beef stock
- 5 ounces baby kale

Directions:

Set your instant pot on Sauté mode, add the oil, heat it up, add the meat, garlic and onion, stir and brown for 5 minutes. Add the rest of the ingredients, put the lid on and cook on High for 20 minutes. Release the pressure naturally for 10 minutes, ladle the soup into bowls and serve.

Nutrition: calories 182, fat 8, fiber 4, carbs 7, protein 12

Scallions and Chicken Soup

Prep time: 10 minutes | Cooking time: 20 minutes | Servings: 4

Ingredients:

- 1 tablespoon olive oil
- 3 scallions, chopped
- 3 garlic cloves, minced
- ¼ cup tomato puree
- 1 pound chicken breast, skinless, boneless and cubed
- 6 cups veggie stock
- 1 tablespoon cilantro, chopped

Directions:

Set your instant pot on Sauté mode, add the oil, heat it up, add scallions, garlic and the chicken, stir and cook for 5 minutes. Add the rest of the ingredients except the cilantro, put the lid on and cook on High for 15 minutes. Release the pressure naturally for 10 minutes, add the cilantro, ladle the soup into bowls and serve.

Nutrition: calories 175, fat 6, fiber 3, carbs 8, protein 14

Chicken and Chilies Soup

Prep time: 10 minutes | Cooking time: 20 minutes | Servings: 4

Ingredients:

- 2 chicken breasts, boneless and skinless and cubed
- 1 tablespoon olive oil
- 3 cups chicken stock
- 14 ounces canned tomatoes, chopped
- A pinch of salt and black pepper
- 4 ounces canned green chilies, chopped
- 2 garlic cloves, minced
- 1 yellow onion, chopped
- 1 teaspoon oregano, dried
- 1 tablespoon cilantro, chopped

Directions:

Set the instant pot on Sauté mode, add the oil, heat it up, add the meat, onion and garlic, stir and cook for 5 minutes. Add the rest of the ingredients except the cilantro, put the lid on and cook on High for 15 minutes. Release the pressure naturally for 10 minutes, ladle the soup into bowls, sprinkle the cilantro on top and serve.

Nutrition: calories 200, fat 8, fiber 4, carbs 7, protein 15

Beef and Broccoli Soup

Prep time: 10 minutes | Cooking time: 25 minutes | Servings: 4

Ingredients:

- 1 and ½ pounds beef stew meat, cubed
- 2 tablespoons olive oil
- A pinch of salt and black pepper
- ½ pound broccoli florets
- 1 yellow onion, chopped
- 6 cups beef stock
- ½ teaspoon rosemary, dried

Directions:

Set your instant pot on Sauté mode, add the oil, heat it up, add the meat and onion, stir and brown for 5 minutes. Add the rest of the ingredients, put the lid on and cook on High for 20 minutes. Release the pressure naturally for 10 minutes, divide the soup into bowls and serve.

Nutrition: calories 152, fat 4, fiber 5, carbs 9, protein 15

Salmon Chowder

Prep time: 10 minutes | Cooking time: 12 minutes | Servings: 4

Ingredients:

- 1 yellow onion, chopped
- 2 celery ribs, chopped
- 1 carrot, grated
- 2 garlic cloves, chopped
- 4 cups chicken stock
- 1 pound salmon fillets, skinless, boneless and cubed
- 2 tablespoons olive oil
- 1 cup corn
- A pinch of salt and black pepper
- 2 cups coconut cream

Directions:

Set your instant pot on Sauté mode, add the oil, heat it up, add the onion, celery, garlic and carrots, stir and sauté for 3 minutes. Add the rest of the ingredients, put the lid on and cook on High for 9 minutes. Release the pressure naturally for 10 minutes, ladle the soup into bowls and serve.

Nutrition: calories 178, fat 7, fiber 4, carbs 8, protein 11

Oregano Turkey Soup

Prep time: 10 minutes | Cooking time: 20 minutes | Servings: 6

Ingredients:

- 1 and ½ pounds turkey breast, skinless, boneless and cubed
- 3 garlic cloves, minced
- 1 yellow onion, chopped
- 6 cups chicken stock
- 1 tablespoon avocado oil
- 2 tomatoes, peeled and cubed
- 1 tablespoon oregano, chopped

Directions:

Set the instant pot on Sauté mode, add the oil, heat it up, add onion, garlic and the meat and brown for 5 minutes. Add the rest of the ingredients, put the lid on and cook on High for 15 minutes. Release the pressure naturally for 10 minutes, ladle the soup into bowls and serve.

Nutrition: calories 221, fat 11, fiber 4, carbs 7, protein 10

Beef and Beets Soup

Prep time: 10 minutes | Cooking time: 20 minutes | Servings: 4

Ingredients:

- 1 pound beef stew meat, cubed
- 3 garlic cloves, minced
- 1 yellow onion, chopped
- 1 tablespoon avocado oil
- 2 beets, peeled and cubed
- 28 ounces beef stock
- 1 cup tomatoes, peeled and crushed
- A pinch of salt and black pepper
- 2 tablespoons parsley, chopped

Directions:

Set your instant pot on Sauté mode, add the oil, heat it up, add the beef, onion and garlic, stir and brown for 5 minutes. Add the remaining ingredients except the parsley, put the lid on and cook on High for 15 minutes. Release the pressure naturally for 10 minutes, add the parsley, stir, ladle the soup into bowls and serve.

Nutrition: calories 210, fat 14, fiber 4, carbs 9, protein 17

Chicken and Mustard Greens Soup

Prep time: 10 minutes | Cooking time: 20 minutes | Servings: 4

Ingredients:

- 1 and ½ pounds chicken breasts, skinless, boneless and cubed
- 2 cups mustard greens
- A pinch of salt and black pepper
- ½ tablespoon basil, dried
- ½ tablespoon oregano, dried
- 6 cups beef stock
- 2 tablespoons olive oil
- 2 yellow onions, chopped
- 2 teaspoons thyme, dried
- 2 garlic cloves, minced

Directions:

Set your instant pot on Sauté mode, add the oil, heat it up, add the meat, onion and garlic, stir and brown for 5 minutes. Add the rest of the ingredients, put the lid on and cook on High for 15 minutes. Release the pressure naturally for 10 minutes, ladle the soup into bowls and serve.

Nutrition: calories 182, fat 7, fiber 4, carbs 9, protein 13

Salmon and Tomato Soup

Prep time: 10 minutes | Cooking time: 15 minutes | Servings: 4

Ingredients:

- 3 cups chicken stock
- 1 pound tomatoes, cubed
- 1 pound salmon fillets, skinless, boneless and cubed
- 1 yellow onion, chopped
- 3 garlic cloves, minced
- ½ cup coconut cream
- 1 tablespoon avocado oil

Directions:

Set your instant pot on sauté mode, add the oil, heat it up, add the onion and garlic, stir and sauté for 5 minutes. Add the rest of the ingredients, put the lid on and cook on High for 10 minutes. Release the pressure naturally for 10 minutes, ladle the soup into bowls and serve.
Nutrition: calories 186, fat 12, fiber 4, carbs 9, protein 11

Cod and Broccoli Soup

Prep time: 5 minutes | Cooking time: 15 minutes | Servings: 4

Ingredients:

- 1 broccoli head, florets separated
- 5 cups chicken stock
- 2 garlic cloves, minced
- 1 yellow onion, chopped
- 1 tablespoon avocado oil
- 1 pound cod fillets, boneless, skinless and cubed
- 2 green onion stalks, chopped

Directions:

Set your instant pot on sauté mode, add the oil, heat it up, add the onion and garlic, stir and sauté for 5 minutes. Add the rest of the ingredients, put the lid on and cook on High for 10 minutes. Release the pressure fast for 5 minutes, ladle the soup into bowls and serve.
Nutrition: calories 201, fat 8, fiber 4, carbs 6, protein 8

Instant Pot Stew Recipes

Shrimp Stew
Prep time: 5 minutes | Cooking time: 12 minutes | Servings: 4

Ingredients:

- 1 pound shrimp, peeled and deveined
- 1 cup chicken stock
- 1 tablespoon olive oil
- 1 tablespoon hot sauce
- 1 tablespoon hot paprika
- 1 tablespoon tomato sauce
- Salt and black pepper to the taste
- ½ bunch parsley, chopped
- 2 garlic cloves, minced
- 1 yellow onion, chopped.

Directions:

Set the instant pot on Sauté mode, add the oil, heat it up, add the onion and garlic, stir and sauté for 2 minutes. Add the rest of the ingredients, put the lid on and cook on High for 10 minutes. Release the pressure fast for 5 minutes, divide the stew into bowls and serve.

Nutrition: calories 176, fat 8, fiber 3, carbs 8, protein 11

Beef and Corn Stew
Prep time: 10 minutes | Cooking time: 30 minutes | Servings: 4

Ingredients:

- 1 tablespoon olive oil
- 1 and ½ pound beef stew meat, cubed
- 1 yellow onion, chopped
- 5 carrots, chopped
- Salt and black pepper to the taste
- 1 cup beef stock
- 1 cup tomato sauce
- ½ cup corn

Directions:

Set your instant pot on Sauté mode, add the oil, heat it up, add the meat and the onion and sauté for 5 minutes. Add the rest of the ingredients, put the lid on and cook on High for 25 minutes. Release the pressure naturally for 10 minutes, divide the stew into bowls and serve.

Nutrition: calories 271, fat 13, fiber 4, carbs 8, protein 14

Beef and Carrots Stew
Prep time: 10 minutes | Cooking time: 25 minutes | Servings: 4

Ingredients:

- 1 and ½ pounds beef stew meat, cubed
- 1 yellow onion, chopped
- 2 tablespoons olive oil
- 2 garlic cloves, chopped
- Salt and black pepper to the taste
- 4 carrots, cut into big chunks
- ½ cup beef stock
- 14 ounces canned tomatoes, chopped

Directions:

Set your instant pot on Sauté mode, add the oil, heat it up, add the meat, onion and garlic, stir and sauté for 5 minutes. Add the rest of the ingredients, put the lid on and cook on High for 20 minutes. Release the pressure naturally for 10 minutes, divide the stew into bowls and serve.

Nutrition: calories 264, fat 12, fiber 4, carbs 9, protein 18

Turkey and Potato Stew

Prep time: 10 minutes | Cooking time: 20 minutes | Servings: 4

Ingredients:

- 1 turkey breast, skinless, boneless and cubed
- 1 teaspoon olive oil
- Salt and black pepper to the taste
- 1 yellow onion, chopped
- 1 celery stalk, chopped
- 2 tablespoons tomato paste
- 2 cups chicken stock
- 2 cups tomatoes, chopped
- 1 and ½ pounds gold potatoes, peeled and cubed

Directions:

Set your instant pot on Sauté mode, add the oil, heat it up, add the meat and onion, stir and cook for 5 minutes. Add the rest of the ingredients, put the lid on and cook on High for 15 minutes. Release the pressure naturally for 10 minutes, divide the stew into bowls and serve.

Nutrition: calories 200, fat 12, fiber 5, carbs 9, protein 16

Chickpeas Stew

Prep time: 10 minutes | Cooking time: 25 minutes | Servings: 4

Ingredients:

- 1 yellow onion, chopped
- 2 garlic cloves, minced
- 1 pound chickpeas, rinsed and drained
- 20 ounces canned tomatoes, chopped
- 1 teaspoon oregano, dried
- 2 tablespoons olive oil
- A pinch of salt and black pepper
- ½ teaspoon red pepper flakes

Directions:

Set the instant pot on Sauté mode, add the oil, heat it up, add onion and the garlic, stir and cook for 5 minutes. Add all the other ingredients, put the lid on and cook on High for 20 minutes. Release the pressure naturally for 10 minutes, divide the stew into bowls and serve.

Nutrition: calories 200, fat 12, fiber 5, carbs 9, protein 10

Lentils and Potato Stew

Prep time: 10 minutes | Cooking time: 20 minutes | Servings: 4

Ingredients:

- 1 yellow onion, chopped
- 2 sweet potatoes, cubed
- 3 garlic cloves, chopped
- 1 celery stalk, chopped
- 1 and ½ cups green lentils
- 2 cups veggie stock
- ½ tablespoon olive oil
- 14 ounces canned tomatoes, chopped
- A pinch of salt and black pepper
- 1 teaspoon turmeric powder
- ½ teaspoon cinnamon powder
- 1 tablespoon cilantro, chopped

Directions:

Set your instant pot on Sauté mode, add the oil, heat it up, add onion, garlic and celery, stir and sauté for 2 minutes. Add salt, pepper, turmeric and cinnamon, stir and cook for 2 minutes more. Add the rest of the ingredients except the cilantro, put the lid on and cook on High for 15 minutes. Release the pressure fast for 5 minutes, add the cilantro, stir the stew, divide it into bowls and serve.

Nutrition: calories 182, fat 8, fiber 3, carbs 10, protein 11

Turmeric Kale Stew

Prep time: 5 minutes | Cooking time: 15 minutes | Servings: 4

Ingredients:

- 1 yellow onion, chopped
- 2 teaspoons olive oil
- 2 carrots, chopped
- 2 garlic cloves, minced
- 1 teaspoon turmeric powder
- A pinch of salt and black pepper
- 6 cups kale, torn
- 2 cups veggie stock
- 1 cup tomato puree

Directions:

Set your instant pot on Sauté mode, add the oil, heat it up, add onion, garlic and carrots, stir and sauté for 2 minutes. Add the rest of the ingredients, put the lid on and cook on High for 10 minutes. Release the pressure fast for 5 minutes, divide the stew into bowls and serve.

Nutrition: calories 172, fat 4, fiber 4, carbs 7, protein 8

Zucchini and Cabbage Stew

Prep time: 10 minutes | Cooking time: 15 minutes | Servings: 4

Ingredients:

- 2 tablespoons olive oil
- 2 zucchinis, sliced
- A pinch of salt and black pepper
- 1 small yellow onion, chopped
- 1 red chili, chopped
- 1 green cabbage head, shredded
- 2 tablespoons tomato sauce
- ¼ cup veggie stock
- 1 teaspoon sweet paprika

Directions:

Set your instant pot on Sauté mode, add the oil, heat it up, the onion, chili and the paprika, stir and sauté for 5 minutes. Add the rest of the ingredients, put the lid on and cook on High for 15 minutes. Release the pressure naturally for 10 minutes, divide the stew into bowls and serve.

Nutrition: calories 165, fat 5, fiber 3, carbs 9, protein 5

Chicken and Cranberries Stew

Prep time: 10 minutes | Cooking time: 25 minutes | Servings: 4

Ingredients:

- 1 tablespoon avocado oil
- 1 yellow onion, chopped
- 3 celery stalks, chopped
- A pinch of salt and black pepper
- 3 cups chicken meat, cooked and shredded
- 1 cup cranberries, dried
- 15 ounces canned tomatoes, chopped
- 5 cups chicken stock
- 1 tablespoon cilantro, chopped

Directions:

Set your instant pot on Sauté mode, add the oil, heat it up, add the onion and celery, stir and sauté for 5 minutes. Add the rest of the ingredients, put the lid on and cook on Low for 20 minutes. Release the pressure naturally for 10 minutes, divide the stew into bowls and serve.

Nutrition: calories 200, fat 12, fiber 4, carbs 8, protein 12

Mushroom and Carrots Stew

Prep time: 10 minutes | Cooking time: 25 minutes | Servings: 6

Ingredients:

- 1 tablespoon olive oil
- 1 red onion, chopped
- 1 teaspoon rosemary, chopped
- 1 and ½ cups chicken stock
- A pinch of salt and black pepper
- ¼ pound white mushrooms, sliced
- 4 carrots, chopped

Directions:

Set your instant pot on Sauté mode, add the oil, heat it up, add the onion and the mushrooms and sauté for 5 minutes. Add the remaining ingredients, put the lid on and cook on Low for 20 minutes. Release the pressure naturally for 10 minutes, divide the stew into bowls and serve.

Nutrition: calories 182, fat 4, fiber 4, carbs 8, protein 12

Artichokes and Beef Stew

Prep time: 10 minutes | Cooking time: 20 minutes | Servings: 4

Ingredients:

- 1 and ½ pounds beef stew meat, cubed
- 1 tablespoon avocado oil
- 1 yellow onion, chopped
- A pinch of salt and black pepper
- 3 carrots, chopped
- 2 garlic cloves, minced
- 10 ounces canned artichokes, drained and chopped
- 1 cup tomatoes, chopped
- 1 cup beef stock
- 1 tablespoon parsley, chopped

Directions:

Set the instant pot on Sauté mode, add the oil, heat it up, add the beef and brown for 3 minutes. Add the rest of the ingredients except the parsley, put the lid on and cook on High for 17 minutes. Release the pressure naturally for 10 minutes, add the parsley, divide the stew into bowls and serve.

Nutrition: calories 231, fat 13, fiber 3, carbs 8, protein 12

Greek Lamb Stew

Prep time: 10 minutes | Cooking time: 20 minutes | Servings: 4

Ingredients:

- 2 pounds lamb shoulder, cubed
- 1 tablespoon garlic, minced
- 14 ounces canned tomatoes, chopped
- 2 yellow onions, chopped
- 1 tablespoon olive oil
- 1 teaspoon oregano, dried
- 1 teaspoon basil, dried
- A pinch of salt and black pepper
- ½ cup parsley, chopped

Directions:

Set the pot on Sauté mode, add the oil, heat it up, add the onions, garlic and the meat, stir and brown for 5 minutes. Add the rest of the ingredients except the parsley, put the lid on and cook on High for 25 minutes. Release the pressure naturally for 10 minutes, add the parsley, divide the stew into bowls and serve.

Nutrition: calories 242, fat 12, fiber 4, carbs 9, protein 15

Lamb and Green Beans Stew

Prep time: 10 minutes | Cooking time: 20 minutes | Servings: 4

Ingredients:

- 1 yellow onion, chopped
- 1 and ½ pounds lamb shoulder, cubed
- A pinch of salt and black pepper
- ½ pound green beans, trimmed and halved
- 2 cups chicken stock
- 2 carrots, chopped
- ¼ cup parsley, minced

Directions:

In your instant pot, combine all the ingredients except the parsley, put the lid on and cook on High for 20 minutes. Release the pressure fast for 6 minutes, divide the stew into bowls and serve.

Nutrition: calories 251, fat 13, fiber 5, carbs 9, protein 15

Sausage and Tomatoes Stew

Prep time: 10 minutes | Cooking time: 20 minutes | Servings: 4

Ingredients:

- 1 pound pork sausage, sliced
- 14 ounces canned tomatoes, chopped
- 1 yellow onions, chopped
- A pinch of salt and black pepper
- 1 tablespoon avocado oil
- ½ cup beef stock

Directions:

Set the instant pot on Sauté mode, add the oil, heat it up, add the onion and the sausage and brown for 5 minutes. Add the rest of the ingredients, put the lid on and cook on Low for 15 minutes. Release the pressure naturally for 10 minutes, divide the stew into bowls and serve.

Nutrition: calories 200, fat 7, fiber 3, carbs 9, protein 12

Rosemary Beef and Parsnips Stew

Prep time: 10 minutes | Cooking time: 30 minutes | Servings: 4

Ingredients:

- 1 pound beef stew meat, cubed
- 2 tablespoons olive oil
- A pinch of salt and black pepper
- ¼ pound parsnips, sliced
- 4 garlic cloves, minced
- 2 cups beef stock
- 1 tablespoon tomato paste
- A bunch of rosemary, chopped

Directions:

Set the instant pot on Sauté mode, add the oil, heat it up, add the beef and the garlic and brown for 5 minutes stirring often. Add the parsnips and the rest of the ingredients, put the lid on and cook on High for 25 minutes. Release the pressure naturally for 10 minutes, divide the stew into bowls and serve.

Nutrition: calories 242, fat 12, fiber 4, carbs 9, protein 13

Italian Chicken and Spinach Stew

Prep time: 10 minutes | Cooking time: 25 minutes | Servings: 4

Ingredients:

- 1 pound chicken breast, skinless, boneless and cubed
- 1 tablespoon olive oil
- 1 yellow onion, chopped
- 2 cups spinach, torn
- 1 cup chicken stock
- ½ cup tomato sauce
- Salt and black pepper to the taste

Directions:

Set your instant pot on Sauté mode, add the oil, heat it up, add the onion and the chicken and brown for 5 minutes. Add the rest of the ingredients, put the lid on and cook on Low for 20 minutes. Release the pressure naturally for 10 minutes, divide the stew into bowls and serve.

Nutrition: calories 263, fat 11, fiber 3, carbs 6, protein 17

Chicken and Okra Stew

Prep time: 10 minutes | Cooking time: 20 minutes | Servings: 4

Ingredients:

- 1 yellow onion, chopped
- 1 pound chicken breast, skinless, boneless and cubed
- 1 garlic clove, minced
- 2 cups chicken stock
- 14 ounces okra
- 1 teaspoon five spice
- 12 ounces tomato sauce
- A pinch of salt and black pepper
- 2 teaspoons avocado oil
- ½ cup parsley, chopped
- Juice of 1 lime

Directions:

Set the instant pot on Sauté mode, add the oil, heat it up, add the meat and the onion and brown for 5 minutes. Add the rest of the ingredients except the parsley, put the lid on and cook on High for 15 minutes. Release the pressure naturally for 10 minutes, add the parsley, divide the stew into bowls and serve.

Nutrition: calories 253, fat 12, fiber 5, carbs 8, protein 16

Peas and Turkey Stew

Prep time: 10 minutes | Cooking time: 25 minutes | Servings: 4

Ingredients:

- 1 turkey breast, skinless, boneless and cubed
- 4 garlic cloves, minced
- 1 tablespoon olive oil
- 2 celery stalks, chopped
- 1 yellow onion, chopped
- 1 cup peas
- 2 bay leaves
- ¼ teaspoon thyme, dried
- A pinch of salt and black pepper
- 1 and ½ cups chicken stock
- 3 tablespoons tomato paste
- 1 tablespoon cilantro, chopped

Directions:

Set your instant pot on sauté mode, add the oil, heat it up, add the meat, garlic and the onion, stir and sauté for 5 minutes. Add the rest of the ingredients except the cilantro, put the lid on and cook on High for 20 minutes. Release the pressure naturally for 10 minutes, discard the bay leaves, add the parsley, divide the stew into bowls and serve.

Nutrition: calories 272, fat 12, fiber 4, carbs 7, protein 11

Turkey and Brussels Sprouts Stew

Prep time: 10 minutes | Cooking time: 25 minutes | Servings: 4

Ingredients:

- 1 pound turkey breast, skinless, boneless and cubed
- 1 pound Brussels sprouts, halved
- 1 shallot, chopped
- 2 garlic cloves, minced
- 1 tablespoon olive oil
- A pinch of salt and black pepper
- 1 tablespoon thyme, chopped
- ½ tablespoon tarragon, chopped
- 1 tablespoon parsley, chopped
- 1 cup chicken stock
- ½ cup tomato sauce

Directions:

Set your instant pot on sauté mode, add the oil, heat it up, add the meat, sprouts, shallot and garlic and brown for 5 minutes. Add the rest of the ingredients, put the lid on and cook on Low for 20 minutes. Release the pressure naturally for 10 minutes, divide the stew into bowls and serve.

Nutrition: calories 239, fat 14, fiber 4, carbs 9, protein 16

Lamb and Peppers Stew

Prep time: 5 minutes | Cooking time: 20 minutes | Servings: 4

Ingredients:

- 1 pound lamb shoulder, cubed
- 2 tablespoons olive oil
- 1 white onion, chopped
- 2 garlic cloves, minced
- 10 ounces mixed peppers, cut into strips
- 2 cups beef stock
- A pinch of salt and black pepper
- 1 tablespoon basil, dried
- 2 tablespoons thyme, chopped

Directions:

Set your instant pot on sauté mode, add the oil, heat it up, add the meat, garlic and onion and sauté for 5 minutes. Add the rest of the ingredients, put the lid on and cook on High for 15 minutes. Release the pressure fast for 5 minutes, divide the stew into bowls and serve.

Nutrition: calories 221, fat 11, fiber 4, carbs 6, protein 14

Cinnamon Pork Stew

Prep time: 10 minutes | Cooking time: 30 minutes | Servings: 4

Ingredients:

- 1 and ½ pounds pork shoulder, cubed
- 1 yellow onion, chopped
- 2 tablespoons olive oil
- 1 teaspoon cinnamon powder
- 2 garlic cloves, chopped
- A pinch of salt and black pepper
- ½ cup beef stock
- 12 ounces canned tomatoes, chopped
- 1 tablespoon basil, chopped

Directions:

Set your instant pot on Sauté mode, add the oil, heat it up, add the meat, onion, garlic and the cinnamon, toss and brown for 5 minutes. Add the rest of the ingredients except the basil, put the lid on and cook on Low for 25 minutes. Release the pressure naturally for 10 minutes, divide the stew into bowls, sprinkle the basil and serve.

Nutrition: calories 231, fat 12, fiber 3, carbs 7, protein 9

Pesto Pork Stew

Prep time: 10 minutes | Cooking time: 30 minutes | Servings: 4

Ingredients:

- 1 yellow onion, chopped
- 1 pound pork stew meat, cubed
- 1 garlic clove, minced
- 1 cup chicken stock
- 12 ounces tomato sauce
- 1 tablespoon olive oil
- Juice of ½ lemon
- 1 tablespoon parsley, chopped
- 1 tablespoon basil pesto

Directions:

Set the instant pot on Sauté mode, add the oil, heat it up, add the meat, onion and garlic and sauté for 5 minutes. Add the rest of the ingredients, put the lid on and cook on Low for 25 minutes. Release the pressure naturally for 10 minutes, divide the stew into bowls and serve.

Nutrition: calories 233, fat 12, fiber 4, carbs 7, protein 15

Beef and Turnips Stew

Prep time: 10 minutes | Cooking time: 40 minutes | Servings: 6

Ingredients:

- 2 pounds beef stew meat, cubed
- 2 cups chicken stock
- 3 garlic cloves, chopped
- 1 cup tomato sauce
- Salt and black pepper to the taste
- 3 turnips, cut into quarters

Directions:

In your instant pot, combine all the ingredients, put the lid on and cook on Low for 40 minutes. Release the pressure naturally for 10 minutes, divide the stew into bowls and serve.

Nutrition: calories 221, fat 12, fiber 4, carbs 7, protein 11

Oregano Lamb and Tomatoes Stew

Prep time: 10 minutes | Cooking time: 40 minutes | Servings: 4

Ingredients:

- 4 lamb shanks
- 2 tablespoons olive oil
- 1 yellow onion, chopped
- 2 garlic cloves, minced
- 1 and ½ cups tomatoes, cubed
- 1 tablespoon oregano, chopped
- A pinch of salt and black pepper
- 2 cups beef stock

Directions:

Set your instant pot on Sauté mode, add the oil, heat it up, add the lamb, and brown for 4 minutes. Add the rest of the ingredients, put the lid on and cook on Low for 35 minutes. Release the pressure naturally for 10 minutes, divide the stew into bowls and serve.

Nutrition: calories 230, fat 14, fiber 4, carbs 7, protein 11

Chili Beef Stew

Prep time: 5 minutes | Cooking time: 20 minutes | Servings: 4

Ingredients:

- 1 pound beef stew meat, ground
- 2 cups beef stock
- 10 ounces Salsa Verde
- 1 teaspoon chili powder
- A pinch of salt and black pepper
- 1 tablespoon cilantro, chopped

Directions:

In your instant pot, combine all the ingredients except the cilantro, put the lid on and cook on High for 20 minutes. Release the pressure fast for 5 minutes, divide the stew into bowls, sprinkle the cilantro on top and serve.

Nutrition: calories 201, fat 7, fiber 4, carbs 7, protein 9

Lemon Kale and Chicken Stew

Prep time: 10 minutes | Cooking time: 20 minutes | Servings: 4

Ingredients:

- 1 pound chicken breast, skinless, boneless and cubed
- 2 cups kale, torn
- ½ cup chicken stock
- ½ cup tomato sauce
- A pinch of salt and black pepper
- 1 tablespoon cilantro, chopped

Directions:

In your instant pot, combine all the ingredients, put the lid on and cook on High for 20 minutes. Release the pressure naturally for 10 minutes, divide the stew into bowls and serve.

Nutrition: calories 192, fat 8, fiber 4, carbs 8, protein 12

Tarragon Beef Stew

Prep time: 10 minutes | Cooking time: 30 minutes | Servings: 4

Ingredients:

- 1 and ½ pounds beef stew meat, cubed
- 3 garlic cloves, minced
- 2 tablespoons olive oil
- 1 cup tomato sauce
- ½ cup beef stock
- 1 tablespoon tarragon, chopped
- A pinch of salt and black pepper

Directions:

Set your instant pot on Sauté mode, add the oil, heat it up, add the meat and the garlic and brown for 5 minutes. Add the rest of the ingredients, put the lid on and cook on Low for 25 minutes. Release the pressure naturally for 10 minutes, divide the stew into bowls and serve.

Nutrition: calories 200, fat 12, fiber 4, carbs 6, protein 9

Bacon and Spinach Stew

Prep time: 10 minutes | Cooking time: 15 minutes | Servings: 4

Ingredients:

- 2 cups bacon, chopped
- 1 teaspoon olive oil
- 1 pound spinach, torn
- ½ cup chicken stock
- 3 tablespoons tomato paste

Directions:

Set your instant pot on sauté mode, add the oil, heat it up, add the bacon and cook for 5 minutes. Add the rest of the ingredients, put the lid on and cook on Low for 12 minutes. Release the pressure naturally for 10 minutes, divide the stew into bowls and serve.

Nutrition: calories 195, fat 4, fiber 5, carbs 9, protein 6

Shrimp and Cod Stew

Prep time: 5 minutes | Cooking time: 15 minutes | Servings: 4

Ingredients:

- 1 pound shrimp, peeled and deveined
- 7 ounces canned tomatoes, chopped
- ½ bunch parsley, chopped
- ¼ cup chicken stock
- 1 pound cod fillets, boneless, skinless and cubed

Directions:

In your instant pot, combine all the ingredients, put the lid on and cook on Low for 12 minutes. Release the pressure fast for 5 minutes, divide the mix into bowls and serve.

Nutrition: calories 160, fat 4, fiber 3, carbs 7, protein 9

Green Beans and Chicken Stew

Prep time: 10 minutes | Cooking time: 15 minutes | Servings: 4

Ingredients:

- 1 tablespoon olive oil
- 2 garlic cloves, minced
- 1 pound chicken breast, skinless, boneless and cubed
- 1 pound green beans, trimmed
- 14 ounces canned tomatoes, chopped

Directions:

Set the instant pot on Sauté mode, add the oil, heat it up, add the meat and garlic and sauté for 5 minutes. Add the rest of the ingredients, put the lid on and cook on High for 15 minutes. Release the pressure naturally for 10 minutes, divide the stew into bowls and serve.

Nutrition: calories 200, fat 8, fiber 5, carbs 8, protein 10

Turmeric Quinoa and Chicken Stew

Prep time: 6 minutes | Cooking time: 20 minutes | Servings: 4

Ingredients:

- 1 tablespoon olive oil
- ½ cup quinoa, rinsed
- 3 cups chicken stock
- 1 pound chicken breast, skinless, boneless and cubed
- ½ teaspoon cumin, ground
- 1 red onion, chopped
- 4 garlic cloves, minced
- ½ teaspoon turmeric powder
- A pinch of salt and black pepper
- 1 teaspoon lemon juice

Directions:

Set the instant pot on sauté mode, add the oil, heat it up, add the meat, onion, garlic, turmeric and cumin, toss and brown for 5 minutes. Add the remaining ingredients, put the lid on and cook on High for 15 minutes. Release the pressure fast for 6 minutes, stir the stew, divide it into bowls and serve.

Nutrition: calories 200, fat 12, fiber 4, carbs 7, protein 14

Lime Pork and Sweet Potato Stew

Prep time: 10 minutes | Cooking time: 30 minutes | Servings: 4

Ingredients:

- 1 yellow onion, chopped
- 1 tablespoon olive oil
- 2 garlic cloves, minced
- 3 sweet potatoes, cubed
- 1 pound pork stew meat, cubed
- 14 ounces canned tomatoes, chopped
- 2 teaspoons curry powder
- Juice of 2 limes
- 1 tablespoon cilantro, chopped

Directions:

Set your instant pot on sauté mode, add the oil, heat it up, add the onion, garlic and the meat, and cook for 5 minutes. Add the remaining ingredients except the cilantro, put the lid on and cook on High for 25 minutes. Release the pressure naturally for 10 minutes, divide the stew into bowls and serve with the cilantro sprinkled on top.

Nutrition: calories 200, fat 12, fiber 4, carbs 7, protein 14

Chili Green Beans and Pea Stew

Prep time: 5 minutes | Cooking time: 15 minutes | Servings: 4

Ingredients:

- 1 yellow onion, chopped
- 1 and ½ tablespoons olive oil
- 5 garlic cloves, minced
- 1 teaspoon sweet paprika
- ¼ teaspoon chili powder
- A pinch of salt and black pepper
- ½ cup tomatoes, chopped
- 2 cups yellow peas
- 1 pound green beans, trimmed and halved
- ½ cup veggie stock
- 1 tablespoon parsley, chopped

Directions:

Set your instant pot on sauté mode, add the oil, heat it up, add the onion, cloves, paprika and chili powder, stir and cook for 5 minutes. Add the rest of the ingredients, put the lid on and cook on High for 10 minutes. Release the pressure fast for 5 minutes, divide the stew into bowls and serve.

Nutrition: calories 212, fat 6, fiber 3, carbs 5, protein 7

Corn and Peas Stew

Prep time: 10 minutes | Cooking time: 15 minutes | Servings: 4

Ingredients:

- 2 tablespoons olive oil
- 2 carrots, chopped
- 1 yellow onion, chopped
- 2 garlic cloves, minced
- 14 ounces canned tomatoes, chopped
- 1 cup corn
- 1 cup peas
- A pinch of salt and black pepper
- 1 tablespoon cilantro, chopped

Directions:

Set your instant pot on sauté mode, add the oil, heat it up, add the onion and the garlic, stir and cook for 5 minutes. Add the rest of the ingredients except the cilantro, put the lid on and cook on High for 10 minutes. Release the pressure naturally for 10 minutes, divide the stew into bowls and serve with the cilantro sprinkled on top.

Nutrition: calories 181, fat 5, fiber 2, carbs 5, protein 10

Potato and Mango Stew

Prep time: 5 minutes | Cooking time: 15 minutes | Servings: 4

Ingredients:

- 1 tablespoon cumin, ground
- A pinch of salt and black pepper
- ½ teaspoon turmeric powder
- 1 mango, peeled and cubed
- 4 gold potatoes, peeled and cubed
- 1 cup veggie stock
- 1 teaspoon sweet paprika
- 2 tablespoons olive oil
- 2 spring onions, chopped

Directions:

Set your instant pot on sauté mode, add the oil, heat it up, add the onion, cumin and turmeric, stir and sauté for 3 minutes. Add the potatoes and the rest of the ingredients, put the lid on and cook on High for 12 minutes. Release the pressure fast for 5 minutes, divide the stew into bowls and serve.

Nutrition: calories 181, fat 9, fiber 4, carbs 6, protein 7

Coconut Cauliflower Stew

Prep time: 5 minutes | Cooking time: 25 minutes | Servings: 4

Ingredients:

- 4 garlic cloves, minced
- 1 yellow onion, chopped
- ½ teaspoon coriander, ground
- ½ teaspoon cayenne pepper
- 2 cups coconut, shredded
- 2 tomatoes, cubed
- 2 cups cauliflower florets
- 1 cup veggie stock
- A pinch of salt and black pepper
- 1 teaspoon olive oil

Directions:

Set your instant pot on sauté mode, add the oil, heat it up, add the onion and the garlic, stir and sauté for 5 minutes. Add the cauliflower and the rest of the ingredients, put the lid on and cook on Low for 15 minutes. Release the pressure fast for 5 minutes, divide the stew into bowls and serve.

Nutrition: calories 198, fat 8, fiber 4, carbs 9, protein 5

Shrimp and Lentils Stew

Prep time: 5 minutes | Cooking time: 20 minutes | Servings: 4

Ingredients:

- 1 tablespoon olive oil
- 1 yellow onion, chopped
- 1 celery stalk, chopped
- 1 teaspoon curry powder
- 1 and ½ cups lentils
- 2 cups chicken stock
- 1 pound shrimp, peeled and deveined
- 2 cups tomatoes, chopped
- Salt and black pepper to the taste

Directions:

Set your instant pot on Sauté mode, add oil, heat it up, add the onion, stir and cook for 5 minutes. Add the rest of the ingredients, put the lid on and cook on Low for 15 minutes. Release the pressure fast for 5 minutes, divide the stew into bowls.

Nutrition: calories 174, fat 7, fiber 3, carbs 5, protein 6

Smoked Chickpeas and Lamb Stew

Prep time: 10 minutes | Cooking time: 30 minutes | Servings: 4

Ingredients:

- 1 tablespoon olive oil
- 2 cups red bell pepper, chopped
- 1 yellow onion, chopped
- 2 teaspoons garlic, minced
- 1 cup chickpeas, rinsed and drained
- 1 cup tomatoes, chopped
- 3 2 teaspoons smoked paprika
- 2 teaspoons marjoram, dried
- 1 pound lamb shoulder, cubed
- A pinch of salt and black pepper

Directions:

Set your instant pot on Sauté mode, add the oil, heat it up, add the onion and the garlic and sauté for 5 minutes. Add the lamb and brown it for 2 minutes. Add the rest of the ingredients, put the lid on and cook on Low for 25 minutes. Release the pressure naturally for 10 minutes, divide the stew into bowls and serve.

Nutrition: calories 200, fat 14, fiber 4, carbs 6, protein 11

Ground Pork Stew

Prep time: 10 minutes | Cooking time: 20 minutes | Servings: 4

Ingredients:

- 1 yellow onion, chopped
- ½ tablespoon olive oil
- 2 and ½ pounds pork meat, ground
- 1 cup tomato paste
- 2 jalapenos, chopped
- 4 tablespoons garlic, minced
- A pinch of salt and black pepper
- 1 teaspoon oregano, dried

Directions:

Set your instant pot on sauté mode, add the oil, heat it up, add the pork, onion and the garlic and brown for 4 minutes. Add the rest of the ingredients, put the lid on and cook on Low for 16 minutes. Release the pressure naturally for 10 minutes, divide the stew into bowls and serve.

Nutrition: calories 177, fat 7, fiber 2, carbs 6, protein 14

Sage Pork Stew

Prep time: 10 minutes | Cooking time: 30 minutes | Servings: 4

Ingredients:

- 1 yellow onion, chopped
- 2 pounds pork stew meat, cubed
- 2 tablespoons olive oil
- 3 carrots, chopped
- 1 cup beef stock
- 2 garlic clove, minced
- Salt and black pepper to the taste
- 1 tablespoon sage, chopped

Directions:

Set your instant pot on sauté mode, add the oil, heat it up, add the meat, onion and garlic and brown for 5 minutes. Add the rest of the ingredients, put the lid on and cook on Low for 25 minutes. Release the pressure naturally for 10 minutes, divide the stew into bowls and serve with sage sprinkled on top.

Nutrition: calories 220, fat 12, fiber 4, carbs 7, protein 16

Salmon and Mushrooms Stew

Prep time: 10 minutes | Cooking time: 20 minutes | Servings: 4

Ingredients:

- 1 and ½ pound salmon fillets, boneless, skinless and cubed
- 1 cup chicken stock
- 2 shallots, chopped
- 10 ounces canned tomatoes, chopped
- A pinch of salt and black pepper
- 1 pound white mushrooms, sliced
- 1 tablespoon thyme, chopped

Directions:

In your instant pot, combine the salmon with the mushrooms and the remaining ingredients, put the lid on and cook on Low for 20 minutes. Release the pressure fast for 5 minutes, divide the stew into bowls and serve.

Nutrition: calories 205, fat 7, fiber 4, carbs 6, protein 10

Saffron Trout and Potato Stew

Prep time: 10 minutes | Cooking time: 10 minutes | Servings: 4

Ingredients:

- 1 cup chicken stock
- 4 sweet potatoes, cubed
- 2 shallots, chopped
- 2 garlic cloves, minced
- ¼ teaspoon saffron powder
- 1 pound trout fillets, boneless, skinless and cubed
- 1 tablespoon chives, chopped
- 1 tablespoon basil, chopped

Directions:

In your instant pot, combine trout with potatoes and the rest of the ingredients except the chives, put the lid on and cook on Low for 12 minutes. Release the pressure fast for 5 minutes, divide the mix into bowls and serve with chives sprinkled on top.

Nutrition: calories 190, fat 8, fiber 4, carbs 5, protein 9

Sausage, Shrimp and Peppers Stew
Prep time: 10 minutes | Cooking time: 20 minutes | Servings: 4

Ingredients:
- ½ pound pork sausage, sliced
- 1 tablespoon olive oil
- 1 yellow onion, chopped
- 1 cup chicken stock
- ¼ cup tomato sauce
- 1 pound shrimp, peeled and deveined
- 1 cup mixed bell peppers, cut into strips
- A pinch of sea salt and pepper

Directions:

Set the instant pot on Sauté mode, add the oil, heat it up, add the sausage and the onion and cook for 3 minutes. Add the rest of the ingredients, put the lid on and cook on Low for 15 minutes. Release the pressure naturally for 10 minutes, divide the stew into bowls and serve.

Nutrition: calories 190, fat 4, fiber 1, carbs 5, protein 6

Zucchini and Okra Stew
Prep time: 5 minutes | Cooking time: 12 minutes | Servings: 4

Ingredients:
- 2 zucchinis, sliced
- 1 and ½ cups tomatoes, chopped
- 1 yellow onion, chopped
- 3 garlic cloves, minced
- 1 tablespoon olive oil
- 2 cups okra, trimmed
- ½ cup basil, chopped
- A pinch of salt and black pepper

Directions:

Set your instant pot on Sauté mode, add the oil, heat it up, add the onion and garlic and sauté for 2 minutes. Add the rest of the ingredients, put the lid on and cook on High for 10 minutes. Release the pressure fast for 5 minutes, divide the stew into bowls and serve.

Nutrition: calories 179, fat 4, fiber 2, carbs 6, protein 9

Orange Pork Stew
Prep time: 10 minutes | Cooking time: 30 minutes | Servings: 4

Ingredients:
- 1 and ½ pounds pork shoulder, cubed
- 3 garlic cloves, minced
- 1 red onion, chopped
- Juice of 1 orange
- A pinch of salt and black pepper
- 1 tablespoon ginger, grated
- 1 teaspoon rosemary, dried
- 1 tablespoon olive oil

Directions:

Set your instant pot on Sauté mode, add the oil, heat it up, add the onion, the meat and the garlic, and brown for 5 minutes. Add the rest of the ingredients, put the lid on and cook on Low for 25 minutes. Release the pressure naturally for 10 minutes, divide the stew into bowls and serve.

Nutrition: calories 200, fat 12, fiber 4, carbs 7, protein 16

Coconut Beef and Cauliflower Stew

Prep time: 5 minutes | Cooking time: 25 minutes | Servings: 4

Ingredients:

- 1 tablespoon olive oil
- 1 pound beef stew meat, cubed
- 1 teaspoon rosemary, chopped
- 1 red onion, chopped
- 1 celery stalk, chopped
- 1 and ½ cups beef stock
- A pinch of salt and black pepper
- ¼ cup coconut cream
- 1 tablespoon oregano, chopped

Directions:

Set your instant pot on Sauté mode, add the oil, heat it up, add the meat and onion and brown for 5 minutes. Add the celery and the rest of the ingredients except the cream, put the lid on and cook on High for 15 minutes. Release the pressure fast for 5 minutes, add the cream, toss, set the pot on sauté mode and cook the stew for 5 minutes more. Divide the stew into bowls and serve.

Nutrition: calories 241, fat 12, fiber 3, carbs 6, protein 14

Ginger Mushroom Stew

Prep time: 5 minutes | Cooking time: 15 minutes | Servings: 4

Ingredients:

- 1 pound cremini mushrooms, sliced
- 1 tablespoon ginger, grated
- 1 and ¼ cups veggie stock
- 2 spring onions, chopped
- 2 garlic cloves, minced
- A pinch of salt and black pepper
- 1 cup tomato sauce
- ¼ cup basil, chopped

Directions:

In your instant pot, combine the mushrooms with the ginger and the rest of the ingredients, put the lid on and cook on High for 15 minutes. Release the pressure fast for 5 minutes, divide the stew into bowls and serve.

Nutrition: calories 140, fat 9, fiber 4, carbs 5, protein 6

Ground Turkey and Beans Stew

Prep time: 10 minutes | Cooking time: 25 minutes | Servings: 4

Ingredients:

- 1 pound turkey meat, ground
- 1 cup red beans, soaked overnight and drained
- 2 tablespoons olive oil
- 3 cups chicken stock
- 4 garlic cloves, minced
- ¼ cup tomato paste

Directions:

Set your instant pot on Sauté mode, add the oil, heat it up, add the meat and the garlic, stir and brown for 5 minutes. Add the rest of the ingredients, put the lid on and cook on High for 20 minutes. Release the pressure naturally for 10 minutes, divide the stew into bowls and serve.

Nutrition: calories 198, fat 9, fiber 4, carbs 7, protein 14

Creamy Red Potato Stew

Prep time: 5 minutes | Cooking time: 30 minutes | Servings: 4

Ingredients:

- 1 tablespoon olive oil
- 2 shallots, chopped
- 1 yellow onion, chopped
- 4 red potatoes, peeled and cubed
- 1 cup chicken stock
- 1 cup coconut cream

Directions:

Set your instant pot on Sauté mode, add the oil, heat it up, add the shallots and sauté for 5 minutes. Add the potatoes and the rest of the ingredients except the cream and dill, put the lid on and cook on Low for 20 minutes. Release the pressure fast for 5 minutes, set the pot on Sauté mode again, add the cream and dill, cook the stew for 5 minutes more, divide into bowls and serve hot.

Nutrition: calories 203, fat 8, fiber 2, carbs 6, protein 11

Chicken and Olives Stew

Prep time: 10 minutes | Cooking time: 35 minutes | Servings: 4

Ingredients:

- 1 pound chicken breast, skinless, boneless and cubed
- 1 tablespoon olive oil
- 1 cup kalamata olives, pitted
- 1 red onion, chopped
- 1 cup chicken stock
- 10 ounces canned tomatoes,
- 1 tablespoon oregano, chopped

Directions:

Set your instant pot on Sauté mode, add the oil, heat it up, add the chicken and the onion and brown for 5 minutes. Add the rest of the ingredients except the oregano, put the lid on and cook on Low for 30 minutes. Release the pressure fast for 6 minutes, add the oregano, stir, divide the stew into bowls and serve right away.

Nutrition: calories 191, fat 9, fiber 3, carbs 6, protein 16

Walnuts Dip

Prep time: 5 minutes | Cooking time: 5 minutes | Servings: 4

Ingredients:

- 8 ounces cream cheese, soft
- 2 tablespoons walnuts, chopped
- A pinch of salt and black pepper
- 1 and ½ teaspoons sweet paprika
- 1 tablespoon lime juice
- 1 cup water

Directions:

In a bowl, combine all the ingredients except the water, blend them well and transfer to a ramekin. Put the water in the instant pot, add the trivet inside, put the ramekin in the trivet, put the lid on and cook on Low for 5 minutes. Release the pressure fast for 5 minutes and serve the dip right away.

Nutrition: calories 132, fat 1, fiber 2, carbs 6, protein 5

Bell Peppers Spread

Prep time: 10 minutes | Cooking time: 15 minutes | Servings: 4

Ingredients:

- 1 pound red bell peppers, deseeded and roughly chopped
- 2 garlic cloves, minced
- 1 tablespoon lemon juice
- 1 tablespoon olive oil
- A pinch of salt and black pepper
- 1 tablespoon basil, chopped

Directions:

In your instant pot, combine the bell peppers with the rest of the ingredients, put the lid on and cook on High for 15 minutes. Release the pressure naturally for 10 minutes, transfer the mix to your blender, pulse well, divide into bowls and serve as a dip.

Nutrition: calories 140, fat 4, fiber 3, carbs 6, protein 6

Stuffed Peppers

Prep time: 10 minutes | Cooking time: 15 minutes | Servings: 4

Ingredients:

- 4 red bell peppers, halved lengthwise and deseeded
- 2 tablespoons parsley, chopped
- 2 tablespoons pumpkin seeds
- 2 cups basil, chopped
- ¼ cup parmesan, grated
- 1 tablespoon garlic, minced
- 2 teaspoons lime juice
- 1 tablespoon olive oil
- 1 cup baby spinach, torn
- 2 cups water

Directions:

In a bowl, mix all the ingredients except the water, toss them and stuff the bell peppers with this mix. Put the water in your instant pot, add the trivet inside and arrange the bell peppers in the pot. Put the lid on and cook on High for 15 minutes. Release the pressure naturally for 10 minutes, arrange the peppers on a platter and serve.

Nutrition: calories 160, fat 9, fiber 4, carbs 6, protein 7

Shrimp Salad

Prep time: 5 minutes | Cooking time: 6 minutes | Servings: 4

Ingredients:

- 1 pound shrimp, peeled and deveined
- 2 cups baby arugula
- 1 tablespoon balsamic vinegar
- 2 tablespoons tomato paste
- 2 spring onions, chopped
- ½ teaspoon olive oil
- ½ teaspoon chili powder
- ½ teaspoon oregano, chopped
- ½ teaspoon garlic, minced

Directions:

Set the instant pot on Sauté mode, add the oil, heat it up, add the onions and sauté for 2 minutes. Add the rest of the ingredients except the arugula and the vinegar, put the lid on and cook on High for 4 minutes. Release the pressure fast for 5 minutes, transfer the shrimp mixture to a bowl, add the arugula and the vinegar, toss and serve as an appetizer.

Nutrition: calories 170, fat 9, fiber 4, carbs 7, protein 6

Chives Salmon Bites

Prep time: 10 minutes | Cooking time: 10 minutes | Servings: 4

Ingredients:

- 1 tablespoon lemon juice
- 1 tablespoon olive oil
- 1 pound salmon fillets, boneless, skinless and cubed
- 2 garlic cloves, minced
- 1 tablespoon chives, chopped
- 1 tablespoon lime zest, grated
- 1 cup water

Directions:

In a bowl, mix the salmon cubes with the rest of the ingredients except the chives and the water and toss. Put the water in your instant pot, add the steamer basket, add the salmon inside, put the lid on and cook on High for 10 minutes. Release the pressure naturally for 10 minutes, arrange the salmon biter on a platter, sprinkle the chives on top and serve.

Nutrition: calories 180, fat 3, fiber 3, carbs 7, protein 9

Eggplant Salad

Prep time: 5 minutes | Cooking time: 10 minutes | Servings: 4

Ingredients:

- 2 eggplants, roughly cubed
- 2 teaspoons cumin, ground
- 2 tablespoons olive oil
- 1 cup tomato, cubed
- ½ cup spring onions, chopped
- 2 tablespoons garlic, minced
- 1 Serrano chili pepper, chopped
- ¼ cup cilantro, chopped

Directions:

Set the instant pot on Sauté mode, add the oil, heat it up, add the onions, garlic and chili pepper and sauté for 2 minutes. Add the rest of the ingredients, put the lid on and cook on High for 8 minutes. Release the pressure fast for 5 minutes, divide the salad into cups and serve as an appetizer.

Nutrition: calories 150, fat 9, fiber 2, carbs 6, protein 6

Basil Shrimp Salad

Prep time: 5 minutes | Cooking time: 6 minutes | Servings: 4

Ingredients:

- ½ cup lime juice
- 1 red onion, chopped
- ½ teaspoon hot sauce
- ½ cup balsamic vinegar
- 1 and ½ pounds shrimp, peeled and deveined
- 1 tablespoon olive oil
- 2 tablespoons basil, chopped

Directions:

Set the instant pot on Sauté mode, add the oil, heat it up, add the onion and sauté for 2 minutes. Add the rest of the ingredients, put the lid on and cook on High for 4 minutes. Release the pressure fast for 5 minutes, divide the shrimp mix into small bowls and serve.

Nutrition: calories 173, fat 9, fiber 3, carbs 5, protein 8

Spinach Dip

Prep time: 5 minutes | Cooking time: 8 minutes | Servings: 4

Ingredients:

- 15 ounces spinach leaves
- 2 tablespoons coconut cream
- 2 tablespoons olive oil
- 4 garlic cloves, roasted and minced
- 2 tablespoons lemon juice

Directions:

In your instant pot, combine all the ingredients except the cream, put the lid on and cook on Low for 8 minutes. Release the pressure fast for 5 minutes, add the cream, blend the mix using an immersion blender, divide into bowls and serve.

Nutrition: calories 183, fat 9, fiber 4, carbs 7, protein 5

Mint Spinach and Shrimp Salad

Prep time: 5 minutes | Cooking time: 10 minutes | Servings: 4

Ingredients:

- 1 pound spinach leaves, torn
- 1 pound shrimp, peeled and deveined
- 1 shallot, sliced
- ½ tablespoons olive oil
- 2 tablespoons mint leaves, chopped
- ½ cup coconut cream
- A pinch of salt and black pepper

Directions:

Set the instant pot on Sauté mode, add the oil, heat it up, add the shallot and sauté for 2 minutes. Add the rest of the ingredients, put the lid on and cook on Low for 8 minutes. Release the pressure fast for 5 minutes, divide the mix into bowls and serve as an appetizer.

Nutrition: calories 180, fat 9, fiber 2, carbs 6, protein 9

Red Beans Spread

*Prep time: 10 minutes | **Cooking time:** 18 minutes | Servings: 4*

Ingredients:

- 1 pound red beans, soaked overnight and drained
- 1 cup red onion, chopped
- 4 cups veggie stock

- 1 tablespoon sweet paprika
- 1 tablespoon lime juice
- 2 tablespoons olive oil
- 2 garlic cloves, minced

Directions:

In your instant pot, combine the beans with the stock, put the lid on and cook on High for 18 minutes. Release the pressure naturally, drain the beans, transfer them to a blender, add ½ cup cooking liquid and the rest of the ingredients and pulse well. Divide the spread into bowls and serve as an appetizer.

Nutrition: calories 210, fat 7, fiber 4, carbs 6, protein 10

Cod Salad

*Prep time: 10 minutes | **Cooking time:** 10 minutes | Servings: 4*

Ingredients:

- 1 teaspoon avocado oil
- 1 pound cod fillets, boneless, skinless and cubed
- A pinch of salt and black pepper
- 2 tomatoes, cubed

- 1 teaspoon oregano, dried
- 1 teaspoon rosemary, dried
- 1 and ½ cups baby arugula
- 1 tablespoon lime juice
- 1 red onion, chopped

Directions:

Set the instant pot on Sauté mode, add the oil, heat it up, add the onion and sauté for 2 minutes. Add the rest of the ingredients except the arugula, put the lid on and cook on High for 8 minutes. Release the pressure naturally for 10 minutes, transfer the cod mix to a bowl, add the arugula, toss and serve.

Nutrition: calories 180, fat 9, fiber 4, carbs 6, protein 8

Pesto Shrimp and Tomato Salad

*Prep time: 10 minutes | **Cooking time:** 8 minutes | Servings: 4*

Ingredients:

- 1 and ½ pounds shrimp, peeled and deveined
- 2 tablespoons parsley, chopped
- 2 tablespoons basil pesto
- 2 teaspoons lime juice

- 1 tablespoon olive oil
- A pinch of salt and black pepper
- ½ pound cherry tomatoes, cubed
- 1 cup baby arugula

Directions:

In your instant pot, combine all the ingredients except the arugula, toss, put the lid on and cook on Low for 8 minutes. Release the pressure naturally for 10 minutes, transfer the mix to a bowl, add the arugula, toss and serve as an appetizer.

Nutrition: calories 177, fat 8, fiber 2, carbs 6, protein 7

Chicken and Peppers Salad

Prep time: 10 minutes | Cooking time: 15 minutes | Servings: 4

Ingredients:

- 1 pound chicken breast, skinless, boneless and cubed
- 1 pound mixed bell peppers, cut into strips
- 2 tablespoons olive oil
- 2 cups red onion, chopped
- 2 tablespoons garlic, chopped
- 1 cup chicken stock
- 1 cup tomatoes, crushed
- 1 tablespoon basil, chopped

Directions:

Set your instant pot on Sauté mode, add the oil, heat it up, add the chicken and the onion and brown for 5 minutes. Add the rest of the ingredients except the basil, put the lid on and cook on High for 10 minutes. Release the pressure naturally for 10 minutes, divide the mix into bowls, sprinkle the basil on top and serve as an appetizer.

Nutrition: calories 221, fat 12, fiber 4, carbs 7, protein 11

Mussels and Spinach Bowls

Prep time: 10 minutes | Cooking time: 10 minutes | Servings: 4

Ingredients:

- 2 pounds mussels, cleaned and scrubbed
- 1 red onion, chopped
- 1 pound baby spinach
- ½ cup chicken stock
- 2 garlic cloves, minced
- 1 teaspoon chili powder
- 1 tablespoon chives, chopped
- 1 tablespoon olive oil

Directions:

Set instant pot on Sauté mode, add the oil, heat it up, add the onion and the garlic, stir and sauté for 2 minutes. Add the rest of the ingredients except the spinach and the chives, put the lid on and cook on Low for 8 minutes. Release the pressure naturally for 10 minutes, transfer the mussels mix to a bowl, add the spinach and the chives and toss. Divide the salad into small bowls and serve as an appetizer.

Nutrition: calories 180, fat 9, fiber 3, carbs 5, protein 7

Tomato Salsa

Prep time: 5 minutes | Cooking time: 7 minutes | Servings: 4

Ingredients:

- 1 and ½ pound cherry tomatoes, cubed
- 2 chili peppers, chopped
- ¼ cup veggie stock
- 2 tablespoons olive oil
- ¼ cup balsamic vinegar
- 2 red onions, chopped
- 1 tablespoon basil, chopped
- 1 tablespoon parsley, chopped
- 1 tablespoon chives, chopped
- 1 cucumber, cubed

Directions:

In your instant pot, combine the tomatoes with the chili peppers and stock, put the lid on and cook on Low for 7 minutes. Release the pressure fast for 5 minutes, transfer the tomatoes to a bowl, add the rest of the ingredients, toss, divide into cups and serve.

Nutrition: calories 140, fat 4, fiber 3, carbs 5, protein 4

Hot Mussels Salad

Prep time: 6 minutes | Cooking time: 10 minutes | Servings: 4

Ingredients:

- 2 pounds mussels, scrubbed
- 1 and ½ cups baby spinach
- 2 tablespoons olive oil
- 1 yellow onion, chopped
- 1 teaspoon hot paprika
- 14 ounces tomatoes, chopped
- 2 teaspoons garlic, minced
- 2 teaspoons oregano, dried
- 1 teaspoon basil, dried
- 1 tablespoon parsley, chopped

Directions:

Set your instant pot on Sauté mode, add the oil, heat it up, add the onion and the garlic and sauté for 2 minutes. Add the rest of the ingredients except the parsley, put the lid on and cook on Low for 7 minutes. Release the pressure fast for 6 minutes, divide the mussels mix into small bowls, sprinkle the parsley on top and serve.

Nutrition: calories 176, fat 4, fiber 3, carbs 6, protein 7

Turkey Salad

Prep time: 10 minutes | Cooking time: 15 minutes | Servings: 4

Ingredients:

- 1 and ½ pounds turkey breast, skinless, boneless and cubed
- 2 tomatoes, cubed
- 2 red bell peppers, cut into strips
- 1 tablespoon olive oil
- 2 red onions, chopped
- ½ cup parsley, chopped
- 20 ounces canned tomatoes, chopped
- 1 tablespoon basil, chopped
- A pinch of salt and black pepper
- 1 cup baby arugula
- ½ cup baby spinach

Directions:

Set your instant pot on Sauté mode, add the oil, heat it up, add the onions and the turkey and sauté for 5 minutes. Add the rest of the ingredients except the basil, arugula and spinach, put the lid on and cook on High for 10 minutes. Release the pressure naturally for 10 minutes, transfer the mix to a bowl, add the arugula, basil and spinach and toss. Divide between plates and serve as an appetizer right away.

Nutrition: calories 181, fat 4, fiber 3, carbs 7, protein 15

Potato and Shrimp Salad

Prep time: 10 minutes | Cooking time: 15 minutes | Servings: 4

Ingredients:

- 1 pound baby red potatoes, peeled and halved
- 1 red onion, chopped
- 1 pound shrimp, peeled and deveined
- 1 tablespoon olive oil

- 1 teaspoon hot paprika
- 1 tablespoon basil, chopped
- A pinch of salt and black pepper
- 1 tablespoon chives, chopped
- 1 cup veggie stock
- 1 teaspoon lemon juice

Directions:

Set your instant pot on Sauté mode, add the oil, heat it up, add the onion and sauté for 2 minutes. Add the potatoes and the rest of the ingredients except the shrimp and chives, put the lid on and cook on High for 10 minutes. Release the pressure naturally for 10 minutes, set the pot on Sauté mode, add the chives and shrimp, cook for 4 minutes more, divide into small bowls and serve cold as an appetizer.

Nutrition: calories 201, fat 9, fiber 4, carbs 7, protein 10

Cheesy Artichokes Spread

Prep time: 10 minutes | Cooking time: 8 minutes | Servings: 8

Ingredients:

- 20 ounces canned artichoke hearts, drained
- 8 ounces cream cheese, soft
- 14 ounces cheddar cheese, grated
- ½ cup chicken stock

- ½ cup coconut cream
- A pinch of salt and black pepper
- 3 garlic cloves, minced
- 1 teaspoon chili powder

Directions:

In your instant pot, combine the artichokes with the stock, garlic, chili powder, salt and pepper, put the lid on and cook on High for 8 minutes. Release the pressure naturally for 10 minutes, transfer the mix to a food processor, add the remaining ingredients, blend well, divide into bowls and serve.

Nutrition: calories 200, fat 8, fiber 2, carbs 6, protein 8

Endives Platter

Prep time: 5 minutes | Cooking time: 12 minutes | Servings: 4

Ingredients:

- 4 endives, halved
- 1 cup water
- 2 garlic cloves, chopped

- ¼ cup olive oil
- 2 tablespoons lemon juice
- 3 garlic cloves

Directions:

Add water to the instant pot, add the steamer basket inside, arrange the endives in the pot, put the lid on and cook on High for 12 minutes. Release the pressure fast for 5 minutes, transfer the endives to a bowl, add the rest of the ingredients, toss, arrange them on a platter and serve.

Nutrition: calories 171, fat 3, fiber 4, carbs 7, protein 5

Wrapped Shrimp

Prep time: 5 minutes | Cooking time: 6 minutes | Servings: 4

Ingredients:

- 1 pound shrimp, peeled and deveined
- 1 cup tomato sauce
- A drizzle of olive oil
- 8 ounces bacon slices
- 1 teaspoon chili powder

Directions:

In a bowl, mix the shrimp with the oil, salt, pepper and chili powder and toss. Set the instant pot on Sauté mode, add the shrimp and cook for 2 minutes. Transfer the shrimp to a bowl, cool it down and wrap each in a bacon slice. Put the tomato sauce in your instant pot, arrange wrapper shrimp inside, put the lid on and cook on High for 4 minutes. Release the pressure fast for 5 minutes, arrange the shrimp on a platter and serve.

Nutrition: calories 162, fat 3, fiber 4, carbs 7, protein 6

Lentils Spread

Prep time: 10 minutes | Cooking time: 20 minutes | Servings: 6

Ingredients:

- 20 ounces tomatoes, crushed
- 3 garlic cloves, minced
- 1 and ½ cups red lentils, rinsed
- A pinch of salt and black pepper
- 1 tablespoon chives, chopped
- 1 tablespoon lemon juice
- 1 and ½ cups low-sodium veggie stock

Directions:

In your instant pot, mix the tomatoes with the lentils, salt, pepper and the stock, put the lid on and cook on High for 20 minutes. Release the pressure naturally for 10 minutes, transfer the lentils mix to a food processor, add the rest of the ingredients except the chives, pulse well, divide into small bowls, sprinkle the chives on top and serve.

Nutrition: calories 167, fat 4, fiber 3, carbs 8, protein 6

Paprika Cranberry Dip

Prep time: 6 minutes | Cooking time: 15 minutes | Servings: 4

Ingredients:

- 2 and ½ teaspoons lemon zest, grated
- 1 teaspoon chili powder
- 1 teaspoon sweet paprika
- 12 ounces cranberries
- ¼ cup orange juice

Directions:

In your instant pot, combine all the ingredients, put the lid on and cook on High for 15 minutes. Release the pressure fast for 6 minutes, blend the mix using an immersion blender, divide into bowls and serve as a dip.

Nutrition: calories 141, fat 2, fiber 4, carbs 5, protein 4

Citrus Onion Spread

Prep time: 5 minutes | Cooking time: 7 minutes | Servings: 4

Ingredients:

- 1 cup cream cheese, soft
- A pinch of salt and black pepper
- 1 tablespoon olive oil
- 6 spring onions, chopped
- Juice of 1 orange
- 1 cup water

Directions:

In a bowl, combine the cream cheese with spring onions and the rest of the ingredients except the water, whisk well and transfer to a ramekin. Add the water in the instant pot, add the trivet inside, place the ramekin in the pot, put the lid on and cook on Low for 7 minutes. Release the pressure fast for 5 minutes and serve the spread right away.

Nutrition: calories 120, fat 2, fiber 3, carbs 5, protein 4

Zucchini and Squash Dip

Prep time: 5 minutes | Cooking time: 15 minutes | Servings: 4

Ingredients:

- 1 yellow onion, chopped
- 1 tablespoon olive oil
- 1 and ½ pounds zucchini, chopped
- 1 butternut squash, peeled and roughly chopped
- ½ cup veggie stock
- 1 tablespoon lemon juice
- 1 tablespoon basil, chopped
- 2 garlic cloves, minced
- 1 tablespoon mint, chopped

Directions:

Set your instant pot on Sauté mode, add the oil, heat it up, add the onion and garlic, stir and cook 4 minutes. Add zucchinis and the rest of the ingredients except the basil and the mint, put the lid on and cook on High for 10 minutes. Release the pressure fast for 5 minutes, blend the mix using an immersion blender, divide into bowls and serve with mint and basil sprinkled on top.

Nutrition: calories 170, fat 5, fiber 3, carbs 4, protein 6

Garlic Cauliflower Dip

Prep time: 10 minutes | Cooking time: 15 minutes | Servings: 4

Ingredients:

- 1 yellow onion, chopped
- 1 tablespoon olive oil
- A pinch of salt and black pepper
- 1 tablespoon rosemary, chopped
- 3 garlic cloves, minced
- ½ cup chicken stock
- 1 pound cauliflower florets
- ½ cup coconut cream
- 1 tablespoons parsley, chopped

Directions:

Set your instant pot on Sauté mode, add the oil, heat it up, add the onion, stir and cook for 5 minutes. Add the rest of the ingredients except the cream and parsley, put the lid on and cook on High for 10 minutes. Release the pressure naturally for 10 minutes, add the cream, blend the mix using an immersion blender, divide into bowls, sprinkle the parsley on top and serve as a party dip.

Nutrition: calories 170, fat 3, fiber 2, carbs 6, protein 7

Broccoli Spread

Prep time: 10 minutes | Cooking time: 12 minutes | Servings: 4

Ingredients:

- 2 tablespoons avocado oil
- 8 garlic cloves, minced
- ½ cup veggie stock
- 6 cups broccoli florets
- A pinch of salt and black pepper
- 3 tablespoons cream cheese, soft

Directions:

Set your instant pot on Sauté mode, add the oil, heat it up, add the garlic and brown for 2 minutes. Add the rest of the ingredients except the cream cheese, put the lid on and cook on Low for 10 minutes. Release the pressure naturally for 10 minutes, transfer the broccoli mix to a blender, add the cream cheese, pulse well, divide into bowls and serve as a party spread.

Nutrition: calories 178, fat 3, fiber 3, carbs 5, protein 8

Cumin Cheese Spread

Prep time: 5 minutes | Cooking time: 8 minutes | Servings: 4

Ingredients:

- 1 teaspoon olive oil
- 1 red onion, chopped
- 2 spring onions, chopped
- 1 cup cream cheese, soft
- 2 teaspoons cumin, ground
- ¼ teaspoon red pepper flakes
- A pinch of salt and black pepper
- 1 cup water

Directions:

In a bowl, combine the cream cheese with spring onions and the rest of the ingredients except the water, whisk really well and put everything in a ramekin. Add the water to your instant pot, add the trivet and put the ramekin inside. Put the lid on, cook on Low for 8 minutes, release the pressure fast for 5 minutes and serve the spread right away.

Nutrition: calories 170, fat 2, fiber 3, carbs 6, protein 8

Leeks and Bell Pepper Spread

Prep time: 10 minutes | Cooking time: 15 minutes | Servings: 6

Ingredients:

- ¼ cup veggie stock
- 1 pound red bell peppers, chopped
- 4 leeks, sliced
- A pinch of salt and black pepper
- 1 tablespoon olive oil
- 1 tablespoon lemon juice
- 2 tablespoons cream cheese
- 2 garlic cloves, minced
- 1 tablespoon cilantro, chopped

Directions:

In your instant pot, combine the bell peppers with the leeks and the rest of the ingredients except the cream cheese and cilantro, put the lid on and cook on High for 15 minutes. Release the pressure naturally for 10 minutes, transfer the mix to a blender, add the cream cheese and pulse well. Divide into bowls and serve as a spread with the cilantro sprinkled on top.

Nutrition: calories 180, fat 4, fiber 3, carbs 7, protein 9

Chicken, Spinach and Avocado Salad

Prep time: 10 minutes | Cooking time: 15 minutes | Servings: 4

Ingredients:

- 1 avocado, pitted, peeled and cubed
- 2 tablespoons Greek yogurt
- 2 tablespoons mayonnaise
- 2 spring onions, chopped
- 1 and ½ cups baby spinach
- 1 cup chicken stock
- A pinch of salt and black pepper
- 1 pound chicken breast, skinless, boneless and cubed

Directions:

In your instant pot, combine the chicken with salt, pepper and the stock, put the lid on and cook on High for 15 minutes. Release the pressure naturally for 10 minutes, drain the chicken, transfer it to a bowl, add the rest of the ingredients, toss, divide into small bowls and serve as an appetizer.

Nutrition: calories 224, fat 12, fiber 4, carbs 7, protein 12

Pesto Barley Bowls

Prep time: 5 minutes | Cooking time: 20 minutes | Servings: 4

Ingredients:

- 1 cup hulled barley, rinsed
- 2 cups veggie stock
- ¾ cup basil pesto
- 1 tablespoon chives, chopped
- 1 red onion, chopped
- 1 celery stalks chopped

Directions:

In your instant pot, combine the barley with the stock, salt and pepper, toss, put the lid on and cook on High for 20 minutes. Release the pressure fast for 5 minutes, stir the barley, transfer to a bowl, add the rest of the ingredients and toss well. Divide into cups and serve as an appetizer.

Nutrition: calories 172, fat 4, fiber 4, carbs 7, protein 9

Balsamic Olives Salsa

Prep time: 5 minutes | Cooking time: 5 minutes | Servings: 4

Ingredients:

- 1 tablespoon balsamic vinegar
- 1 tablespoon olive oil
- 1 cup cherry tomatoes, halved
- 2 green onions, chopped
- 2 cups kalamata olives, pitted and chopped
- 1 handful basil leaves, chopped
- 1 handful parsley leaves, chopped

Directions:

Set your instant pot on Sauté mode, add the oil, heat it up, add the tomatoes and the rest of the ingredients, toss, put the lid on and cook on High for 5 minutes. Release the pressure fast for 5 minutes, divide the salsa into bowls and serve cold as an appetizer.

Nutrition: calories 152, fat 2, fiber 3, carbs 6, protein 7

Cauliflower Bites

Prep time: 10 minutes | Cooking time: 10 minutes | Servings: 4

Ingredients:

- 1 cup veggie stock
- 1 pound cauliflower florets
- A pinch of salt and black pepper
- ¼ teaspoon mustard seeds
- ¼ teaspoon cumin, ground
- 1 teaspoon ginger, grated
- 1 tablespoon chana dal
- 2 garlic cloves, minced
- 2 teaspoons olive oil
- ¼ teaspoon garam masala
- ¼ teaspoon turmeric powder
- 1 tablespoon chives, chopped

Directions:

Set your instant pot on Sauté mode, add the oil, heat it up, add mustard seeds, cumin, ginger, garlic, turmeric and garam masala, toss and cook for 2 minutes. Add the cauliflower, stock, salt and pepper, put the lid on and cook on High for 8 minutes. Release the pressure naturally for 10 minutes, arrange the cauliflower bites on a platter and serve with the chives sprinkled on top.

Nutrition: calories 154, fat 2, fiber 3, carbs 4, protein 4

Almonds and Barley Salad

Prep time: 5 minutes | Cooking time: 20 minutes | Servings: 4

Ingredients:

- 1 cup barley
- 1 teaspoon fennel seeds
- ½ cup almonds, toasted and chopped
- 2 cups veggie stock
- 1 tablespoon cilantro, chopped
- 1 cup tomatoes, cubed
- 1 cup avocado, peeled, pitted and cubed
- 1 cup mango, peeled and cubed
- A pinch of salt and black pepper

Directions:

In your instant pot, combine the barley with fennel seeds, stock, salt and pepper, put the lid on and cook on High for 20 minutes. Release the pressure naturally for 10 minutes, transfer the barley to a bowl, add the rest of the ingredients and toss well. Divide the mix into small bowls and serve as an appetizer.

Nutrition: calories 142, fat 2, fiber 3, carbs 5, protein 7

Orange Broccoli Bites

Prep time: 10 minutes | Cooking time: 12 minutes | Servings: 4

Ingredients:

- Zest of 1 orange, grated
- Juice of 2 oranges
- 2 garlic cloves, minced
- 2 teaspoons avocado oil
- 2 tablespoons ginger, grated
- 1 pound broccoli florets
- 2/3 cup scallions, chopped
- A pinch of salt and black pepper
- ½ cups veggie stock

Directions:

Set your instant pot on Sauté mode, add the oil, heat it up, add garlic, ginger, scallions, salt and pepper and cook for 2 minutes. Add the broccoli and the rest of the ingredients, put the lid on and cook on High for 10 minutes. Release the pressure naturally for 10 minutes, arrange the broccoli on a platter and serve as an appetizer.

Nutrition: calories 142, fat 2, fiber 3, carbs 5, protein 8

Lentils Salsa

Prep time: 10 minutes | Cooking time: 12 minutes | Servings: 4

Ingredients:

- 1 and ½ cups chicken stock
- 1 cup lentils
- ½ teaspoon thyme, dried
- ¼ cup spring onions, chopped
- ¼ teaspoon chili powder
- 1 cup cherry tomatoes, cubed
- ¼ cup red bell pepper, chopped
- 2 tablespoons olive oil
- 1 tablespoon garlic, minced
- 1 tablespoon oregano, chopped
- Juice of 1 lime
- 2 tablespoons parsley, chopped
- A pinch of salt and black pepper

Directions:

In your instant pot, combine the lentils with the stock, thyme, salt and pepper, put the lid on and cook on High for 12 minutes. Release the pressure naturally for 10 minutes, drain the lentils, transfer them to a bowl, add the rest of the ingredients, toss and serve as an appetizer.

Nutrition: calories 162, fat 4, fiber 3, carbs 5, protein 7

Black Beans and Avocado Spread

Prep time: 10 minutes | Cooking time: 30 minutes | Servings: 6

Ingredients:

- 16 ounces black beans, soaked overnight and drained
- 2 tablespoons chili powder
- 1 yellow onion, chopped
- 4 garlic cloves, minced
- 2 teaspoons cumin, ground
- 2 avocados, peeled, pitted and chopped
- 2 quarts water
- 3 tablespoons olive oil
- A pinch of salt and black pepper

Directions:

In your instant pot, mix the beans with the water, salt and pepper, put the lid on and cook on High for 30 minutes. Release the pressure naturally for 10 minutes, drain the beans, transfer them to a blender, add the rest of the ingredients, pulse well, divide into bowls and serve.

Nutrition: calories 152, fat 3, fiber 4, carbs 5, protein 9

Lime Green Beans and Olives Salad

Prep time: 5 minutes | Cooking time: 12 minutes | Servings: 4

Ingredients:

- 2 cups green beans, trimmed and halved
- 2 teaspoons avocado oil
- 1 red onion, chopped
- 2 garlic cloves, minced
- 1 and ½ cups black olives, pitted
- 1 tablespoon chili powder
- 1 teaspoon smoked paprika
- ½ cup veggie stock
- Juice of 1 lime
- Zest of 1 lime, grated

Directions:

Set your instant pot on Sauté mode, add the oil, heat it up, add the onion and garlic, stir and sauté for 2 minutes. Add the rest of the ingredients, put the lid on and cook on High for 10 minutes. Release the pressure fast for 5 minutes, divide the mix into small bowls and serve as an appetizer.

Nutrition: calories 140, fat 2, fiber 3, carbs 5, protein 4

Rosemary Artichoke Hearts

Prep time: 10 minutes | Cooking time: 15 minutes | Servings: 4

Ingredients:

- 1 pound artichoke hearts
- 1 tablespoon olive oil
- 1 tablespoon rosemary, chopped
- 4 garlic cloves, minced
- A pinch of salt and black pepper
- 1 cup chicken stock
- 2 tablespoons lemon juice

Directions:

Set your instant pot on Sauté mode, add the oil, heat it up, add the garlic and sauté for 2 minutes. Add the artichokes and the rest of the ingredients, put the lid on and cook on High for 13 minutes. Release the pressure naturally for 10 minutes, arrange the artichokes on a platter and serve.

Nutrition: calories 132, fat 2, fiber 3, carbs 4, protein 4

Shrimp and Avocado Platter

Prep time: 5 minutes | Cooking time: 5 minutes | Servings: 4

Ingredients:

- 1 pound shrimp, peeled and deveined
- 1 tablespoon balsamic vinegar
- 1 tablespoon olive oil
- 2 spring onions, chopped
- 2 avocados, peeled, pitted and cut into wedges
- 4 parsley springs, chopped
- ½ cup chicken stock
- 2 teaspoons Creole seasoning
- ½ teaspoon sweet paprika
- 1 tablespoon chives, chopped
- 2 tablespoons cilantro, chopped

Directions:

Set your instant pot on Sauté mode, add the oil, heat it up, add the spring onions, Creole seasoning and sweet paprika, stir and sauté for 2 minutes. Add the shrimp and the rest of the ingredients except the chives and the avocados, put the lid on and cook on High for 3 minutes. Release the pressure fast for 5 minutes, transfer the shrimp mix to a platter, add the avocado and the chivies, toss a bit and serve as an appetizer.

Nutrition: calories 200, fat 5, fiber 2, carbs 5, protein 7

Lime Fava Bean Dip

Prep time: 10 minutes | Cooking time: 20 minutes | Servings: 4

Ingredients:

- 1 and ½ cups fava beans, soaked overnight and drained
- 2 garlic cloves, minced
- 2 cups chicken stock
- 2 teaspoons tahini
- 2 tablespoons olive oil
- 2 teaspoons cumin powder
- Zest of 1 lime
- Juice of 1 lime
- A pinch of salt and black pepper
- 1 teaspoon sweet paprika

Directions:

Set your instant pot on Sauté mode, add the oil, heat it up, add the garlic and cook for 1 minute. Add the beans and the rest of the ingredients except the tahini paste and lime juice, stir, put the lid on and cook on High for 28 minutes. Release the pressure naturally for 10 minutes, drain the beans, transfer them to a blender, add the lime juice and the tahini paste, pulse well, divide into bowls and serve.

Nutrition: calories 123, fat 5, fiber 3, carbs 5, protein 8

Beans and Chickpeas Dip

Prep time: 10 minutes | Cooking time: 25 minutes | Servings: 6

Ingredients:

- 1 pound fava bean, soaked overnight and drained
- 1 cup chickpeas, rinsed
- 1 cup red onion, chopped
- 4 and ½ cups water
- ¼ cup olive oil
- 1 garlic clove, minced
- 2 tablespoons lemon juice
- A pinch of salt and black pepper

Directions:

In your instant pot, combine the beans with the chickpeas, salt, pepper and the water, put the lid on and cook on High for 25 minutes. Release the pressure naturally for 10 minutes, transfer the mix to a blender, add the rest of the ingredients, pulse well, divide into bowls and serve.

Nutrition: calories 200, fat 4, fiber 3, carbs 5, protein 9

Okra and Tomatoes Salsa

Prep time: 10 minutes | Cooking time: 15 minutes | Servings: 4

Ingredients:

- 2 cups okra
- 4 garlic cloves, chopped
- 1 red onion, chopped
- 1 tablespoon olive oil
- 1 pound cherry tomatoes, halved
- 1 tablespoon basil, chopped
- 1 tablespoon oregano, chopped
- 1 cucumber, cubed
- A pinch of salt and black pepper
- Juice of 2 lemons
- ¼ teaspoon red chili flakes

Directions:

Set your instant pot on Sauté mode, add the oil, heat it up, add the garlic, onion, salt and pepper, stir and sauté for 2 minutes. Add the rest of the ingredients except the cucumber, put the lid on and cook on High for 13 minutes. Release the pressure naturally for 10 minutes, transfer the mix to a bowl, add the cucumber and toss. Cool down, divide into small bowls and serve.

Nutrition: calories 143, fat 5, fiber 3, carbs 5, protein 8

Italian Sweet Potato Spread

Prep time: 10 minutes | Cooking time: 15 minutes | Servings: 6

Ingredients:

- 1 pound sweet potato, peeled and chopped
- 1 cup tomato puree
- 3 garlic cloves, minced
- ½ teaspoon smoked paprika
- 1 tablespoon chives, chopped
- A pinch of salt and black pepper

Directions:

In your instant pot, combine all the ingredients except the chives, put the lid on and cook on High for 15 minutes. Release the pressure naturally for 10 minutes, blend the mix using an immersion blender, divide into bowls, sprinkle the chives on top and serve.

Nutrition: calories 120, fat 2, fiber 3, carbs 5, protein 7

Oregano Chili Dip

Prep time: 10 minutes | Cooking time: 210minutes | Servings: 6

Ingredients:

- 6 red chilies, seedless and chopped
- 2 garlic cloves, minced
- A pinch of salt and black pepper
- 1 cup tomato sauce
- ½ teaspoon oregano, dried
- 2 tablespoons balsamic vinegar

Directions:

In your instant pot, combine all the ingredients, put the lid on and cook on High for 10 minutes. Release the pressure naturally for 10 minutes, blend the mix using an immersion blender, divide into bowls and serve as a party dip.

Nutrition: calories 100, fat 1, fiber 2, carbs 4, protein 4

Smoked Tomato Dip

Prep time: 10 minutes | Cooking time: 12 minutes | Servings: 4

Ingredients:

- 1 tablespoon olive oil
- 2 cups tomato puree
- 1 red onion, chopped
- 4 tablespoons balsamic vinegar
- 2 garlic cloves, minced
- A pinch of salt and black pepper
- 1 teaspoon liquid smoke
- ½ teaspoon cumin, ground

Directions:

Set your instant pot on Sauté mode, add the oil, heat it up, add the onion, stir and cook for 3 minutes. Add the rest of the ingredients, put the lid on and cook on High for 9 minutes. Release the pressure naturally for 10 minutes, blend the mix using an immersion blender, divide into bowls and serve cold as a party dip.

Nutrition: calories 100, fat 2, fiber 1, carbs 4, protein 6

Green Beans and Ginger Bowls

Prep time: 5 minutes | Cooking time: 10 minutes | Servings: 4

Ingredients:

- ½ cup veggie stock
- 1 tablespoon olive oil
- 4 spring onions, chopped
- 1-inch ginger piece, grated
- 1 pound green beans, trimmed
- 1 tablespoon cilantro, chopped
- Juice of 1 orange

Directions:

In your instant pot, combine the green beans with the stock and the rest of the ingredients, put the lid on and cook on High for 10 minutes. Release the pressure naturally for 10 minutes, divide the green beans mix into bowls and serve cold.

Nutrition: calories 121, fat 5, fiber 3, carbs 5, protein 6

Zucchini Spread

Prep time: 10 minutes | Cooking time: 10 minutes | Servings: 4

Ingredients:

- 1 yellow onion, chopped
- 1 tablespoon olive oil
- 2 pounds zucchini, chopped
- A pinch of salt and black pepper
- ½ cup veggie stock
- 1 bunch basil, chopped
- 2 garlic cloves, minced

Directions:

Set your instant pot on Sauté mode, add the oil, heat it up, add the onion, garlic, salt and pepper, stir and sauté for 2 minutes. Add the rest of the ingredients, stir, put the lid on and cook on High for 8 minutes. Release the pressure fast for 5 minutes, blend everything using an immersion blender, transfer to a bowl and serve cold.

Nutrition: calories 110, fat 2, fiber 3, carbs 6, protein 4

Chili Mango and Shallot Dip

Prep time: 10 minutes | Cooking time: 10 minutes | Servings: 4

Ingredients:

- 2 shallots, chopped
- 1 tablespoon olive oil
- 2 tablespoons ginger, grated
- 2 mangos, peeled and chopped
- 2 red hot chilies, chopped
- A pinch of salt and black pepper
- 1 and ¼ apple cider vinegar

Directions:

Set your instant pot on Sauté mode, add the oil, heat it up, add ginger and shallot, stir and cook for 2 minutes. Add the rest of the ingredients, put the lid on and cook on High for 8 minutes. Release the pressure naturally for 10 minutes, blend everything using an immersion blender, divide into bowls and serve as a party dip.

Nutrition: calories 100, fat 1, fiber 2, carbs 4, protein 6

Balsamic Spring Onions Dip

Prep time: 5 minutes | Cooking time: 8 minutes | Servings: 4

Ingredients:

- 3 red hot peppers, chopped
- A pinch of salt and black pepper
- 1 tablespoon balsamic vinegar
- 1 cup spring onions, chopped
- 1 teaspoon sweet paprika
- ½ cup veggie stock

Directions:

In your instant pot, combine all the ingredients, put the lid on and cook on High for 8 minutes. Release the pressure fast for 5 minutes, blend the mix using an immersion blender, divide into small bowls and serve.

Nutrition: calories 90, fat 1, fiber 1, carbs 2, protein 3

Cream Cheese and Beef Spread

Prep time: 10 minutes | Cooking time: 20 minutes | Servings: 4

Ingredients:

- 1 yellow onion, chopped
- 1 tablespoon olive oil
- 1 pound beef, ground
- A pinch of salt and black pepper
- ½ teaspoon garlic powder
- ½ teaspoon rosemary, chopped
- 2 ounces cream cheese
- ½ cup cheddar cheese, shredded

Directions:

Set your instant pot on sauté mode, add the oil, heat it up, add the onion, beef and garlic powder, stir and brown for 5 minutes. Add the rest of the ingredients, stir, put the lid on and cook on High for 15 minutes. Release the pressure naturally for 10 minutes, stir the mix, divide into bowls and serve as a party spread.

Nutrition: calories 200, fat 12, fiber 3, carbs 6, protein 9

Carrot Spread

Prep time: 10 minutes | Cooking time: 10 minutes | Servings: 4

Ingredients:

- ¼ cup veggie stock
- A pinch of salt and black pepper
- 1 teaspoon onion powder
- ½ teaspoon garlic powder
- ½ teaspoon oregano, dried
- 1 pound carrots, sliced
- ½ cup coconut cream

Directions:

In your instant pot, combine all the ingredients except the cream, put the lid on and cook on High for 10 minutes. Release the pressure naturally for 10 minutes, transfer the carrots mix to food processor, add the cream, pulse well, divide into bowls and serve cold.

Nutrition: calories 124, fat 1, fiber 2, carbs 5, protein 8

Chicken Wings Platter

Prep time: 10 minutes | Cooking time: 20 minutes | Servings: 4

Ingredients:

- 2 pounds chicken wings
- ½ cup tomato sauce
- A pinch of salt and black pepper
- 1 teaspoon smoked paprika
- 1 tablespoon cilantro, chopped
- 1 tablespoon chives, chopped

Directions:

In your instant pot, combine the chicken wings with the sauce and the rest of the ingredients, stir, put the lid on and cook on High for 20 minutes. Release the pressure naturally for 10 minutes, arrange the chicken wings on a platter and serve as an appetizer.

Nutrition: calories 203, fat 13, fiber 3, carbs 5, protein 8

Stuffed Chicken

Prep time: 10 minutes | Cooking time: 30 minutes | Servings: 4

Ingredients:

- 4 chicken breasts, skinless, boneless and butterflied
- 1 ounce spring onions, chopped
- ½ pound white mushrooms, sliced
- 1 teaspoon hot paprika
- A pinch of salt and black pepper
- 1 cup tomato sauce

Directions:

Flatten chicken breasts with a meat mallet and place them on a plate. In a bowl, mix the spring onions with the mushrooms, paprika, salt and pepper and stir well. Divide this on each chicken breast half, roll them and secure with a toothpick. Add the tomato sauce in the instant pot, put the chicken rolls inside as well. put the lid on and cook on High for 30 minutes. Release the pressure naturally for 10 minutes, arrange the stuffed chicken breasts on a platter and serve.

Nutrition: calories 221, fat 12, fiber 3, carbs 6, protein 11

Cinnamon Baby Back Ribs Platter

Prep time: 10 minutes | Cooking time: 40 minutes | Servings: 4

Ingredients:

- 1 rack baby back ribs
- 2 teaspoons smoked paprika
- 2 teaspoon chili powder
- A pinch of salt and black pepper
- 1 teaspoon garlic powder
- 1 teaspoon onion powder
- 1 teaspoon cinnamon powder
- ½ teaspoon cumin seeds
- A pinch of cayenne pepper
- 1 cup tomato sauce
- 3 garlic cloves, minced

Directions:

In your instant pot, combine the baby back ribs with the rest of the ingredients, put the lid on and cook on High for 30 minutes. Release the pressure naturally for 10 minutes, arrange the ribs on a platter and serve as an appetizer.

Nutrition: calories 222, fat 12, fiber 4, carbs 6, protein 14

Buttery Carrot Sticks

Prep time: 10 minutes | Cooking time: 15 minutes | Servings: 4

Ingredients:

- 1 pound carrot, cut into sticks
- 4 garlic cloves, minced
- ¼ cup chicken stock
- 1 teaspoon rosemary, chopped
- A pinch of salt and black pepper
- 2 tablespoons olive oil
- 2 tablespoons ghee, melted

Directions:

Set the instant pot on Sauté mode, add the oil and the ghee, heat them up, add the garlic and brown for 1 minute. Add the rest of the ingredients, put the lid on and cook on High for 14 minutes. Release the pressure naturally for 10 minutes, arrange the carrot sticks on a platter and serve.

Nutrition: calories 142, fat 4, fiber 2, carbs 5, protein 7

Cajun Walnuts and Olives Bowls

Prep time: 10 minutes | Cooking time: 1 hour | Servings: 2

Ingredients:

- ½ pound walnuts, chopped
- A pinch of salt and black pepper
- 1 and ½ cups black olives, pitted
- ½ tablespoon Cajun seasoning
- 2 garlic cloves, minced
- 1 red chili pepper, chopped
- ¼ cup veggie stock
- 2 tablespoon tomato puree

Directions:

In your instant pot, combine the walnuts with the olives and the rest of the ingredients, put the lid on and cook on High 10 minutes. Release the pressure fast for 5 minutes, divide the mix into small bowls and serve as an appetizer.

Nutrition: calories 105, fat 1, fiber 1, carbs 4, protein 7

Mango Salsa

Prep time: 10 minutes | Cooking time: 10 minutes | Servings: 2

Ingredients:

- 2 mangoes, peeled and cubed
- ½ tablespoon sweet paprika
- 2 garlic cloves, minced
- 2 tablespoons cilantro, chopped
- 1 tablespoon spring onions, chopped
- 1 cup cherry tomatoes, cubed
- 1 cup avocado, peeled, pitted and cubed
- A pinch of salt and black pepper
- 1 tablespoon olive oil
- ¼ cup tomato puree
- ½ cup kalamata olives, pitted and sliced

Directions:

In your instant pot, combine the mangoes with the paprika and the rest of the ingredients except the cilantro, put the lid on and cook on High for 5 minutes. Release the pressure fast for 5 minutes, divide the mix into small bowls, sprinkle the cilantro on top and serve.

Nutrition: calories 123, fat 4, fiber 1, carbs 3, protein 5

Hot Asparagus Sticks

Prep time: 10 minutes | Cooking time: 10 minutes | Servings: 2

Ingredients:

- 1 and ½ pounds asparagus, trimmed
- 2 tablespoons olive oil
- 2 tablespoons cayenne pepper sauce
- A pinch of salt and black pepper
- 1 cup water

Directions:

In a bowl, mix the asparagus with the other ingredients except the water and toss. Put the water in your instant pot, add the steamer basket, put the asparagus sticks inside, put the lid on and cook on High for 6 minutes. Release the pressure fast for 5 minutes, arrange the asparagus on a platter and serve.

Nutrition: calories 181, fat 6, fiber 3, carbs 4, protein 4

Pork Bites

Prep time: 10 minutes | Cooking time: 30 minutes | Servings: 4

Ingredients:

- 1 pound pork roast, cubed and browned
- 1 tablespoon Italian seasoning
- 1 cup beef stock
- 2 tablespoons water
- 1 tablespoon sweet paprika
- 2 tablespoons tomato sauce
- 1 tablespoon rosemary, chopped

Directions:

In your instant pot, combine the pork cubes with the seasoning and the rest of the ingredients except the rosemary, toss, put the lid on and cook on High for 30 minutes. Release the pressure naturally for 10 minutes, arrange the pork cubes on a platter, sprinkle the rosemary on top and serve.

Nutrition: calories 242, fat 12, fiber 2, carbs 6, protein 14

Salmon and Citrus Sauce

Prep time: 5 minutes | Cooking time: 12 minutes | Servings: 4

Ingredients:

- 4 salmon fillets, boneless
- 4 spring onions, chopped
- 1 tablespoon olive oil
- 1 tablespoon ginger, grated
- Salt and black pepper to the taste
- Juice of 1 orange
- 1 tablespoon cilantro, chopped

Directions:

Set the instant pot on sauté mode, add the oil, heat it up, add the spring onions and ginger and cook for 2 minutes. Add the salmon fillets and the rest of the ingredients, put the lid on and cook on High for 10 minutes. Release the pressure fast for 5 minutes, divide the salmon and the sauce between plates and serve.

Nutrition: calories 200, fat 12, fiber 3, carbs 6, protein 11

Fish Bowls

Prep time: 5 minutes | Cooking time: 10 minutes | Servings: 4

Ingredients:

- 1 pound white fish fillets, boneless, skinless and cubed
- 1 cup black olives, pitted and chopped
- 1 pound cherry tomatoes, halved
- 2 garlic cloves, minced
- 1 tablespoon olive oil
- Salt and black pepper to the taste
- 1 tablespoon oregano, chopped
- 1 tablespoon parsley, chopped

Directions:

Set the instant pot on Sauté mode, add the oil, heat it up, add the fish and sear for 1 minute on each side. Add the rest of the ingredients, put the lid on and cook on High for 8 minutes. Release the pressure fast for 5 minutes, divide everything into bowls and serve.

Nutrition: calories 132, fat 9, fiber 2, carbs 5, protein 11

Trout Curry

Prep time: 10 minutes | Cooking time: 12 minutes | Servings: 4

Ingredients:

- 1 pound trout fillets, boneless, skinless and cubed
- 1 tomato, chopped
- 1 and ½ coconut milk
- 2 red onions, sliced
- 2 garlic clovs, minced
- 1 tablespoons coriander, ground
- 1 tablespoon ginger, grated
- ½ teaspoon turmeric powder
- A pinch of salt and black pepper
- 2 tablespoons lemon juice

Directions:

Set your instant pot on Sauté mode, add the oil, heat it up, add the onions, garlic and ginger and sauté for 2 minutes. Add the fish and the rest of the ingredients, put the lid on and cook on High for 10 minutes. Release the pressure naturally for 10 minutes, divide the curry into bowls and serve.

Nutrition: calories 200, fat 12, fiber 2, carbs 6, protein 11

Trout and Capers Sauce

Prep time: 10 minutes | Cooking time: 12 minutes | Servings: 4

Ingredients:

- 4 trout fillets, boneless
- 1 cup cherry tomatoes, halved
- 2 garlic cloves, minced
- 2 tablespoons capers, drained and chopped
- Salt and black pepper to the taste
- 1 tablespoon parsley, chopped
- 1 tablespoon olive oil
- ½ cup veggie stock

Directions:

Set the instant pot on Sauté mode, add the oil, heat it up, add the garlic, capers, salt and pepper and sauté for 2 minutes. Add the rest of the ingredients, put the lid on and cook on High for 10 minutes. Release the pressure naturally for 10 minutes, divide the trout and sauce between plates and serve.

Nutrition: calories 200, fat 12, fiber 2, carbs 6, protein 9

Paprika Salmon

Prep time: 10 minutes | Cooking time: 10 minutes | Servings: 4

Ingredients:

- 4 salmon fillets, boneless
- 1 tablespoon parsley, chopped
- ½ cup fish stock
- ½ teaspoon oregano, dried
- 2 teaspoons sweet paprika
- 2 garlic cloves, chopped
- A pinch of salt and black pepper

Directions:

In your instant pot, combine the salmon with the stock and the rest of the ingredients, put the lid on and cook on High for 10 minutes. Release the pressure naturally for 10 minutes, divide the salmon mix between plates and serve.

Nutrition: calories 211, fat 13, fiber 2, carbs 7, protein 11

Lemon Cod and Scallions

Prep time: 10 minutes | Cooking time: 12 minutes | Servings: 4

Ingredients:

- 4 cod fillets, boneless
- Zest of 1 lemon, grated
- Juice of ½ lemon
- 4 scallions, chopped
- 1 teaspoon white wine vinegar
- 1 cup chicken stock
- ¼ cup parsley, chopped
- A pinch of salt and black pepper

Directions:

In your instant pot, combine the cod with the lemon zest and the rest of the ingredients, put the lid on and cook on High for 12 minutes. Release the pressure naturally for 10 minutes, divide the cod mix between plates and serve.

Nutrition: calories 200, fat 12, fiber 4, carbs 6, protein 8

Shrimp and Parsley Mix

Prep time: 5 minutes | Cooking time: 4 minutes | Servings: 4

Ingredients:

- 1 and ½ pounds shrimp, peeled and deveined
- A pinch of salt and black pepper
- 1 tablespoon parsley, chopped
- 2 tablespoons tomato sauce
- ½ tablespoon sweet paprika, chopped
- 2 garlic cloves, minced

Directions:

In your instant pot, combine the shrimp with the rest of the ingredients, put the lid on and cook on High for 4 minutes. Release the pressure fast for 5 minutes, divide the mix into bowls and serve.

Nutrition: calories 232, fat 7, fiber 3, carbs 7, protein 9

Cod and Cauliflower Rice

Prep time: 5 minutes | Cooking time: 12 minutes | Servings: 4

Ingredients:

- 4 cod fillets, boneless
- A pinch of salt and black pepper
- 1 cup cauliflower, riced
- 1 cup chicken stock
- 2 tablespoons tomato puree
- 1 tablespoon cilantro, chopped

Directions:

In your instant pot, combine all the ingredients, put the lid on and cook on High for 12 minutes. Release the pressure fast for 5 minutes, divide the mix between plates and serve.

Nutrition: calories 232, fat 9, fiber 2, carbs 6, protein 8

Salmon And Baby Carrots

Prep time: 10 minutes | Cooking time: 12 minutes | Servings: 4

Ingredients:

- 4 salmon fillets, boneless
- ½ cup veggie stock
- 2 garlic cloves, minced
- 1 red onion, minced
- 1 tablespoon avocado oil
- 2 cups baby carrots, trimmed
- A pinch of salt and black pepper
- 1 tablespoon rosemary, chopped

Directions:

Set the instant pot on Sauté mode, add the oil, heat it up, add the onion and garlic and sauté for 2 minutes. Add the rest of the ingredients, put the lid on and cook on High for 10 minutes. Release the pressure naturally for 10 minutes, divide the salmon and carrots mix between plates and serve.

Nutrition: calories 200, fat 13, fiber 3, carbs 6, protein 11

Spicy Trout

Prep time: 5 minutes | Cooking time: 12 minutes | Servings: 4

Ingredients:

- 4 trout fillets, boneless
- 2 tablespoons chili pepper, minced
- Juice of 1 lime
- ½ cup veggie stock
- A pinch of salt and black pepper
- A pinch of cayenne pepper
- 1 tablespoon chives, chopped

Directions:

In your instant pot, mix the trout fillets with the rest of the ingredients except the chives, put the lid on and cook on High for 10 minutes. Release the pressure fast for 5 minutes, arrange the trout between plates, sprinkle the chives on top and serve with a side salad.

Nutrition: calories 200, fat 12, fiber 2, carbs 6, protein 9

Thyme Cod and Tomatoes

Prep time: 10 minutes | Cooking time: 15 minutes | Servings: 4

Ingredients:

- 4 cod fillets, boneless
- 1 red onion, chopped
- 3 tomatoes, roughly chopped
- 2 tablespoons thyme, chopped
- 3 tablespoons olive oil
- A pinch of salt and black pepper
- 2 tablespoons tomato puree

Directions:

Set the instant pot on Sauté mode, add the oil, heat it up, add the onion, salt and pepper, toss and cook for 2 minutes. Add the cod and the rest of the ingredients, put the lid on and cook on High for 10 minutes. Release the pressure naturally for 10 minutes, divide the whole mix between plates and serve.

Nutrition: calories 200, fat 12, fiber 2, carbs 5, protein 6

Salmon Cakes and Sauce

Prep time: 10 minutes | Cooking time: 15 minutes | Servings: 4

Ingredients:

- 1 teaspoon olive oil
- 1 egg, whisked
- 1 pound salmon meat, minced
- 2 tablespoons lemon zest, grated
- 1 teaspoon lemon juice
- A pinch of salt and black pepper
- 1 cup tomato sauce

Directions:

In a bowl, combine the salmon with the egg and the rest of the ingredients except the tomato sauce and the oil, stir well and shape medium cakes out of this mix. Set the instant pot on Sauté mode, add the oil, heat it up, add the salmon cakes and cook them for 2 minutes on each side. Add the tomato sauce, put the lid on and cook on High for 8 minutes. Release the pressure naturally for 10 minutes, divide the mix between plates and serve.

Nutrition: calories 192, fat 9, fiber 2, carbs 8, protein 7

Sea Bass and Artichokes

Prep time: 10 minutes | Cooking time: 15 minutes | Servings: 4

Ingredients:

- 1 pound sea bass, skinless, boneless and cubed
- 1 yellow onion, chopped
- 12 ounces canned artichokes, roughly chopped
- 1 and ½ cups coconut cream
- A pinch of salt and black pepper
- 1 tablespoon cilantro, chopped

Directions:

In your instant pot, combine the sea bass with the rest of the ingredients except the cilantro, put the lid on and cook on High for 15 minutes. Release the pressure naturally for 10 minutes, divide the mix into bowls, sprinkle the cilantro on top and serve.

Nutrition: calories 210, fat 9, fiber 2, carbs 6, protein 7

Cod and Strawberries Sauce

Prep time: 5 minutes | Cooking time: 15 minutes | Servings: 4

Ingredients:

- 6 cod fillets, boneless
- 2 tablespoons olive oil
- 2 shallots, minced
- 2 garlic cloves, minced
- 2 tablespoons parsley, chopped
-
- 1 cup strawberries, chopped
- 2 tablespoons lemon juice
- A pinch of salt and black pepper
- 2 tablespoons balsamic vinegar

Directions:

Set the instant pot on Sauté mode, add the oil, heat it up, add the shallots and the garlic and sauté for 2 minutes. Add the berries, vinegar, salt and pepper, toss, and cook for 2 minutes more. Add the fish, put the lid on and cook on High for 10 minutes. Release the pressure fast for 5 minutes, divide the mix between plates, sprinkle the parsley on top, drizzle the lemon juice all over and serve.

Nutrition: calories 200, fat 10, fiber 2, carbs 5, protein 9

Tilapia and Lemon Sauce

Prep time: 10 minutes | Cooking time: 20 minutes | Servings: 4

Ingredients:

- 1 pound tilapia fillets, boneless and cubed
- 2 tablespoons parsley, chopped
- 2 tablespoons lemon juice
- 1 teaspoon lemon zest, grated
- 2 garlic cloves, minced
- 1 shallot, chopped
- 1 tablespoon avocado oil
- ½ pint coconut cream
- A pinch of salt and black pepper

Directions:

Set the instant pot on Sauté mode, add the oil, heat it up, add the garlic and the shallot and cook for 2 minutes. Add the tilapia and the remaining ingredients, put the lid on and cook on Low for 15 minutes. Release the pressure naturally for 10 minutes, divide everything between plates and serve.

Nutrition: calories 200, fat 13, fiber 3, carbs 6, protein 11

Shrimp and Chicken Mix

Prep time: 5 minutes | Cooking time: 10 minutes | Servings: 4

Ingredients:

- 1 pound chicken breast, skinless, boneless and cubed
- 1 pound shrimp, peeled and deveined
- 2 tablespoons olive oil
- 2 tablespoons garlic, chopped
- 2 cups red bell peppers, chopped
- 1 and ½ cups chicken stock
- 1 tablespoon Creole seasoning
- 1 cup tomatoes, crushed
- 1 tablespoon parsley, chopped

Directions:

Set your instant pot on Sauté mode, add the oil, heat it up, add the garlic and the bell peppers and sauté for 2 minutes. Add the shrimp and the rest of the ingredients except the parsley, put the lid on and cook on High for 8 minutes. Release the pressure fast for 5 minutes, divide the mix between plates and serve with the parsley sprinkled on top.

Nutrition: calories 211, fat 12, fiber 3, carbs 6, protein 7

Tuna and Tomatoes

Prep time: 10 minutes | Cooking time: 10 minutes | Servings: 4

Ingredients:

- ½ cup red onion, chopped
- 1 tablespoon olive oil
- 14 ounces canned tomatoes, chopped
- 1 tablespoon oregano, chopped
- A pinch of salt and black pepper
- 14 ounces tuna fillets, boneless, skinless and cubed
- 1 tablespoon parsley, chopped

Directions:

Set your instant pot on Sauté mode, add the oil, heat it up, add the onion and sauté for 2 minutes. Add the tomatoes, oregano, salt and pepper, stir and cook for 2 minutes more. Add the tuna, put the lid on and cook on High for 6 minutes. Release the pressure naturally for 10 minutes, divide the mix between plates, sprinkle the parsley on top and serve.

Nutrition: calories 200, fat 12, fiber 2, carbs 6, protein 13

Tuna and Olives

Prep time: 5 minutes | Cooking time: 8 minutes | Servings: 4

Ingredients:

- 14 ounces canned tuna, drained
- 1 cup black olives, pitted
- 1 cup tomato sauce
- 1 tablespoon chives, chopped

Directions:

In your instant pot, combine the tuna with the rest of the ingredients, put the lid on and cook on High for 8 minutes. Release the pressure fast for 5 minutes, divide the mix into bowls and serve.

Nutrition: calories 200, fat 9, fiber 3, carbs 7, protein 10

Turmeric Trout and Lemongrass

Prep time: 5 minutes | Cooking time: 8 minutes | Servings: 4

Ingredients:

- 4 trout fillets, boneless
- 3 garlic cloves, minced
- 2 shallots chopped
- 1 teaspoon turmeric powder
- 1 tablespoon chili paste
- 2 lemongrass sticks, chopped
- 1 tablespoon ginger, grated
- 2 tablespoons olive oil
- 1 and ½ tablespoons tomato sauce

Directions:

In your blender, mix the lemongrass with ginger, chili paste, garlic, turmeric and shallots and pulse well. Set the instant pot on Sauté mode, add the oil, heat it up, add the lemongrass and turmeric mix and cook for 1 minute. Add the fish and the tomato sauce, toss gently, put the lid on and cook on High for 7 minutes. Release the pressure fast for 5 minutes, divide the mix between plates and serve.

Nutrition: calories 211, fat 13, fiber 4, carbs 7, protein 10

Ginger Mackerel

Prep time: 10 minutes | Cooking time: 15 minutes | Servings: 4

Ingredients:

- 2 pounds mackerel, cut into chunks
- 1 cup tomato sauce
- 2 garlic cloves, minced
- 1 shallot, sliced
- 2 tablespoons ginger piece, grated
- 1 sweet onion, thinly sliced
- 1 tablespoon balsamic vinegar
- A pinch of salt and black pepper
- 1 tablespoon parsley, chopped

Directions:

Set your instant pot on Sauté mode, add the mackerel, tomato sauce and the rest of the ingredients except the parsley, put the lid on and cook on Low for 15 minutes. Release the pressure naturally for 10 minutes, divide the mix into bowls, sprinkle the parsley on top and serve.

Nutrition: calories 220, fat 12, fiber 3, carbs 6, protein 13

Chives Trout

Prep time: 5 minutes | Cooking time: 15 minutes | Servings: 4

Ingredients:

- 4 trout fillets, boneless
- Juice and rind of 1 lemon
- 2 tablespoons chives, chopped
- A pinch of salt and black pepper
- 1 tablespoon olive oil
- 1 shallot, chopped

Directions:

Set the instant pot on Sauté mode, add the oil, heat it up, add the shallot and cook for 2 minutes. Add the trout and the rest of the ingredients, put the lid on and cook on High for 10 minutes. Release the pressure fast for 5 minutes, divide the mix between plates and serve.

Nutrition: calories 200, fat 12, fiber 3, carbs 6, protein 11

Shrimp and Spinach

Prep time: 5 minutes | Cooking time: 6 minutes | Servings: 4

Ingredients:

- 2 pounds shrimp, peeled and deveined
- 1 cup radishes, cubed
- 1 white onion, chopped
- 1 pound baby spinach
- ½ cup chicken stock
- 2 garlic cloves, minced
- 1 tablespoon olive oil

Directions:

Set instant pot on Sauté mode, add the oil, heat it up, add the onion and the garlic and cook for 1 minute. Add the shrimp and the rest of the ingredients, put the lid on and cook on High for 5 minutes. Release the pressure fast for 5 minutes, divide the mix into bowls and serve.

Nutrition: calories 182, fat 10, fiber 2, carbs 5, protein 6

Sea Bass and Radish Mix

Prep time: 10 minutes | Cooking time: 12 minutes | Servings: 4

Ingredients:

- 2 cups canned tomatoes, crushed
- 1 red onion, chopped
- 2 chili peppers, chopped
- 2 tablespoons avocado oil
- ¼ cup balsamic vinegar
- 1 pound sea bass fillets, boneless, skinless and cubed
- 1 cup radishes, cubed
- 2 teaspoons red pepper flakes
- A pinch of salt and black pepper
- ½ cup basil, chopped

Directions:

Set your instant pot on Sauté mode, add the oil, heat it up, add the onion, pepper flakes and chili peppers, stir and cook for 2 minutes. Add the sea bass and the rest of the ingredients except the basil, put the lid on and cook on High for 10 minutes. Release the pressure naturally for 10 minutes, divide the sea bass mix between plates, sprinkle the basil on top and serve.

Nutrition: calories 192, fat 11, fiber 3, carbs 6, protein 9

Oregano Mussels

Prep time: 10 minutes | Cooking time: 5 minutes | Servings: 4

Ingredients:

- 2 pounds mussels, cleaned and scrubbed
- 2 tablespoons avocado oil
- 1 shallot, chopped
- ½ teaspoon red pepper flakes
- 14 ounces tomatoes, chopped
- 2 teaspoons garlic, minced
- 2 tablespoons oregano, chopped

Directions:

Set your instant pot on Sauté mode, add the oil, heat it up, add the shallot, garlic and pepper flakes, stir and cook for 2 minutes. Add the mussels and the rest of the ingredients, put the lid on and cook on High for 6 minutes. Release the pressure naturally for 10 minutes, divide the mussels mix into bowls and serve.

Nutrition: calories 132, fat 5, fiber 3, carbs 6, protein 6

Shrimp and Olives

Prep time: 5 minutes | Cooking time: 6 minutes | Servings: 4

Ingredients:

- 1 and ½ pound shrimp, peeled and deveined
- 1 cup kalamata olives, pitted
- ½ cup black olives, pitted
- 2 spring onions, chopped
- 1 tablespoon olive oil
- 1 yellow onion, chopped
- 1 and ½ cups tomato puree
- 1 tablespoon sweet paprika

Directions:

Set your instant pot on Sauté mode, add the oil, heat it up, add the yellow and spring onions, stir and cook for 2 minutes. Add the shrimp and the rest of the ingredients, put the lid on and cook on High for 4 minutes. Release the pressure fast for 5 minutes, divide everything into bowls and serve.

Nutrition: calories 162, fat 6, fiber 1, carbs 6, protein 8

Parsley Tuna and Shrimp

Prep time: 10 minutes | Cooking time: 15 minutes | Servings: 4

Ingredients:

- 1 tablespoon olive oil
- 1 pound shrimp, peeled and deveined
- 2 tuna fillets, boneless, skinless and cubed
- 3 garlic cloves, minced
- ¼ cup parsley, chopped
- ¼ cup tomato puree
- 1 tablespoon lime juice

Directions:

Set the instant pot on Sauté mode, add the oil, heat it up, add the garlic and cook for 1 minute. Add the shrimp, tuna and the rest of the ingredients, put the lid on and cook on Low for 15 minutes. Release the pressure naturally for 10 minutes, divide the mix into bowls and serve.

Nutrition: calories 199, fat 7, fiber 4, carbs 7, protein 12

Shrimp and Tilapia Warm Salad
Prep time: 10 minutes | Cooking time: 8 minutes | Servings: 4

Ingredients:
- 1 and ½ pounds big shrimp, peeled and deveined
- 1 and ½ pounds tilapia fillets, boneless, skinless and cubed
- 2 red onions, chopped
- 1 tablespoon avocado oil
- 3 garlic cloves, minced
- ½ cup basil, chopped
- 20 ounces caned tomatoes, chopped
- ½ teaspoon marjoram, dried
- A pinch of salt and black pepper
- 1 and ½ cups baby spinach

Directions:

Set your instant pot on Sauté mode, add the oil, heat it up, add the garlic and the onions, stir and sauté for 2 minutes. Add the shrimp, fish and the rest of the ingredients, put the lid on and cook on High for 6 minutes. Release the pressure naturally for 10 minutes, divide the salad into bowls and serve warm.

Nutrition: calories 200, fat 14, fiber 3, carbs 8, protein 10

Mussels and Sweet Potatoes
Prep time: 10 minutes | Cooking time: 15 minutes | Servings: 4

Ingredients:
- 30 mussels, cleaned and scrubbed
- 1 pound sweet potatoes, peeled and cubed
- 1 yellow onion, chopped
- 10 ounces tomato sauce
- 2 tablespoons parsley, chopped
- 1 tablespoon olive oil

Directions:

Set your instant pot on Sauté mode, add the oil, heat it up, add the onion and sauté for 2 minutes. Add the mussels and the rest of the ingredients, put the lid on and cook on High for 12 minutes. Release the pressure naturally for 10 minutes, divide the mix between plates and serve.

Nutrition: calories 200, fat 12, fiber 3, carbs 7, protein 10

Shrimp and Celery Mix
Prep time: 5 minutes | Cooking time: 6 minutes | Servings: 4

Ingredients:
- 1 and ½ pounds shrimp, peeled and deveined
- 2 celery stalks, roughly chopped
- ½ cup chicken stock
- 1 tablespoon lemon juice

Directions:

In your instant pot, combine the shrimp and celery with the rest of the ingredients, put the lid on and cook on High for 6 minutes. Release the pressure fast for 5 minutes, divide into bowls and serve.

Nutrition: calories 172, fat 11, fiber 4, carbs 7, protein 9

Avocado and Salmon Salad

Prep time: 5 minutes | Cooking time: 6 minutes | Servings: 4

Ingredients:

- 1 and ½ pounds salmon fillets, boneless, skinless and cubed
- 2 tablespoons olive oil
- 1 cup shallots, chopped
- 2 tablespoons parsley, chopped
- 4 garlic cloves, minced
- ½ cup chicken stock
- 1 cup tomato sauce
- 1 teaspoon sage, chopped
- 2 avocados, peeled, pitted and cubed

Directions:

Set your instant pot on Sauté mode, add the oil, heat it up, add the shallots and garlic and sauté for 2 minutes. Add the salmon and the rest of the ingredients, put the lid on and cook on High for 4 minutes.

Nutrition: calories 200, fat 12, fiber 2, carbs 6, protein 11

Trout and Broccoli Mix

Prep time: 10 minutes | Cooking time: 15 minutes | Servings: 4

Ingredients:

- 1 pound trout fillets, boneless
- 2 cups broccoli florets
- ½ cup tomatoes, cubed
- 2 tablespoons olive oil
- A pinch of salt and black pepper
- 2 tablespoons basil, chopped
- A pinch of red pepper, crushed
- Juice of 1 lime
- 1 and ¼ cups chicken stock

Directions:

In your instant pot, combine the trout with the broccoli and the rest of the ingredients, put the lid on and cook on High for 12 minutes. Release the pressure naturally for 10 minutes, divide everything between plates and serve.

Nutrition: calories 211, fat 14, fiber 3, fiber 6, carbs 11

Shrimp and Corn

Prep time: 10 minutes | Cooking time: 10 minutes | Servings: 4

Ingredients:

- 1 and ½ pounds shrimp, peeled and deveined
- 8 ounces corn
- 1 tablespoon old bay seasoning
- 1 and ½ cups tomato puree
- A pinch of salt and black pepper
- 2 sweet onions, cut into wedges
- 1 tablespoon parsley, chopped

Directions:

In your instant pot, combine the shrimp with the corn and the rest of the ingredients except the parsley, put the lid on and cook on Low for 10 minutes. Release the pressure naturally for 10 minutes, divide the mix into bowls and serve with the parsley sprinkled on top.

Nutrition: calories 200, fat 11, fiber 2, carbs 6, protein 8

Cardamom and Chili Salmon

Prep time: 10 minutes | Cooking time: 15 minutes | Servings: 4

Ingredients:

- 4 salmon fillets, boneless and cubed
- 3 cardamom pods
- 2 red onions, roughly cubed
- 1 red chili, chopped
- 3 green chilies, chopped
- 1 tablespoon garlic paste
- 4 tomatoes, chopped
- A pinch of salt and black pepper
- ½ cup coconut cream

Directions:

In a blender, combine the cardamom with the chilies, garlic paste, tomatoes, salt and pepper and pulse well. Set the instant pot on Sauté mode, add the chilies mix, heat it up, add the salmon, onions and the cream, put the lid on and cook on High for 12 minutes. Release the pressure naturally for 10 minutes, divide the mix into bowls and serve.

Nutrition: calories 224, fat 13, fiber 3, carbs 7, protein 11

Shrimp and Mushroom Curry

Prep time: 10 minutes | Cooking time: 10 minutes | Servings: 4

Ingredients:

- 1 pound shrimp, peeled and deveined
- 1 cup tomato puree
- 1 tablespoon lemon juice
- A pinch of salt and black pepper
- ½ teaspoon curry powder
- 1 and ½ cups mushrooms, sliced
- 1 yellow onion, chopped
- 2 tablespoons olive oil

Directions:

Set your instant pot on Sauté mode, add the oil, heat it up, add the onion and the mushrooms and sauté for 3 minutes. Add the rest of the ingredients, put the lid on and cook on High for 7 minutes. Release the pressure naturally for 10 minutes, divide the mix into bowls and serve.

Nutrition: calories 221, fat 12, fiber 3, carbs 6, protein 8

Tilapia and Dill Sauce

Prep time: 10 minutes | Cooking time: 10 minutes | Servings: 4

Ingredients:

- 1 pound tilapia, boneless, skinless and cubed
- 2 tablespoons olive oil
- 1 yellow onion, chopped
- 1 cup chicken stock
- ¾ cup coconut milk
- 1 tablespoon dill, chopped

Directions:

Set your instant pot on Sauté mode, add the oil, heat it up, add the onion, stir and cook for 3 minutes. Add the rest of the ingredients, put the lid on and cook on High for 7 minutes. Release the pressure fast for 5 minutes, divide the mix into bowls and serve.

Nutrition: calories 231, fat 11, fiber 3, carbs 6, protein 9

Mussels and Chives Mix

Prep time: 5 minutes | Cooking time: 15 minutes | Servings: 4

Ingredients:

- 2 pounds mussels, cleaned
- 1 pound tomatoes, peeled and chopped
- 1 cup chicken stock
- A pinch of salt and black pepper
- 2 tablespoons olive oil
- 1 red onion, chopped
- 1 teaspoon coriander powder
- 1 tablespoon chives, chopped

Directions:

Set the instant pot on Sauté mode, add the oil, heat it up, add the onion and sauté for 5 minutes. Add the rest of the ingredients, put the lid on and cook on High for 10 minutes. Release the pressure fast for 5 minutes, divide the mix into bowls and serve.

Nutrition: calories 192, fat 9, fiber 4, carbs 7, protein 9

Chili Tuna Bites

Prep time: 6 minutes | Cooking time: 10 minutes | Servings: 4

Ingredients:

- 1 pound tuna, skinless, boneless and cubed
- 2 teaspoons chili powder
- 2 teaspoons balsamic vinegar
- 1 cup tomato sauce
- A pinch of salt and black pepper
- 2 tablespoons olive oil

Directions:

Set the pot on Sauté mode, add the oil, heat it up, add the tuna and sear for 1 minute on each side. Add the rest of the ingredients, put the lid on and cook on High for 8 minutes. Release the pressure fast for 6 minutes, divide the mix into bowls and serve.

Nutrition: calories 232, fat 8, fiber 2, carbs 6, protein 11

Shrimp, Mango and Arugula Mix

Prep time: 5 minutes | Cooking time: 6 minutes | Servings: 4

Ingredients:

- 1 pounds shrimp, peeled and deveined
- 2 tablespoons olive oil
- 2 spring onions, chopped
- 1 mango, peeled and cubed
- 2 cups baby arugula
- 2 tablespoons balsamic vinegar
- 1 cup chicken stock
- 1 tablespoon parsley, chopped

Directions:

Set the instant pot on Sauté mode, add the oil, heat it up, add the onions and cook for 1 minute. Add the rest of the ingredients, except the arugula and the parsley, put the lid on and cook on High for 5 minutes. Release the pressure fast for 5 minutes, transfer the mix to a bowl, add the arugula and the parsley, toss well and serve.

Nutrition: calories 232, fat 5, fiber 1, carbs 5, protein 8

Mustard Shrimp Mix

Prep time: 5 minutes | Cooking time: 8 minutes | Servings: 4

Ingredients:

- 1 and ½ pounds shrimp, peeled and deveined
- A pinch of salt and black pepper
- 1 tablespoon mustard
- 1 tablespoon olive oil
- 1 teaspoon turmeric powder
- 1 tablespoon parsley, chopped
- ½ pound baby spinach

Directions:

Set the instant pot on Sauté mode, add the oil, heat it up, add all the ingredients except the shrimp and the spinach and whisk well. Add the shrimp, put the lid on and cook on Low for 8 minutes. Release the pressure fast for 5 minutes, divide the mix between plates and serve.

Nutrition: calories 222, fat 9, fiber 2, carbs 6, protein 7

Shrimp and Squash Mix

Prep time: 10 minutes | Cooking time: 15 minutes | Servings: 4

Ingredients:

- 1 pound shrimp, peeled and deveined
- 2 tablespoons olive oil
- 1 garlic clove, minced
- 10 ounces canned tomatoes, chopped
- 1 butternut squash, peeled and cubed
- ¼ teaspoon basil, dried
- 1 tablespoon parsley, chopped
- ½ cup chicken stock

Directions:

Set your instant pot on Sauté mode, add the oil, heat it up, add the garlic, stir and brown for 2 minutes. Add the rest of the ingredients, put the lid on and cook on High for 2 minutes. Release the pressure naturally for 10 minutes, divide the mix into bowls and serve.

Nutrition: calories 200, fat 7, fiber 3, carbs 6, protein 8

Clams and Shrimp Mix

Prep time: 10 minutes | Cooking time: 10 minutes | Servings: 4

Ingredients:

- 1 pound shrimp, peeled and deveined
- ½ cup chicken stock
- ½ pound clams
- A pinch of salt and black pepper
- 1 tablespoon lemon juice

Directions:

In your instant pot, combine all the ingredients, put the lid on and cook on Low for 10 minutes. Release the pressure naturally for 10 minutes, divide the mix into bowls and serve.

Nutrition: calories 198, fat 7, fiber 2, carbs 6, protein 7

Herbed Shrimp Mix

Prep time: 10 minutes | Cooking time: 10 minutes | Servings: 4

Ingredients:

- 2 tablespoons avocado oil
- 2 garlic cloves, minced
- 1 shallot, chopped
- ½ cup chicken stock
- A pinch of salt and black pepper
- 1 pound shrimp, peeled and deveined
- ¼ cup tarragon, chopped
- ¼ cup parsley, chopped
- ¼ cup oregano, chopped

Directions:

Set your instant pot on Sauté mode, add the oil, heat it up, add the garlic and the shallot and sauté for 2 minutes. Add the rest of the ingredients, put the lid on and cook on Low for 8 minutes. Release the pressure naturally for 10 minutes, divide the mix into bowls and serve.

Nutrition: calories 221, fat 8, fiber 3, carbs 6, protein 7

Salmon and Potatoes

Prep time: 10 minutes | Cooking time: 15 minutes | Servings: 4

Ingredients:

- 1 and ½ pounds salmon fillets, boneless, skinless and cubed
- 1 pound baby red potatoes, halved
- 3 garlic cloves, crushed
- 2 tablespoons parsley, chopped
- 1 cup chicken stock
- A pinch of salt and black pepper
- 2 tablespoon olive oil

Directions:

Set the instant pot on Sauté mode, add the oil, heat it up, add the garlic and sauté for 2 minutes. Add the rest of the ingredients, put the lid on and cook on High for 13 minutes. Release the pressure naturally for 10 minutes, divide the mix between plates and serve.

Nutrition: calories 235, fat 8, fiber 4, carbs 7, protein 9

Shrimp and Crab Mix

Prep time: 10 minutes | Cooking time: 15 minutes | Servings: 4

Ingredients:

- 1 tablespoon olive oil
- 1 pound shrimp, peeled and deveined
- 1 and ½ cups crab meat
- 1 cup white onion, chopped
- 1 cup chicken stock
- 1 cup green bell pepper, chopped
- 4 garlic cloves, chopped
- 6 plum tomatoes, chopped
- A pinch of cayenne pepper
- 1 teaspoon thyme, dried
- 1 teaspoon sweet paprika
- A pinch of salt and black pepper

Directions:

Set the instant pot on Sauté mode, add the oil, heat it up, add the onion, garlic and bell pepper, stir and cook for 2 minutes. Add the shrimp and the rest of the ingredients, put the lid on and cook on High for 10 minutes. Release the pressure naturally for 10 minutes, divide everything into bowls and serve.

Nutrition: calories 211, fat 8, fiber 4, carbs 8, protein 8

Crab and Arugula Mix

Prep time: 10 minutes | Cooking time: 8 minutes | Servings: 4

Ingredients:

- 1 pound crab meat
- 1 cup veggie stock
- 2 tablespoons avocado oil
- 1 tablespoon hot sauce
- 1 tablespoon smoked paprika
- A pinch of salt and black pepper
- ½ bunch parsley, chopped
- 2 garlic cloves, minced
- 1 and ½ cups arugula

Directions:

Set the instant pot on Sauté mode, add the oil, heat it up, add the garlic and cook for 1 minute. Add the crab and the rest of the ingredients except the arugula, put the lid on and cook on High for 7 minutes. Release the pressure naturally for 10 minutes, transfer the mix to a bowl, add the arugula, toss and serve.

Nutrition: calories 193, fat 7, fiber 3, carbs 6, protein 6

Marinated Salmon

Prep time: 15 minutes | Cooking time: 12 minutes | Servings: 4

Ingredients:

- 4 salmon fillets, skinless and boneless
- ¼ cup olive oil
- Juice of 1 lemon
- 4 garlic cloves, minced
- 2 thyme springs, chopped
- 1 tablespoon rosemary, chopped
- A pinch of salt and black pepper
- 1 cup water

Directions:

In a bowl, mix the salmon with the oil and the rest of the ingredients except the water, toss and keep in the fridge for 10 minutes. Put the water in the instant pot, add the steamer basket, arrange the salmon fillets inside, put the lid on and cook on High for 12 minutes. Release the pressure fast for 5 minutes, divide the salmon between plates and serve with a side salad.

Nutrition: calories 200, fat 11, fiber 4, carbs 5, protein 12

Shrimp and Carrots

Prep time: 10 minutes | Cooking time: 6 minutes | Servings: 4

Ingredients:

- 1 pound shrimp, peeled and deveined
- 1 cup carrots, sliced
- 1 cup chicken stock
- 1 tablespoon olive oil
- 1 red onion, chopped
- 1 tablespoon chives, chopped

Directions:

Set the instant pot on Sauté mode, add the oil, heat it up, add the onion and sauté for 2 minutes. Add the shrimp and the rest of the ingredients except the chives, put the lid on and cook on High for 4 minutes. Release the pressure naturally for 10 minutes, divide the mix into bowls, sprinkle the chives on top and serve.

Nutrition: calories 200, fat 12, fiber 3, carbs 7, protein 9

Creamy Coconut Trout

Prep time: 5 minutes | Cooking time: 15 minutes | Servings: 4

Ingredients:

- 1 pound trout fillets, boneless, skinless and cubed
- 1 tablespoon red chili powder
- A pinch of salt and black pepper
- 1 cup coconut cream
- 4 garlic cloves, minced
- 2 tablespoons olive oil
- ¼ teaspoon mustard seeds
- 1 tablespoon cilantro, chopped

Directions:

Set the instant pot on Sauté mode, add the oil, heat it up, add the garlic, chili powder, salt and pepper, stir and cook for 2 minutes. Add the trout and the rest of the ingredients, put the lid on and cook on High for 13 minutes. Release the pressure fast for 5 minutes, divide the mix into bowls and serve.

Nutrition: calories 232, fat 10, fiber 4, carbs 6, protein 9

Lime Tuna and Peas

Prep time: 10 minutes | Cooking time: 15 minutes | Servings: 4

Ingredients:

- 1 pound tuna, skinless, boneless and cubed
- 1 pound fresh peas
- 1 and ½ cups tomatoes, crushed
- 1 yellow onion, chopped
- A drizzle of olive oil
- Salt and black pepper to the taste

Directions:

Set your instant pot on Sauté mode, add the oil, heat it up, add the onion, stir and cook for 2 minutes Add the tuna and the rest of the ingredients, put the lid on and cook on High for 10 minutes. Release the pressure naturally for 10 minutes, divide the mix into bowls and serve.

Nutrition: calories 182, fat 7, fiber 3, carbs 6, protein 9

Coriander Salmon

Prep time: 15 minutes | Cooking time: 10 minutes | Servings: 4

Ingredients:

- 1 pound salmon, skinless, boneless and cubed
- 2 garlic cloves, minced
- 2 green chilies, chopped
- 1 yellow onion, chopped
- ½ tablespoon lime juice
- 1 tablespoon coriander powder
- A pinch of salt and black pepper
- 1 tablespoon avocado oil
- 1 cup chicken stock

Directions:

Set your instant pot on Sauté mode, add the oil, heat it up, add the onion, garlic, chilies and coriander, stir and cook for 2 minutes. Add the rest of the ingredients, put the lid on and cook on High for 13 minutes. Release the pressure naturally for 10 minutes, divide the mix between plates and serve with a side salad.

Nutrition: calories 210, fat 8, fiber 3, carbs 6, protein 14

Dill Beef Roast

Prep time: 10 minutes | Cooking time: 50 minutes | Servings: 4

Ingredients:

- 2 and ½ pounds beef brisket
- 2 garlic cloves, minced
- 2 red onions, thinly sliced
- 1 celery stalk, chopped

- 2 tablespoons dill, chopped
- 1 teaspoon cinnamon powder
- Salt and black pepper to the taste
- 2 and ½ cups beef stock

Directions:

In your instant pot, combine the beef with the garlic and the rest of the ingredients, put the lid on and cook on High for 50 minutes. Release the pressure naturally for 10 minutes, transfer the beef to a cutting board, slice and divide between plates.

Serve with a side salad.

Nutrition: calories 254, fat 12, fiber 2, carbs 6, protein 16

Beef Roast and Mushrooms

Prep time: 10 minutes | Cooking time: 40 minutes | Servings: 4

Ingredients:

- 1 and ½ pounds beef roast
- 2 carrots, sliced
- ½ cup beef stock
- ½ pound mushrooms, sliced

- 2 garlic cloves, minced
- ¼ teaspoon rosemary, dried
- A pinch of salt and black pepper
- 1 teaspoon smoked paprika

Directions:

In your instant pot, combine the beef with carrots, stock and the rest of the ingredients, put the lid on and cook on High for 40 minutes. Release the pressure naturally for 10 minutes, slice the roast, divide it and the veggies mix between plates and serve.

Nutrition: calories 243, fat 15, fiber 3, carbs 6, protein 20

Coconut Curry Beef

Prep time: 10 minutes | Cooking time: 30 minutes | Servings: 4

Ingredients:

- 2 pounds beef stew meat, cubed
- 2 tablespoons olive oil
- 2 and ½ tablespoons curry powder
- 2 yellow onions, chopped

- 2 garlic cloves, minced
- 10 ounces coconut milk
- 2 tablespoons cilantro, chopped
- A pinch of salt and black pepper

Directions:

Set your instant pot on Sauté mode, add the oil, heat it up, add onions and garlic, stir and sauté for 4 minutes. Add the meat and brown for 5 minutes more. Add the rest of the ingredients, put the lid on and cook on High for 25 minutes. Release the pressure naturally for 10 minutes, divide everything between plates and serve.

Nutrition: calories 263, fat 14, fiber 3, carbs 6, protein 16

Beef and Avocado Mix

Prep time: 10 minutes | Cooking time: 30 minutes | Servings: 4

Ingredients:

- 1 and ½ pound beef, cubed
- 1 yellow onion, chopped
- 2 tablespoons avocado oil
- 2 avocados, peeled, pitted and roughly chopped
- 2 garlic cloves, minced
- 1 cup tomato puree
- A pinch of salt and black pepper
- 1 and ½ cups beef stock
- 1 tablespoon cilantro, chopped

Directions:

Set your instant pot on Sauté mode, add oil, heat it up, add the meat and brown for 5 minutes. Add the onion and garlic and sauté for 3-4 minutes more. Add the rest of the ingredients except the cilantro, put the lid on and cook on High for 25 minutes. Release the pressure naturally for 10 minutes, divide the mix between plates, sprinkle the cilantro on top and serve.

Nutrition: calories 264, fat 14, fiber 4, carbs 7, protein 15

Spicy Beef and Green Beans

Prep time: 10 minutes | Cooking time: 40 minutes | Servings: 4

Ingredients:

- 1 and ½ pounds beef, cubed
- 1 sweet onion, chopped
- A pinch of salt and black pepper
- 16 ounces green beans, trimmed and halved
- 1 and ½ cups beef stock
- 6 garlic cloves, chopped
- 6 jalapeno peppers, diced
- 2 tablespoons avocado oil
- 1 tablespoon parsley, chopped

Directions:

Set your instant pot on Sauté mode, add the oil, heat it up, add the beef, and brown for 5 minutes. Add the onion, garlic and jalapenos and cook for 3 minutes. Add the rest of the ingredients except the parsley, put the lid on and cook on High for 30 minutes. Release the pressure naturally for 10 minutes, divide the mix between plates, sprinkle the parsley on top and serve.

Nutrition: calories 263, fat 12, fiber 4, carbs 6, protein 16

Beef and Kidney Beans Mix

Prep time: 10 minutes | Cooking time: 35 minutes | Servings: 4

Ingredients:

- 1 and ½ pound beef, cubed
- 1 yellow onion, chopped
- 2 tablespoons olive oil
- A pinch of salt and black pepper
- 1 tablespoon sweet paprika
-
- ½ teaspoon chili powder
- 1 and ½ cups beef stock
- 2 garlic cloves, minced
- 8 ounces kidney beans, soaked overnight and drained
- 8 ounces canned tomatoes, chopped

Directions:

Set your instant pot on Sauté mode, add the oil, heat it up, add the meat and brown for 5 minutes. Add the onion, garlic, chili, paprika, salt and pepper and sauté for 5 minutes more. Add the rest of the ingredients, put the lid on and cook on High for 25 minutes. Release the pressure naturally for 10 minutes,, divide the mix between plates and serve.

Nutrition: calories 263, fat 14, fiber 4, carbs 6, protein 18

Beef and Artichokes

Prep time: 10 minutes | Cooking time: 45 minutes | Servings: 6

Ingredients:

- 2 pounds beef roast, cubed
- 1 tablespoon olive oil
- A pinch of salt and black pepper
- 2 cups beef stock
- 12 ounces canned artichokes, drained
- 1 tablespoon capers, drained and chopped
- 2 tomatoes, cubed
- 1 tablespoon parsley, chopped
- ½ teaspoon smoked paprika
- 1 yellow onion, chopped
- 4 garlic cloves, minced

Directions:

Set the instant pot on Sauté mode, add the oil, heat it up, add the onion and the garlic and sauté for 5 minutes. Add the meat and brown for 5 minutes more. Add the rest of the ingredients, put the lid on and cook on High for 35 minutes. Release the pressure naturally for 10 minutes, divide the mix between plates and serve.

Nutrition: calories 264, fat 14, fiber 4, carbs 6, protein 17

Lemony Beef Mix

Prep time: 10 minutes | Cooking time: 35 minutes | Servings: 4

Ingredients:

- 2 tablespoons avocado oil
- 1 and ½ pounds beef stew meat, cubed
- 1 red onion, chopped
- 2 tablespoons lemon juice
- 2 garlic cloves, minced
- 2 cups beef stock
- A pinch of salt and black pepper
- ½ teaspoon thyme, dried
- ½ bunch basil, chopped

Directions:

Set the instant pot on Sauté mode, add the oil, heat it up, add the meat, onion and garlic and cook for 5 minutes. Add the rest of the ingredients, put the lid on and cook on High for 30 minutes. Release the pressure naturally for 10 minutes, divide the mix between plates and serve.

Nutrition: calories 263, fat 14, fiber 3, carbs 7, protein 20

Beef and Shallots Sauce

Prep time: 10 minutes | Cooking time: 35 minutes | Servings: 4

Ingredients:

- 6 shallots, chopped
- 2 pounds beef stew meat, cubed
- 2 cups beef stock
- 2 garlic cloves, minced
- 2 tablespoons chives, chopped
- 1 teaspoon sage, dried
- ½ teaspoon oregano, dried
- A pinch of salt and black pepper
- 2 tablespoons olive oil

Directions:

Set your instant pot on Sauté mode, add the oil, heat it up, add the garlic and the shallots and sauté for 5 minutes. Add the meat and brown for 5 minutes more. Add the rest of the ingredients, put the lid on and cook on High for 25 minutes. Release the pressure naturally for 10 minutes, divide the beef and shallots sauce between plates and serve.

Nutrition: calories 263, fat 14, fiber 5, carbs 7, protein 15

Cheesy Beef and Carrots

Prep time: 10 minutes | Cooking time: 30 minutes | Servings: 4

Ingredients:

- 1 and ½ pound beef stew meat, cubed
- 12 ounces mozzarella cheese, shredded
- 1 tablespoon olive oil
- 1 red onion, chopped
- 2 spring onions, chopped
- 4 carrots, sliced
- 1 and ½ cups beef stock
- 1 tablespoon parsley, chopped
- A pinch of salt and black pepper

Directions:

Set your instant pot on Sauté mode, add the oil, heat it up, add the red and spring onion and cook for 2 minutes. Add the meat and brown it for 5 minutes. Add the rest of the ingredients except the parsley and the cheese, put the lid on and cook on High for 22 minutes. Release the pressure naturally for 10 minutes, sprinkle the cheese all over the beef mix, leave aside for a few minutes, divide everything between plates and serve.

Nutrition: calories 253, fat 14, fiber 3, carbs 7, protein 17

Beef and Zucchini Mix

Prep time: 10 minutes | Cooking time: 30 minutes | Servings: 4

Ingredients:

- 2 tablespoons chili paste
- 1 cup beef stock
- 1 tablespoon olive oil
- 2 pounds beef steak, cubed
- ¼ teaspoon red pepper flakes
- A pinch of salt and black pepper
- 3 zucchinis, cubed
- 2 spring onions, chopped

Directions:

Set your instant pot on Sauté mode, add the oil, heat it up, add the meat and brown for 5 minutes. Add the chili paste and the rest of the ingredients except the zucchinis and the spring onion, put the lid on and cook on High for 20 minutes. Release the pressure fast for 5 minutes, add the zucchinis, put the lid back on and cook on High for 5 minutes more. Release the pressure fast for 5 minutes more, divide the mix between plates, sprinkle the spring onion on top and serve.

Nutrition: calories 276, fat 14, fiber 3, carbs 7, protein 20

Cinnamon Beef and Asparagus

Prep time: 10 minutes | Cooking time: 30 minutes | Servings: 4

Ingredients:

- 2 pounds chuck roast, cubed
- 1 tablespoon avocado oil
- 1 yellow onion, chopped
- 1 cup beef stock
- 1 pound asparagus, trimmed and halved
- 2 teaspoons sweet paprika
- 1 and ½ teaspoons cinnamon powder
- 1 tablespoon chives, chopped

Directions:

Set your instant pot on Sauté mode, add the oil, heat it up, add the onion and sauté for 2 minutes. Add the meat and brown for 3 minutes more. Add the rest of the ingredients except the asparagus and the chives, toss, put the lid on and cook on High for 20 minutes. Release the pressure naturally for 10 minutes, set the pot on Sauté mode again, add the asparagus and the chives, toss gently and cook for 5 minutes more. Divide the mix between plates and serve.

Nutrition: calories 287, fat 16, fiber 4, carbs 6, protein 20

Beef and Red Cabbage Mix

Prep time: 10 minutes | Cooking time: 40 minutes | Servings: 4

Ingredients:

- 2 and ½ pounds beef roast, cubed
- 2 cups beef stock
- 3 garlic cloves, chopped
- 1 red cabbage head, shredded
- A pinch of salt and black pepper
- 1 cup tomato puree
- 1 tablespoon cilantro, chopped

Directions:

In your instant pot, combine the beef with the rest of the ingredients except the cabbage and the cilantro, toss, put the lid on and cook on High for 30 minutes. Release the pressure fast for 5 minutes, add the cabbage, put the lid back on and cook on High for 10 minutes more. Release the pressure fast for 5 more minutes, divide the beef and cabbage mix between plates, sprinkle the cilantro on top and serve.

Nutrition: calories 264, fat 8, fiber 3, carbs 6, protein 17

Cheesy Lamb

Prep time: 10 minutes | Cooking time: 30 minutes | Servings: 4

Ingredients:

- 1 and ½ pound lamb shanks
- 2 tablespoons olive oil
- 1 yellow onion, chopped
- 2 garlic cloves, minced
- 2 tablespoons tomato sauce
- 1 teaspoon rosemary, dried
- 2 cups beef stock
- A pinch of salt and black pepper
- ¼ cup goat cheese, crumbled
- 1 tablespoon cilantro, chopped

Directions:

Set your instant pot on Sauté mode, add the oil, heat it up, add the meat and brown for 3 minutes. Add the onion, garlic and rosemary and cook for 2 minutes more. Add the rest of the ingredients except the cheese and cilantro, put the lid on and cook on High for 25 minutes. Release the pressure naturally for 10 minutes, add the cheese and the cilantro, leave the mix aside for a few minutes, divide everything between plates and serve.

Nutrition: calories 275, fat 13, fiber 4, carbs 7, protein 20

Sage Lamb Ribs

Prep time: 10 minutes | Cooking time: 25 minutes | Servings: 4

Ingredients:

- 4 lamb ribs
- 4 garlic cloves, minced
- 1 tablespoon sage, chopped
- 1 and ½ cups veggie stock
- 2 tablespoons olive oil
- A pinch of salt and black pepper
- 2 tomatoes, cubed

Directions:

Set your instant pot on Sauté mode, add the oil, heat it up, add the lamb, garlic, sage, salt and pepper and brown for 5 minutes. Add the stock and the tomatoes, put the lid on and cook on High for 20 minutes. Release the pressure naturally for 10 minutes, divide the lamb between plates and serve.

Nutrition: calories 263, fat 12, fiber 4, carbs 7, protein 12

Herbed Lamb Shanks

Prep time: 10 minutes | Cooking time: 40 minutes | Servings: 4

Ingredients:

- 4 lamb shanks
- 2 tablespoons olive oil
- A pinch of salt and black pepper
- 1 teaspoon marjoram, dried
- 1 teaspoon rosemary, dried
- 1 teaspoon sage, dried
- 1 teaspoon thyme, dried
- 3 garlic cloves, minced
- 2 cups veggie stock

Directions:

Set your instant pot on Sauté mode, add the oil, heat it up, add the meat and brown for 4 minutes. Add the rest of the ingredients, put the lid on and cook on High for 35 minutes. Release the pressure naturally for 10 minutes, divide the lamb between plates and serve with a side salad.

Nutrition: calories 263, fat 12, fiber 3, carbs 7, protein 10

Coconut Lamb Curry

Prep time: 10 minutes | Cooking time: 30 minutes | Servings: 4

Ingredients:

- 2 pounds lamb shoulder, cubed
- 1 cup coconut milk
- ½ cup coconut cream
- 3 tablespoons curry powder
- 2 tablespoons avocado oil
- 1 red onion, chopped
- A pinch of salt and black pepper
- 1 tablespoon parsley, chopped

Directions:

Set your instant pot on Sauté mode, add the oil, heat it up, add the onion, stir and cook for 5 minutes. Add the meat and brown for 4 minutes more. Add the rest of the ingredients, put the lid on and cook on High for 20 minutes. Release the pressure naturally for 10 minutes, divide the mix between plates and serve.

Nutrition: calories 233, fat 7, fiber 2, carbs 6, protein 12

Lamb Chops and Peas

Prep time: 10 minutes | Cooking time: 40 minutes | Servings: 4

Ingredients:

- 4 lamb chops
- A pinch of salt and black pepper
- 2 tablespoons olive oil
- 2 red onions, chopped
- 2 garlic cloves, minced
- 1 cup green peas
- 12 ounces tomatoes, chopped
- 2 tablespoons parsley, chopped

Directions:

Set your instant pot on Sauté mode, add the oil, heat it up, add the lamb and brown for 2 minutes. Add the onion and garlic and sauté for 3 minutes more. Add the rest of the ingredients, put the lid on and cook on High for 30 minutes. Release the pressure naturally for 10 minutes, divide the mix between plates and serve.

Nutrition: calories 235, fat 12, fiber 5, carbs 7, protein 10

Spiced Lamb Bites

Prep time: 10 minutes | Cooking time: 25 minutes | Servings: 4

Ingredients:

- 2 pounds lamb shoulder, cubed
- A drizzle of olive oil
- 3 tablespoons almonds, toasted and chopped
- 1 and ½ cups veggie stock
- 2 yellow onions, chopped
- 2 garlic cloves, minced
- A pinch of salt and black pepper
- 1 teaspoon cumin powder
- 1 teaspoon ginger powder
- 1 teaspoon cinnamon powder

Directions:

In a bowl, mix the meat with the oil, salt, pepper, cumin, ginger and cinnamon and toss well. In your instant pot, combine the meat with the almonds and the remaining ingredients, put the lid on and cook on High for 25 minutes. Release the pressure naturally for 10 minutes, divide the spiced lamb between plates and serve with a side salad.

Nutrition: calories 211, fat 9, fiber 2, carbs 6, protein 12

Lamb and Bok Choy

Prep time: 10 minutes | Cooking time: 35 minutes | Servings: 4

Ingredients:

- 1 and ½ pounds lamb shoulder, cubed
- 1 cup bok choy, roughly chopped
- 4 tomatoes, chopped
- 1 red onion, chopped
- 2 garlic cloves, minced
- 2 tablespoons tomato paste
- 1 teaspoon avocado oil
- A pinch of salt and black pepper
- A handful parsley, chopped

Directions:

Set your instant pot on Sauté mode, add the oil, heat it up, add the meat and brown for 2 minutes. Add the onion and garlic and cook for 3 minutes. Add the rest of the ingredients except the parsley, put the lid on and cook on High for 30 minutes. Release the pressure naturally for 10 minutes, divide everything between plates, sprinkle the parsley on top and serve.

Nutrition: calories 254, fat 12, fiber 3, carbs 6, protein 16

Lamb and Sweet Potatoes

Prep time: 10 minutes | Cooking time: 35 minutes | Servings: 4

Ingredients:

- 1 and ½ pounds lamb shoulder, cubed
- 1 carrot, chopped
- 1 yellow onion, chopped
- 3 garlic cloves, crushed
- A pinch of salt and black pepper
- 2 sweet potatoes, cubed
- 1 cup chicken stock
- 2 tablespoons avocado oil

Directions:

Set your instant pot on Sauté mode, add the oil, heat it up, add the onion and garlic and sauté for 2 minutes. Add the meat and brown for 3 minutes. Add the rest of the ingredients, put the lid on and cook on High for 30 minutes. Release the pressure naturally for 10 minutes, divide the mix between plates and serve.

Nutrition: calories 274, fat 9, fiber 5, carbs 6, protein 12

Lamb and Quinoa

Prep time: 10 minutes | Cooking time: 25 minutes | Servings: 4

Ingredients:
- 1 and ½ cups quinoa
- 1 lamb shoulder, cubed
- 2 yellow onions, chopped
- 2 cups beef stock
- ¼ cup tomato sauce
- 1 tablespoon chives, chopped
- A pinch of salt and black pepper

Directions:

In your instant pot, mix the quinoa with the lamb and the rest of the ingredients except the chives, put the lid on and cook on High for 25 minutes. Release the pressure naturally for 10 minutes, divide the mix between plates and serve.

Nutrition: calories 232, fat 10, fiber 5, carbs 7, protein 11

Provencal Lamb Shanks

Prep time: 10 minutes | Cooking time: 30 minutes | Servings: 4

Ingredients:
- 4 lamb chops
- 2 spring onions, chopped
- 2 cups canned tomatoes, chopped
- 2 garlic cloves, minced
- 1 and ½ teaspoons herbs de Provence
- A pinch of salt and black pepper
- 1 cup veggie stock

Directions:

In your instant pot, combine the lamb chops with the rest of the ingredients, put the lid on and cook on High for 30 minutes. Release the pressure naturally for 10 minutes, divide the mix between plates and serve.

Nutrition: calories 243, fat 11, fiber 4, carbs 6, protein 10

Salsa Lamb Mix

Prep time: 10 minutes | Cooking time: 35 minutes | Servings: 4

Ingredients:
- 1 and ½ pounds lamb shoulder, cubed
- 1 and ½ cups salsa Verde
- 3 garlic cloves, minced
- 1 red onion, chopped
- 2 tablespoons olive oil
- A pinch of salt and black pepper
- ½ bunch cilantro, chopped

Directions:

Set your instant pot on Sauté mode, add the oil, heat it up, add the onion and garlic, stir and cook for 5 minutes. Add the meat and the rest of the ingredients, put the lid on and cook on High for 30 minutes. Release the pressure naturally for 10 minutes, divide the mix between plates and serve.

Nutrition: calories 232, fat 12, fiber 4, carbs 6, protein 9

Turmeric Lamb Shanks

Prep time: 10 minutes | Cooking time: 30 minutes | Servings: 4

Ingredients:

- 4 lamb shanks
- A pinch of salt and black pepper
- 3 teaspoons turmeric powder
- 1 teaspoon cinnamon powder
- 1 tablespoon ginger, grated
- 2 tomatoes, chopped
- 2 garlic cloves, minced
- 2 and ½ cups veggie stock
- 1 teaspoon coriander, chopped

Directions:

Set your instant pot on Sauté mode, add the oil, heat it up, add the lamb and garlic and brown for 5 minutes. Add the rest of the ingredients, put the lid on and cook on High for 25 minutes. Release the pressure naturally for 10 minutes, divide everything between plates and serve.

Nutrition: calories 232, fat 9, fiber 3, carbs 6, protein 10

Balsamic Pork Chops

Prep time: 5 minutes | Cooking time: 25 minutes | Servings: 4

Ingredients:

- 4 pork chops
- 2 tablespoons balsamic vinegar
- 2 tablespoons olive oil
- A pinch of salt and black pepper
- 1 tablespoon rosemary, chopped
- ½ cup beef stock

Directions:

Set your instant pot on Sauté mode, add the oil, heat it up, add pork chops and brown for 2 minutes on each side. Add the rest of the ingredients, put the lid on and cook on High for 20 minutes. Release the pressure fast for 5 minutes, divide everything between plates and serve with a side salad.

Nutrition: calories 200, fat 11, fiber 3, carbs 6, protein 15

Pork Chops and Apples

Prep time: 5 minutes | Cooking time: 25 minutes | Servings: 4

Ingredients:

- 4 pork chops
- 2 tablespoons avocado oil
- 1 garlic clove, minced
- 2 tablespoons lemon juice
- 2 green apples, cored and cubed
- 1 yellow onion, chopped
- ½ cup beef stock
- A pinch of salt and black pepper
- 1 tablespoon parsley, chopped

Directions:

Set your instant pot on Sauté mode, add the oil, heat it up, add the onion and garlic and sauté for 2 minutes. Add the pork chops and cook for 3 minutes. Add the rest of the ingredients except the parsley, put the lid on and cook on High for 20 minutes. Release the pressure fast for 5 minutes, divide everything between plates and serve.

Nutrition: calories 210, fat 5, fiber 3, carbs 8, protein 12

Pork and Parsley Sauce

Prep time: 10 minutes | Cooking time: 20 minutes | Servings: 4

Ingredients:

- 4 pork chops
- 2 tablespoons olive oil
- 2 teaspoons chili powder
- 1 cup coconut cream
- 2 garlic cloves, minced
- Salt and black pepper to the taste
- 1 small bunch parsley, chopped

Directions:

In a blender, combine the parsley with the oil, cream, garlic, chili powder, salt and pepper and pulse well. Put the pork chops in your instant pot, add the parsley sauce, toss, put the lid on and cook on High for 20 minutes. Release the pressure naturally for 10 minutes, divide the mix between plates and serve.

Nutrition: calories 248, fat 11, fiber 3, carbs 6, protein 15

Tomato Pork Chops

Prep time: 10 minutes | Cooking time: 25 minutes | Servings: 4

Ingredients:

- 4 pork chops
- 1 cup veggie stock
- ¼ cup tomato puree
- 4 teaspoons sweet paprika
- A pinch of salt and black pepper

Directions:

In your instant pot, combine the pork chops with the rest of the ingredients, put the lid on and cook on High for 25 minutes. Release the pressure naturally for 10 minutes, divide everything between plates and serve.

Nutrition: calories 233, fat 9, fiber 3, carbs 7, protein 14

Pork and Endives

Prep time: 10 minutes | Cooking time: 25 minutes | Servings: 4

Ingredients:

- 4 pork chops
- 2 tablespoons olive oil
- A pinch of salt and black pepper
- 2 garlic cloves, minced
- 1 yellow onion, chopped
- 1 cup chicken stock
- 2 endives, sliced
- ¼ cup tomato sauce
- 1 tablespoon parsley, chopped

Directions:

Set your instant pot on Sauté mode, add the oil, heat it up, add the onion and garlic and sauté for 2 minutes. Add the meat and cook for 3 minutes more. Add the rest of the ingredients, put the lid on and cook on High for 20 minutes. Release the pressure naturally for 10 minutes, divide the mix between plates and serve.

Nutrition: calories 227, fat 14, fiber 4, carbs 6, protein 16

Sesame Pork Chops

Prep time: 10 minutes | Cooking time: 25 minutes | Servings: 4

Ingredients:

- 4 pork chops
- 2 teaspoons sesame seeds
- 1 tablespoon olive oil
- 1 teaspoon chili powder
- 1 teaspoon sweet paprika
- 1 cup tomato sauce
- 1 tablespoon chives, chopped

Directions:

Set your instant pot on Sauté mode, add the oil, heat it up, add the pork chops and brown for 5 minutes. Add the rest of the ingredients except the sesame seeds, put the lid on and cook on High for 20 minutes. Release the pressure naturally for 10 minutes, divide the pork chops between plates, sprinkle the sesame seeds on top and serve.

Nutrition: calories 236, fat 12, fiber 2, carbs 7, protein 15

Pork and Fennel

Prep time: 10 minutes | Cooking time: 25 minutes | Servings: 4

Ingredients:

- 1 and ½ pounds pork loin, cubed
- 1 cup stock
- 2 fennel bulbs, sliced
- 2 tablespoons lemon juice
- 2 tablespoons olive oil
- ¼ cup garlic powder
- 1 tablespoon sweet paprika
- A pinch of salt and black pepper

Directions:

Set the instant pot on Sauté mode, add the oil, heat it up, add the meat and brown for 5 minutes. Add the rest of the ingredients, put the lid on and cook on High for 20 minutes. Release the pressure naturally for 10 minutes, divide the mix between plates and serve.

Nutrition: 273, fat 12, fiber 4, carbs 7, protein 17

Pork Chops and Cauliflower Rice

Prep time: 10 minutes | Cooking time: 25 minutes | Servings: 4

Ingredients:

- 2 cups beef stock
- 1 tablespoon peppercorns, crushed
- 1 cup cauliflower rice
- 4 garlic cloves, minced
- 4 pork chops
- 1 red onion, chopped
- 2 tablespoons olive oil
- A pinch of salt and black pepper

Directions:

Set your instant pot on sauté mode, add the oil, heat it up, add the onion and the garlic and sauté for 2 minutes. Add the meat and brown for 3 minutes. Add the rest of the ingredients, put the lid on and cook on High for 20 minutes. Release the pressure naturally for 10 minutes, divide the mix between plates and serve.

Nutrition: calories 244, fat 12, fiber 2, carbs 5, protein 16

Rosemary Pork and Green Beans

Prep time: 10 minutes | Cooking time: 25 minutes | Servings: 4

Ingredients:

- 1 and ½ pound pork loin, sliced
- 1 pound green beans, trimmed
- 1 and ½ cup veggie stock
- 3 garlic cloves, minced
- 1 yellow onion, chopped
- 1 bunch rosemary, chopped
- A pinch of salt and black pepper

Directions:

In your instant pot, combine the meat with green beans and the rest of the ingredients, put the lid on and cook on High for 25 minutes. Release the pressure naturally for 10 minutes, divide the mix between plates and serve.

Nutrition: calories 254, fat 14, fiber 3, carbs 6, protein 17

Mustard Pork Ribs

Prep time: 10 minutes | Cooking time: 30 minutes | Servings: 4

Ingredients:

- 2 pounds country style pork ribs
- A pinch of salt and black pepper
- 1 tablespoon smoked paprika
- 2 tablespoons Dijon mustard
- 1 tablespoon sage, chopped
- 1 tablespoon olive oil
- 1 and ½ cups beef stock
- 1 tablespoon cilantro, chopped

Directions:

Set your instant pot on Sauté mode, add the oil, heat it up, add the ribs and the rest of the ingredients except the stock and the cilantro, toss and brown for 5 minutes. Add the stock, put the lid on and cook on High for 25 minutes. Release the pressure naturally for 10 minutes, divide the ribs between plates, sprinkle the parsley on top and serve.

Nutrition: calories 263, fat 14, fiber 3, carbs 6, protein 20

Pesto Pork Chops

Prep time: 10 minutes | Cooking time: 25 minutes | Servings: 4

Ingredients:

- 4 pork chops
- A pinch of salt and black pepper
- 1 teaspoon onion powder
- ½ teaspoon sweet paprika
- 1 yellow onion, chopped
- 4 tablespoons basil pesto
- 1 and ½ cups beef stock
- A pinch of cayenne pepper

Directions:

In a bowl, mix the pork chops with the pesto and the rest of the ingredients except the stock and rub well. Put the pork chops in your instant pot, add the stock, put the lid on and cook on High for 25 minutes. Release the pressure naturally for 10 minutes, divide the pork chops between plates and serve with a side salad.

Nutrition: calories 283, fat 13, fiber 4, carbs 6, protein 16

Oregano and Spring Onions Pork

Prep time: 10 minutes | Cooking time: 35 minutes | Servings: 4

Ingredients:

- 4 green onions, chopped
- 4 pork chops
- 2 teaspoons olive oil
- 3 garlic cloves, minced
- 1 tablespoon oregano, chopped
- 1 and ½ cups beef stock
- 2 tablespoons tomato sauce
- 1 tablespoon cilantro, chopped

Directions:

Set your instant pot on Sauté mode, add the oil, heat it up, add the onions and garlic and sauté for 2 minutes. Add the meat and brown for 3 minutes. Add the rest of the ingredients, put the lid on and cook on High for 30 minutes. Release the pressure naturally for 10 minutes, divide the pork chops between plates and serve.

Nutrition: calories 253, fat 14, fiber 2, carbs 6, protein 18

Pork and Collard Greens

Prep time: 10 minutes | Cooking time: 25 minutes | Servings: 4

Ingredients:

- 1 and ½ pound pork loin, cubed
- 1 tablespoon avocado oil
- 1 yellow onion, chopped
- A pinch of salt and black pepper
- ¼ cup tomato paste
- 1 pound collard greens
- 1 tablespoon cilantro, chopped

Directions:

Set your instant pot on Sauté mode, add the oil, heat it up, add the onion and cook for 2 minutes. Add the meat and brown for another 3 minutes. Add the rest of the ingredients except the cilantro, put the lid on and cook on High for 20 minutes. Release the pressure naturally for 10 minutes, divide everything between plates and serve.

Nutrition: calories 264, fat 14, fiber 3, carbs 6, protein 17

Pork Chops and Bell Peppers

Prep time: 10 minutes | Cooking time: 35 minutes | Servings: 4

Ingredients:

- 2 tablespoons olive oil
- 4 pork chops
- A pinch of salt and black pepper
- 1 red bell pepper, roughly chopped
- 1 green bell pepper, roughly chopped
- 3 garlic cloves, minced
- 1 red onion, chopped
- 2 cups beef stock
- 1 tablespoon parsley, chopped

Directions:

Set your instant pot on Sauté mode, add the oil, heat it up, add the pork chops and brown for 2 minutes. Add the garlic and the onion and brown for 3 minutes more. Add all the other ingredients except the parsley, put the lid on and cook on High for 30 minutes. Release the pressure naturally for 10 minutes, divide the mix between plates, sprinkle the parsley on top and serve.

Nutrition: calories 273, fat 13, fiber 2, carbs 6, protein 15

Orange and Cinnamon Pork

Prep time: 10 minutes | Cooking time: 35 minutes | Servings: 4

Ingredients:

- 4 pork chops
- 3 garlic cloves, minced
- 1 tablespoon cinnamon powder
- Juice of 1 orange
- A pinch of salt and black pepper
- 1 tablespoon ginger, grated
- ½ cup beef stock
- 1 teaspoon rosemary, dried

Directions:

In your instant pot, combine all the ingredients, put the lid on and cook on High for 35 minutes. Release the pressure naturally for 10 minutes, divide the mix between plates and serve.

Nutrition: calories 274, fat 14, fiber 2, carbs 6, protein 16

Pork, Corn and Green Beans

Prep time: 10 minutes | Cooking time: 35 minutes | Servings: 4

Ingredients:

- 2 pounds pork shoulder, boneless and cubed
- 2 garlic cloves, minced
- A pinch of salt and black pepper
- 1 cup corn
- 1 cup green beans, trimmed and halved
- 1 cup beef stock
- 1 teaspoon cumin, ground

Directions:

In your instant pot, combine the pork with the garlic and the rest of the ingredients, put the lid on and cook on High for 35 minutes. Release the pressure naturally for 10 minutes, divide the mix between plates and serve.

Nutrition: calories 264, fat 14, fiber 2, carbs 8, protein 12

Cocoa Pork

Prep time: 10 minutes | Cooking time: 30 minutes | Servings: 4

Ingredients:

- 4 pork chops
- A pinch of salt and black pepper
- 2 tablespoons cocoa powder
- 2 tablespoons hot sauce
- 1 cup beef stock
- 2 teaspoons chili powder
- ¼ teaspoon cumin, ground
- 1 tablespoon parsley, chopped

Directions:

In your instant pot, combine the pork chops with the rest of the ingredients, put the lid on and cook on High for 30 minutes. Release the pressure naturally for 10 minutes, divide the mix between plates and serve with a side salad.

Nutrition: calories 200, fat 9, fiber 2, carbs 6, protein 12

Pork Shoulder and Celery

Prep time: 10 minutes | Cooking time: 30 minutes | Servings: 4

Ingredients:

- 2 pounds pork shoulder, boneless and cubed
- 2 tablespoons avocado oil
- A pinch of salt and black pepper
- 2 tablespoons chili powder
- 2 celery stalks, chopped
- 4 garlic cloves, minced
- 1 and ½ cups beef stock
- 1 tablespoon sage, chopped

Directions:

Set your instant pot on Sauté mode, add the oil, heat it up, add the garlic and cook for 2 minutes. Add the meat and brown for 3 minutes more. Add the rest of the ingredients, put the lid on and cook on High for 25 minutes. Release the pressure naturally for 10 minutes, divide everything between plates and serve.

Nutrition: calories 234, fat 11, fiber 3, carbs 7, protein 15

Pork and Brussels Sprouts

Prep time: 10 minutes | Cooking time: 30 minutes | Servings: 4

Ingredients:

- 2 pounds pork shoulder, cubed
- 1 and ½ cups beef stock
- 2 cups Brussels sprouts, trimmed and halved
- 2 tablespoons olive oil
- 1 tablespoon parsley, chopped
- 1 tablespoon sweet paprika

Directions:

Set your instant pot on Sauté mode, add the oil, heat it up, add the meat and brown for 5 minutes. Add the rest of the ingredients, put the lid on and cook on High for 25 minutes. Release the pressure naturally for 10 minutes, divide the mix between plates and serve.

Nutrition: calories 273, fat 14, fiber 2, carbs 6, protein 15

Balsamic Sprouts and Pork Chops

Prep time: 10 minutes | Cooking time: 30 minutes | Servings: 4

Ingredients:

- 1 and ½ pound pork chops
- 1 pound Brussels sprouts,
- 2 tablespoons Cajun seasoning
- 1 cup beef stock
- 1 tablespoon parsley, chopped

Directions:

In your instant pot, combine all the ingredients, put the lid on and cook on High for 30 minutes. Release the pressure naturally for 10 minutes, divide everything between plates and serve.

Nutrition: calories 292, fat 12, fiber 3, carbs 7, protein 16

Pork, Spinach and Dill

Prep time: 10 minutes | Cooking time: 25 minutes | Servings: 4

Ingredients:

- 1 and ½ pounds pork stew meat, cubed
- 2 tablespoons olive oil
- ½ cup yellow onion, chopped

- 2 cups baby spinach
- 2 tomatoes, cubed
- 1 and ½ cups beef stock
- 1 tablespoon dill, chopped

Directions:

Set the instant pot on Sauté mode, add the oil, heat it up, add the onion and the meat and brown for 3 minutes. Add the rest of the ingredients, put the lid on and cook on High for 20 minutes. Release the pressure naturally for 10 minutes, divide everything between plates and serve.

Nutrition: calories 277, fat 14, fiber 3, carbs 7, protein 17

Pork and Tomato Meatloaf

Prep time: 10 minutes | Cooking time: 30 minutes | Servings: 4

Ingredients:

- ½ cup coconut milk
- ½ cup almond meal
- 1 yellow onion, minced
- A pinch of salt and black pepper

- 2 eggs, whisked
- 2 pounds pork meat, ground
- ½ cup tomato sauce
- 1 tablespoon chives, chopped

Directions:

In a bowl, mix the pork meat with the rest of the ingredients except the water and stir well. Shape a meatloaf and put it in a loaf pan that fits the instant pot. Add the water to your instant pot, add the steamer basket, put the pan inside, put the lid on and cook on High for 30 minutes. Release the pressure naturally for 10 minutes, cool the meatloaf down, slice and serve.

Nutrition: calories 274, fat 12, fiber 4, carbs 7, protein 16

Pork and Ginger Broccoli

Prep time: 10 minutes | Cooking time: 30 minutes | Servings: 4

Ingredients:

- 1 and ½ pounds pork stew meat, cubed
- 1 tablespoon olive oil
- 2 cups broccoli florets
- 1 tablespoon ginger, grated

- ¾ cup parmesan, grated
- A pinch of salt and black pepper
- ¼ cup tomato puree
- 1 and ½ cups beef stock
- 1 tablespoon basil, chopped

Directions:

Set the instant pot on Sauté mode, add the oil, heat it up, add the meat and brown for 5 minutes. Add the broccoli and the rest of the ingredients except the parmesan and the basil, put the lid on and cook on High for 25 minutes. Release the pressure fast for 5 minutes, sprinkle the parmesan and the basil all over, and leave aside for 5 minutes more. Divide the mix between plates and serve.

Nutrition: calories 269, fat 12, fiber 3, carbs 5, protein 16

Nutmeg Pork

Prep time: 10 minutes | Cooking time: 30 minutes | Servings: 4

Ingredients:

- 1 and ½ pounds pork meat, cubed
- 2 tablespoons parsley, chopped
- 2 garlic cloves, minced
- A pinch of salt and black pepper
- 1 cup beef stock
- 2 teaspoons nutmeg, ground
- ½ teaspoon sweet paprika
- 2 tablespoons olive oil

Directions:

Set the instant pot on Sauté mode, add the oil, heat it up, add the meat and garlic and brown for 5 minutes. Add the rest of the ingredients, put the lid on and cook on High for 25 minutes. Release the pressure naturally for 10 minutes, divide everything between plates and serve.

Nutrition: calories 293, fat 14, fiber 4, carbs 6, protein 18

Tarragon Pork Mix

Prep time: 10 minutes | Cooking time: 30 minutes | Servings: 4

Ingredients:

- 1 red onion, chopped
- 1 tablespoon tarragon, chopped
- ½ teaspoon oregano, dried
- A pinch of salt and black pepper
- 1 and ½ pound pork stew meat, cubed
- 1 tablespoon olive oil
- 1 cup tomato puree

Directions:

Set the instant pot on Sauté mode, add the oil, heat it up, add the meat and the onion and brown for 5 minutes. Add the rest of the ingredients, put the lid on and cook on High for 25 minutes. Release the pressure naturally for 10 minutes, divide the mix between plates and serve.

Nutrition: calories 263, fat 12, fiber 3, carbs 6, protein 13

Pork Roast and Creamy Potatoes

Prep time: 10 minutes | Cooking time: 40 minutes | Servings: 4

Ingredients:

- 2 pounds pork shoulder, sliced
- 2 sweet potatoes, peeled and cubed
- 2 red onions, chopped
- 1 cup coconut cream
- 1 teaspoon chili powder
- ½ teaspoon rosemary, chopped
- 1 tablespoon olive oil
- 1 cup beef stock
- 1 tablespoon parsley, chopped
- A pinch of salt and black pepper

Directions:

Set your instant pot on Sauté mode, add the oil, heat it up, add the meat and onions and brown for 5 minutes. Add the potatoes and the rest of the ingredients except the parsley and the coconut cream, put the lid on and cook on High for 25 minutes. Release the pressure naturally for 10 minutes, set the pot on Sauté mode again, add the cream, toss and cook for 10 minutes more. Divide the mix between plates, sprinkle the parsley on top and serve.

Nutrition: calories 263, fat 14, fiber 3, carbs 7, protein 19

Pork and Balsamic Asparagus

Prep time: 10 minutes | Cooking time: 35 minutes | Servings: 4

Ingredients:

- 2 pounds pork roast
- 4 garlic cloves, minced
- 1 yellow onions, chopped
- 1 cup beef stock
- 1 bunch asparagus, trimmed
- 2 tablespoons balsamic vinegar
- A pinch of salt and black pepper
- 1 teaspoon smoked paprika
- 1 tablespoon basil, chopped
- 1 teaspoon chives, chopped
- 1 tablespoon olive oil

Directions:

Set your instant pot on sauté mode, add the oil, heat it up, add the onion and garlic and sauté for 2 minutes. Add the meat and brown for 5 minutes more. Add the stock, salt, pepper and the basil, put the lid on and cook on High for 20 minutes. Release the pressure naturally for 10 minutes, set the pot on sauté mode again, add the asparagus, vinegar and the chives, cook for 7 minutes more, divide everything between plates and serve.

Nutrition: calories 253, fat 14, fiber 4, carbs 7, protein 17

Beef and Lamb Mix

Prep time: 5 minutes | Cooking time: 35 minutes | Servings: 4

Ingredients:

- 1 pound beef stew meat, cubed
- 1 pound lamb shoulder, cubed
- 4 garlic cloves, minced
- 2 red bell peppers, cut into strips
- 1 tablespoon olive oil
- 2 celery stalks, chopped
- 2 carrots, chopped
- ¼ teaspoon thyme, dried
- A pinch of salt and black pepper
- 1 tablespoon oregano, chopped
- 1 and ½ cups beef stock

Directions:

Set your instant pot on Sauté mode, add the oil, heat it up, add the garlic and the meat and brown for 5 minutes. Add the rest of the ingredients, put the lid on and cook on High for 30 minutes. Release the pressure fast for 5 minutes, divide the mix between plates and serve.

Nutrition: calories 272, fat 14, fiber 3, carbs 7, protein 17

Kale Pork Meatloaf

Prep time: 10 minutes | Cooking time: 25 minutes | Servings: 4

Ingredients:

- 1 and ½ pound pork meat, ground
- 1 yellow onion, chopped
- 2 eggs, whisked
- 3 garlic cloves, minced
- 1 and ½ teaspoons basil, dried
- A pinch of salt and black pepper
- 1 cup kale, chopped
- ¼ cup almond milk
- Cooking spray
- 2 cups water

Directions:

In a bowl, combine the meat with the onion and the rest of the ingredients except the cooking spray and the water and stir really well. Grease a loaf pan that fits the instant pot with the cooking spray, shape the meatloaf and put it in the pan. dd the water to the instant pot, add the steamer basket, put the meatloaf inside, put the lid on and cook on High for 25 minutes. Release the pressure naturally for 10 minutes, cool the meatloaf down, slice and serve.

Nutrition: calories 273, fat 13, fiber 4, carbs 7, protein 19

Chili and Oregano Pork Roast

Prep time: 10 minutes | Cooking time: 35 minutes | Servings: 4

Ingredients:

- 1 yellow onion, chopped
- 1 and ½ pounds pork roast
- 12 ounces tomatoes, crushed
- 4 garlic cloves, minced
- 2 tablespoons chili powder
- 1 teaspoon oregano, dried
- 1 tablespoon olive oil
- A pinch of salt and black pepper
- 1 tablespoon apple cider vinegar
- 1 cup beef stock

Directions:

Set the instant pot on sauté mode, add the oil, heat it up, add the onion and garlic and sauté for 5 minutes. Add the meat and the rest of the ingredients, put the lid on and cook on High for 30 minutes. Release the pressure naturally for 10 minutes, divide the mix between plates and serve.

Nutrition: calories 261, fat 14, fiber 4, carbs 6, protein 14

Beef and Sun-Dried Tomatoes

Prep time: 10 minutes | Cooking time: 25 minutes | Servings: 4

Ingredients:

- 1 and ½ pounds beef stew meat, cubed
- 1 yellow onion, chopped
- 1 and ½ cups sun-dried tomatoes, chopped
- 3 garlic cloves, minced
- 1 cup beef stock
- 1 teaspoon sweet paprika
- 1 tablespoon olive oil
- A pinch of salt and black pepper

Directions:

Set your instant pot on Sauté mode, add the oil, heat it up, add the onion and garlic and cook for 2 minutes. Add the meat and brown for 3 minutes. Add the rest of the ingredients, put the lid on and cook on High for 20 minutes. Release the pressure naturally for 10 minutes, divide the mix between plates and serve.

Nutrition: calories 239, fat 16, fiber 3, carbs 6, protein 18

Pork and Mint Rice

Prep time: 10 minutes | Cooking time: 40 minutes | Servings: 4

Ingredients:

- 2 pounds pork stew meat, cubed
- 1 tablespoon olive oil
- 4 cups beef stock
- 1 yellow onion, chopped
- 2 cups wild rice
- ½ cup mint, chopped
- 4 garlic cloves, minced
- 1 tablespoon rosemary, chopped

Directions:

Set your instant pot on sauté mode, add the oil, heat it up, add the onion and the garlic and sauté for 5 minutes. Add the meat and brown for 5 minutes more. Add the remaining ingredients, put the lid on and cook on High for 30 minutes. Release the pressure naturally for 10 minutes, divide the mix between plates and serve.

Nutrition: calories 239, fat 16, fiber 4, carbs 6, protein 16

Meatballs and Coconut Sauce

Prep time: 10 minutes | Cooking time: 20 minutes | Servings: 4

Ingredients:

- 1 pound pork meat, ground
- 1 yellow onion, chopped
- 1 egg, whisked
- 4 garlic cloves, minced
- 1 teaspoon basil
- 1 tablespoon olive oil
- A pinch of salt and black pepper
- 1 teaspoon sweet paprika
- 2 cups coconut cream
- 1 teaspoon parsley, chopped

Directions:

In a bowl, combine the pork with the onion and the other ingredients except the oil, cream and parsley, stir well and shape medium meatballs out of this mix. Set the instant pot on Sauté mode, add the oil, heat it up, add the meatballs and brown for 2 minutes on each side. Add the cream and the parsley, put the lid on and cook on High for 15 minutes. Release the pressure naturally for 10 minutes, divide the meatballs and sauce between plates and serve.

Nutrition: calories 264, fat 10, fiber 3, carbs 6, protein 18

Pork and Cherries Sauce

Prep time: 5 minutes | Cooking time: 25 minutes | Servings: 4

Ingredients:

- 4 pork chops
- A pinch of salt and black pepper
- 1 cup beef stock
- 1 cup cherries, pitted
- 1 tablespoon parsley, chopped
- 1 tablespoon balsamic vinegar
- 1 tablespoon avocado oil

Directions:

Set the instant pot on Sauté mode, add the oil, heat it up, add the pork chops and brown for 2 minutes on each side. Add the rest of the ingredients, put the lid on and cook on High for 20 minutes. Release the pressure fast for 5 minutes, divide everything between plates and serve.

Nutrition: calories 226, fat 11, fiber 4, carbs 6, protein 16

Lamb and Couscous

Prep time: 10 minutes | Cooking time: 40 minutes | Servings: 4

Ingredients:

- 4 lamb chops
- 1 and ½ cups couscous
- 3 cups veggie stock
- 1 tablespoon almonds, toasted and chopped
- A pinch of salt and black pepper
- 1 tablespoon oregano, chopped
- 1 tablespoon basil, chopped
- 1 tablespoon olive oil
- 2 celery stalks, chopped

Directions:

Set your instant pot on sauté mode, add the oil, heat it up, add the meat and brown for 3 minutes on each side. Add the rest of the ingredients except the almonds, put the lid on and cook on Low for 40 minutes. Release the pressure naturally for 10 minutes, divide everything between plates, sprinkle the almonds on top and serve.

Nutrition: calories 247, fat 15, fiber 4, carbs 6, protein 15

Beef and Green Beans Rice

Prep time: 10 minutes | Cooking time: 45 minutes | Servings: 4

Ingredients:

- 1 and ½ pounds beef stew meat, cubed
- 1 tablespoon olive oil
- A pinch of salt and black pepper
- 1 tablespoon sweet paprika
- 1 and ½ cups green beans, trimmed and halved
- 1 cup wild rice
- 3 cups beef stock
- 1 tablespoon cilantro, chopped

Directions:

Set your instant pot on Sauté mode, add the oil, heat it up, add the meat and brown for 5 minutes. Add the rest of the ingredients, put the lid on and cook on Low for 40 minutes. Release the pressure naturally for 10 minutes, divide the mix between plates and serve.

Nutrition: calories 238, fat 13, fiber 3, carbs 6, protein 15

Pork and Sage Mushrooms

Prep time: 10 minutes | Cooking time: 30 minutes | Servings: 4

Ingredients:

- 2 and ½ pounds pork stew meat, cubed
- 1 tablespoon sage, chopped
- 1 and ½ cups cremini mushrooms, sliced
- 1 yellow onion, chopped
- 2 tablespoons olive oil
- A pinch of salt and black pepper
- 1 teaspoon sweet paprika

Directions:

Set your instant pot on Sauté mode, add the oil, heat it up, add the onion and the meat and brown for 5 minutes. Add the rest of the ingredients, put the lid on and cook on High for 25 minutes. Release the pressure naturally for 10 minutes, divide the mix between plates and serve.

Nutrition: calories 221, fat 12, fiber 4, carbs 7, protein 18

Pork and Balsamic Onions

Prep time: 10 minutes | Cooking time: 35 minutes | Servings: 4

Ingredients:
- 4 pork chops
- 2 tablespoons balsamic vinegar
- 1 tablespoon olive oil
- 1 tablespoon sweet paprika
- 1 tablespoon cilantro, chopped
- 1 cup beef stock
- 2 cups yellow onions, chopped

Directions:

Set your instant pot on Sauté mode, add the oil, heat it up, add the onions, vinegar, and the paprika, stir and sauté for 10 minutes. Add the meat and the stock, put the lid on and cook on High for 20 minutes. Release the pressure naturally for 10 minutes, divide the mix between plates, sprinkle the cilantro on top and serve.

Nutrition: calories 271, fat 12, fiber 2, carbs 6, protein 15

Pork and Walnuts Mix

Prep time: 10 minutes | Cooking time: 30 minutes | Servings: 4

Ingredients:
- 4 pork chops
- 1 tablespoon avocado oil
- 1 shallot, chopped
- 3 garlic cloves, minced
- 1 tablespoon walnuts, chopped
- 2 red chilies, chopped
- A pinch of salt and black pepper
- 1 cup beef stock

Directions:

Set your instant pot on Sauté mode, add the oil, heat it up, add the meat, shallots and the garlic and brown for 5 minutes. Add the rest of the ingredients, put the lid on and cook on High for 25 minutes. Release the pressure naturally for 10 minutes, divide everything between plates and serve.

Nutrition: calories 240, fat 12, fiber 3, carbs 5, protein 16

Chili Flakes Lamb Chops

Prep time: 10 minutes | Cooking time: 40 minutes | Servings: 4

Ingredients:
- 4 lamb chops
- 1 cup veggie stock
- 1 teaspoon dill, dried
- 1 teaspoon garlic powder
- 1 teaspoon chili flakes, crushed
- 1 tablespoon chives, chopped
- 1 tablespoon olive oil
- A pinch of salt and black pepper

Directions:

Set your instant pot on Sauté mode, add the oil, heat it up, add the lamb chops and brown for 2 minutes on each side. Add the rest of the ingredients, put the lid on and cook on Low for 35 minutes. Release the pressure naturally for 10 minutes, divide the mix between plates and serve.

Nutrition: calories 238, fat 10, fiber 2, carbs 5, protein 15

Chili Beef and Lemongrass

Prep time: 10 minutes | Cooking time: 40 minutes | Servings: 4

Ingredients:

- 2 pounds beef stew meat, cubed
- 1 cup beef stock
- 2 teaspoons chili powder
- 1 lemongrass stick, minced
- 2 garlic cloves, minced
- A pinch of salt and black pepper

Directions:

In your instant pot, combine the beef with the other ingredients, put the lid on and cook on Low for 40 minutes. Release the pressure naturally for 10 minutes, divide the mix between plates and serve.

Nutrition: calories 231, fat 14, fiber 3, carbs 5, protein 14

Ginger Pork and Collard Greens

Prep time: 10 minutes | Cooking time: 40 minutes | Servings: 4

Ingredients:

- 4 pork chops
- 1 pound collard greens
- 1 tablespoon ginger, grated
- 4 garlic cloves, minced
- 1 tablespoon olive oil
- 1 cup tomato sauce
- A pinch of salt and black pepper

Directions:

Set your instant pot on Sauté mode, add the oil, heat it up, add the pork chops and the garlic and brown for 2 minutes on each side. Add the rest of the ingredients, put the lid on and cook on Low for 35 minutes. Release the pressure naturally for 10 minutes, divide the mix between plates and serve.

Nutrition: calories 242, fat 13, fiber 2, carbs 4, protein 15

Baby Back Ribs and Carrots

Prep time: 10 minutes | Cooking time: 40 minutes | Servings: 4

Ingredients:

- 4 tablespoons tomato sauce
- 1 rack baby back ribs
- A pinch of salt and black pepper
- 4 carrots, sliced

Directions:

In your instant pot, combine all the ingredients, put the lid on and cook on High for 40 minutes. Release the pressure naturally for 10 minutes, divide the ribs between plates and serve.

Nutrition: calories 300, fat 14, fiber 3, carbs 5, protein 15

Pork Chops and Leeks

Prep time: 10 minutes | Cooking time: 35 minutes | Servings: 4

Ingredients:

- 4 pork chops
- 4 garlic cloves, minced
- 1 shallot, chopped
- 2 tablespoons avocado oil
- A pinch of salt and black pepper
- 2 leeks, sliced
- 1 cup coconut cream
- ½ cup beef stock

Directions:

Set your instant pot on Sauté mode, add the oil, heat it up, add the shallots and the garlic and sauté for 2 minutes. Add the meat and brown for 3 minutes more. Add the rest of the ingredients, put the lid on and cook on High for 30 minutes. Release the pressure naturally for 10 minutes, divide everything between plates and serve.

Nutrition: calories 291, fat 15, fiber 3, carbs 6, protein 14

Pork Chops and Chervil

Prep time: 5 minutes | Cooking time: 25 minutes | Servings: 4

Ingredients:

- 4 pork chops, boneless
- 1 tablespoon avocado oil
- 1 tablespoon chervil, chopped
- A pinch of salt and black pepper
- 1 yellow onion, chopped
- 1 cup beef stock
- ½ cup tomato sauce
- 4 garlic cloves, minced

Directions:

Set the instant pot on Sauté mode, add the oil, heat it up, add the onion and garlic and sauté for 2 minutes. Add the meat and brown for 3 minutes more. Add the rest of the ingredients, put the lid on and cook on High for 20 minutes. Release the pressure fast for 5 minutes, divide the mix between plates and serve.

Nutrition: calories 300, fat 14, fiber 2, carbs 4, protein 15

Lemongrass Turkey

Prep time: 10 minutes | Cooking time: 25 minutes | Servings: 4

Ingredients:

- 1 bunch lemongrass, chopped
- 4 garlic cloves, minced
- 2 tablespoons balsamic vinegar
- 1 tablespoon oregano, chopped

- 1 cup coconut milk
- 2 turkey breasts, skinless, boneless and cubed
- A pinch of salt and black pepper
- ¼ cup cilantro, chopped

Directions:

In your food processor, mix the lemongrass with the rest of the ingredients except the turkey and the coconut milk and pulse well. In your instant pot, combine the turkey with the lemongrass mix and the coconut milk, put the lid on and cook on High for 25 minutes. Release the pressure naturally for 10 minutes, divide everything between plates and serve with the cilantro sprinkled on top.

Nutrition: calories 263, fat 12, fiber 3, carbs 6, protein 14

Cilantro Stuffed Chicken Breast

Prep time: 10 minutes | Cooking time: 25 minutes | Servings: 4

Ingredients:

- 2 chicken breasts, skinless, boneless, halved and flattened
- 1 cup cilantro, chopped
- 1 teaspoon sweet paprika

- 2 spring onions, chopped
- A pinch of salt and black pepper
- 1 cup tomato sauce
- 1 tablespoon olive oil

Directions:

Arrange the chicken breasts on a working surface, divide the cilantro, onion and paprika on each and season with salt and pepper. Roll each chicken breast half and secure with a toothpick. Set the instant pot on Sauté mode, add the oil, heat it up, add the stuffed chicken and sear for 2 minutes on each side. Add the tomato sauce, put the lid on and cook on High for 20 minutes. Release the pressure naturally for 10 minutes, divide everything between plates and serve.

Nutrition: calories 162, fat 8, fiber 2, carbs 5, protein 9

Turkey Bites and Mustard Sauce

Prep time: 10 minutes | Cooking time: 25 minutes | Servings: 4

Ingredients:

- 2 tablespoons olive oil
- 1 big turkey breast, skinless, boneless and cubed
- ¾ cup chicken stock
- ¼ cup lime juice

- 3 tablespoons Dijon mustard
- 2 tablespoons sweet paprika
- 1 tablespoon oregano, chopped
- A pinch of salt and black pepper

Directions:

Set your instant pot on sauté mode, add the oil, heat it up, add the meat and brown for 5 minutes. Add the stock and the rest of the ingredients except the oregano, toss well, put the lid on and cook on High for 20 minutes. Release the pressure naturally for 10 minutes, divide the mix between plates, sprinkle the oregano on top and serve.

Nutrition: calories 200, fat 9, fiber 2, carbs 5, protein 10

Orange and Oregano Chicken

Prep time: 10 minutes | Cooking time: 20 minutes | Servings: 4

Ingredients:

- 2 chicken breasts, skinless, boneless and halved
- 1 cup orange juice
- ½ cup chicken stock
- 1 tablespoon oregano, chopped
- A pinch of salt and black pepper
- 1 teaspoon chili powder

Directions:

In your instant pot, combine the chicken with the orange juice and the rest of the ingredients, put the lid on and cook on High for 20 minutes. Release the pressure naturally for 10 minutes, divide the chicken and the orange sauce between plates and serve.

Nutrition: calories 200, fat 7, fiber 2, carbs 6, protein 11

Cinnamon and Turmeric Chicken

Prep time: 5 minutes | Cooking time: 20 minutes | Servings: 4

Ingredients:

- 2 chicken breasts, skinless, boneless and cubed
- 2 tablespoons olive oil
- ½ teaspoon turmeric, ground
- ½ teaspoon cinnamon, ground
- 1 teaspoon sweet paprika
- 1 red onion, chopped
- 2 tablespoons tomato paste
- 1 cup chicken stock
- ½ cup parsley, chopped

Directions:

Set your instant pot on Sauté mode, add the oil, heat it up, add the onion and the meat and brown for 5 minutes. Add the rest of the ingredients except the parsley, toss, put the lid on and cook on High for 15 minutes. Release the pressure fast for 5 minutes, divide the chicken mix between plates, sprinkle the parsley on top and serve.

Nutrition: calories 210, fat 8, fiber 2, carbs 6, protein 11

Mozzarella Chicken Thighs

Prep time: 10 minutes | Cooking time: 20 minutes | Servings: 4

Ingredients:

- 1 cup chicken stock
- A pinch of salt and black pepper
- 8 chicken thighs, boneless and skinless
- 1 yellow onion, chopped
- 1 tablespoon hot paprika
- 1 tablespoon chives, chopped
- 1 cup mozzarella, shredded
- 1 tablespoon olive oil

Directions:

Set your instant pot on Sauté mode, add the oil, heat it up, add the onion and the chicken thighs and brown for 5 minutes. Add the rest of the ingredients except the chives and mozzarella, put the lid on and cook on High for 15 minutes. Release the pressure fast for 5 minutes, sprinkle the chives and the mozzarella all over and leave the mix aside for 5 minutes more. Divide everything between plates and serve.

Nutrition: calories 220, fat 8, fiber 2, carbs 5, protein 11

Sweet Basil and Paprika Chicken

Prep time: 10 minutes | Cooking time: 25 minutes | Servings: 4

Ingredients:

- 2 chicken breasts, skinless, boneless and halved
- Salt and black pepper to the taste
- 2 tablespoons coconut sugar

- 2 teaspoons sweet paprika
- ½ cup chicken stock
- 1 tablespoon basil, chopped

Directions:

Set the instant pot on Sauté mode, add the sugar and the rest of the ingredients except the chicken, stir and simmer for 5 minutes. Whisk the mix again, add the chicken breasts, toss a bit, put the lid on and cook on High for 20 minutes. Release the pressure naturally for 10 minutes, divide the mix between plates and serve.

Nutrition: calories 192, fat 12, fiber 3, carbs 5, protein 12

Thai Chili Chicken

Prep time: 10 minutes | Cooking time: 20 minutes | Servings: 4

Ingredients:

- 2 chicken breasts, skinless, boneless and halved
- 1 cup lime juice
- 2 tablespoons avocado oil

- 2 Thai chilies, minced
- 1 teaspoon ginger, grated
- 2 teaspoons cilantro, chopped
- 1 cup chicken stock

Directions:

Set the instant pot on Sauté mode, add the oil, heat it up, add the chilies and the ginger and cook for 2 minutes. Add the chicken and brown for 3 minutes more. Add the rest of the ingredients, put the lid on and cook on High for 15 minutes. Release the pressure naturally for 10 minutes, divide the mix between plates and serve.

Nutrition: calories 200, fat 7, fiber 1, carbs 5, protein 12

Cumin and Cardamom Turkey

Prep time: 10 minutes | Cooking time: 20 minutes | Servings: 4

Ingredients:

- 1 turkey breast, skinless, boneless and cubed
- A pinch of salt and black pepper
- 1 cup chicken stock
- 1 yellow onion, chopped

- 3 garlic cloves, minced
- 1 and ½ teaspoons cumin, ground
- 1 teaspoon cardamom, ground
- 1 tablespoon chives, chopped

Directions:

In your instant pot, combine the turkey with salt, pepper, the stock and the rest of the ingredients except the chives, put the lid on and cook on High for 20 minutes. Release the pressure naturally for 10 minutes, divide the mix between plates and serve.

Nutrition: calories 231, fat 7, fiber 2, carbs 6, protein 12

Turkey and Eggplant Mix

Prep time: 10 minutes | Cooking time: 20 minutes | Servings: 4

Ingredients:

- 1 big turkey breast, skinless, boneless and cubed
- A pinch of salt and black pepper
- 1 big eggplant, roughly cubed
- 2 tablespoons avocado oil
- 1 red onion, chopped
- 10 ounces tomato sauce
- 1 tablespoon oregano, dried
- 1 teaspoon basil, dried

Directions:

Set your instant pot on Sauté mode, add the oil, heat it up, add the onion and the turkey and brown for 5 minutes. Add the eggplant and the rest of the ingredients, put the lid on and cook on High for 15 minutes. Release the pressure naturally for 10 minutes, divide everything between plates and serve.

Nutrition: calories 252, fat 12, fiber 4, carbs 7, protein 13

Chicken and Peppercorns

Prep time: 5 minutes | Cooking time: 20 minutes | Servings: 4

Ingredients:

- 2 chicken breasts, skinless, boneless and cubed
- A pinch of salt and black pepper
- 1 teaspoon black peppercorns, crushed
- 4 garlic cloves, minced
- 1 cup chicken stock
- 1 tablespoon cilantro, chopped

Directions:

In your instant pot, mix the chicken with the rest of the ingredients except the cilantro, put the lid on and cook on High for 20 minutes. Release the pressure fast for 5 minutes, divide everything between plates and serve with the cilantro sprinkled on top.

Nutrition: calories 221, fat 14, fiber 3, carbs 7, protein 14

Turkey and Tomato Sauce

Prep time: 10 minutes | Cooking time: 25 minutes | Servings: 4

Ingredients:

- 1 turkey breast, skinless, boneless and cut into strips
- 2 tablespoons olive oil
- 1 yellow onion, chopped
- 4 ounces tomato sauce
- A handful cilantro, chopped
- A pinch of salt and black pepper
- ½ pound cherry tomatoes, halved
- 1 tablespoon parsley, chopped

Directions:

Set your instant pot on Sauté mode, add the oil, heat it up, add the onion and the meat and brown for 5 minutes. Add the tomato sauce and the rest of the ingredients except the parsley, put the lid on and cook on High for 20 minutes. Release the pressure naturally between plates, divide the turkey mix between plates, and serve with the parsley sprinkled on top.

Nutrition: calories 263, fat 14, fiber 1, carbs 8, protein 12

Ginger Turkey and Potatoes

Prep time: 10 minutes | Cooking time: 25 minutes | Servings: 4

Ingredients:

- 1 turkey breast, skinless, boneless and sliced
- A pinch of salt and black pepper
- 1 tablespoon avocado oil
- 1 tablespoon ginger, grated
- 1 tablespoon sweet paprika
- 2 gold potatoes, peeled and cubed
- 2 garlic cloves, minced
- 1 and ½ cups chicken stock
- 2 green onions, chopped
- 1 tablespoon cilantro, chopped

Directions:

Set your instant pot on Sauté mode, add the oil, heat it up, add the ginger, paprika, garlic and the meat and brown for 5 minutes. Add the rest of the ingredients, put the lid on and cook on High for 20 minutes. Release the pressure naturally for 10 minutes, divide everything between plates and serve.

Nutrition: calories 263, fat 12, fiber 3, carbs 6, protein 14

Turkey and Carrots Mix

Prep time: 10 minutes | Cooking time: 20 minutes | Servings: 4

Ingredients:

- 1 big turkey breast, skinless, boneless and sliced
- 1 tablespoon olive oil
- 1 pound baby carrots
- 1 teaspoon chili powder
- 1 teaspoon oregano, dried
- 1 and ½ cups chicken stock
- 2 tablespoons tomato sauce
- A pinch of salt and black pepper

Directions:

Set the instant pot on Sauté mode, add the oil, heat it up, add the meat and brown for 5 minutes. Add the carrots and the rest of the ingredients, put the lid on and cook on High for 15 minutes. Release the pressure naturally for 10 minutes, divide the mix between plates and serve.

Nutrition: calories 253, fat 13, fiber 2, carbs 7, protein 16

Creamy Turkey

Prep time: 10 minutes | Cooking time: 20 minutes | Servings: 4

Ingredients:

- 1 big turkey breast, skinless, boneless and cubed
- 1 yellow onion, chopped
- 4 garlic cloves, minced
- ¼ cup parsley, chopped
- A pinch of salt and black pepper
- 1 teaspoon oregano, dried
- 1 cup coconut milk
- 1 cup chicken stock
- 2 tablespoons olive oil

Directions:

Set your instant pot on Sauté mode, add the oil, heat it up, add the onion, garlic and the turkey and brown for 5 minutes. Add the rest of the ingredients, toss, put the lid on and cook on High for 15 minutes. Release the pressure naturally for 10 minutes, divide everything between plates and serve.

Nutrition: calories 234, fat 14, fiber 4, carbs 7, protein 15

Sage Turkey and Sweet Potatoes

Prep time: 5 minutes | Cooking time: 30 minutes | Servings: 4

Ingredients:

- 1 turkey breast, skinless, boneless and sliced
- 1 yellow onion, chopped
- 3 garlic cloves, minced
- 1 cup chicken stock
- A pinch of salt and black pepper
- 2 tablespoons olive oil
- 1 tablespoon sage, chopped
- 2 sweet potatoes, cubed
- 1 tablespoon chives, chopped

Directions:

Set pot on Sauté mode, add the oil, heat it up, add the onion, garlic and the turkey and brown for 5 minutes. Add the stock and the rest of the ingredients, put the lid on and cook on High for 25 minutes. Release the pressure fast for 5 minutes, divide the turkey and the sweet potatoes between plates and serve.

Nutrition: calories 263, fat 13, fiber 2, carbs 7, protein 15

Chicken and Ginger Asparagus

Prep time: 10 minutes | Cooking time: 20 minutes | Servings: 4

Ingredients:

- 4 chicken breasts, skinless, boneless and halved
- 1 asparagus bunch, trimmed and steamed
- 1 cup tomato sauce
- 1 cup chicken stock
- ½ teaspoon chili powder
- 1 teaspoon basil, chopped
- 1 teaspoon oregano, chopped
- A pinch of salt and black pepper

Directions:

In your instant pot, mix the chicken with the tomato sauce and the rest of the ingredients except the asparagus, put the lid on and cook on High for 15 minutes. Release the pressure naturally for 10 minutes, set the pot on Sauté mode again, add the asparagus, cook for 5 minutes more, divide everything between plates and serve.

Nutrition: calories 200, fat 13, fiber 2, carbs 5, protein 16

Balsamic Chicken

Prep time: 5 minutes | Cooking time: 20 minutes | Servings: 4

Ingredients:

- 2 chicken breasts, skinless, boneless and halved
- 1 and ½ cups chicken stock
- A pinch of salt and black pepper
- 1 tablespoon mustard
- 3 garlic cloves, minced
- 1 tablespoon balsamic vinegar
- 1 tablespoon avocado oil

Directions:

Set the instant pot on Sauté mode, add the oil, heat it up, add the garlic and the chicken and brown for 2 minutes. Add the stock and the rest of the ingredients, put the lid on and cook on High for 18 minutes. Release the pressure fast for 5 minutes, divide the mix between plates and serve.

Nutrition: calories 200, fat 12, fiber 2, carbs 6, protein 15

Turkey and Ginger Rice

Prep time: 5 minutes | Cooking time: 25 minutes | Servings: 4

Ingredients:

- 1 big turkey breast, skinless, boneless and sliced
- 1 shallot, sliced
- 1 tablespoon olive oil
- 3 garlic cloves, minced
- A pinch of salt and black pepper
- 2 cups chicken stock
- 1 cup wild rice
- 1 tablespoon ginger, grated
- 1 green bell pepper, chopped
- 1 cup coconut milk
- 1 and ½ teaspoon turmeric powder
- 1 tablespoon cilantro, chopped

Directions:

Set the instant pot on Sauté mode, add the oil, heat it up, add the shallots and the garlic and sauté for 2 minutes. Add the meat and brown for 2 minutes more. Add the stock, rice and the rest of the ingredients, put the lid on and cook on High for 20 minutes. Release the pressure fast for 5 minutes.

Nutrition: calories 253, fat 14, fiber 2, carbs 7, protein 16

Rosemary Chicken and Green Beans

Prep time: 10 minutes | Cooking time: 20 minutes | Servings: 4

Ingredients:

- 4 garlic cloves, chopped
- 2 chicken breasts, skinless and halved
- 1 yellow onion, sliced
- 1 teaspoon rosemary, dried
- 1 cup chicken stock
- A pinch of salt and black pepper
- 1 cup tomato puree
- 1 cup green beans, trimmed and halved

Directions:

In your instant pot, mix the chicken with the rest of the ingredients, put the lid on and cook on High for 20 minutes. Release the pressure naturally for 10 minutes, divide the mix between plates and serve.

Nutrition: calories 273, fat 13, fiber 3, carbs 7, protein 17

Turkey and Endives

Prep time: 10 minutes | Cooking time: 25 minutes | Servings: 4

Ingredients:

- 1 big turkey breast, skinless, boneless and sliced
- 1 cup chicken stock
- 2 scallions, chopped
- 2 endives, halved lengthwise
- Juice of 1 lemon
- 1 tablespoon olive oil
- 1 cup tomatoes, cubed
- 1 tablespoon chives, chopped

Directions:

Set the instant pot on Sauté mode, add the oil, heat it up, add the scallions and the turkey and brown for 5 minutes. Add the stock, endives and the rest of the ingredients except the chives, put the lid on and cook on High for 20 minutes. Release the pressure naturally for 10 minutes, divide the mix between plates and serve with the chives sprinkled on top.

Nutrition: calories 276, fat 15, fiber 3, carbs 7, protein 16

Turkey and Thyme Sauce

Prep time: 10 minutes | Cooking time: 25 minutes | Servings: 4

Ingredients:

- 1 big turkey breast, skinless, boneless and sliced
- 2 tablespoons avocado oil
- 1 and ½ cups chicken stock
- A pinch of salt and black pepper
- 1 tablespoon cilantro, chopped
- 1 cup orange juice
- 1 bunch thyme, chopped

Directions:

Set your instant pot on Sauté mode, add the oil, heat it up, add the meat and brown for 5 minutes. Add the stock and the rest of the ingredients, put the lid on and cook on High for 20 minutes. Release the pressure naturally for 10 minutes, divide the mix between plates and serve.

Nutrition: calories 252, fat 15, fiber 2, carbs 6, protein 15

Cumin Chicken and Lemon

Prep time: 10 minutes | Cooking time: 25 minutes | Servings: 4

Ingredients:

- 2 chicken breasts, skinless, boneless and halved
- 1 tablespoon olive oil
- 1 and ½ tablespoons lemon zest, grated
- 1 tablespoon lemon juice
- 1 cup chicken stock
- 1 tablespoon cumin, ground
- A pinch of salt and black pepper
- 1 tablespoon parsley, chopped

Directions:

Set the instant pot on Sauté mode, add the oil, heat it up, add the chicken, cumin and lemon zest, and brown for 5 minutes. Add the rest of the ingredients, put the lid on and cook on High for 20 minutes. Release the pressure naturally for 10 minutes, divide everything between plates and serve.

Nutrition: calories 234, fat 12, fiber 3, carbs 5, protein 7

Hot Turkey and Kalamata Olives

*Prep time: 10 minutes | **Cooking time:** 25 minutes | Servings: 4*

Ingredients:

- 1 big turkey breast, skinless, boneless and sliced
- 4 tablespoons hot sauce
- 1 cup chicken stock
- 2 tablespoons tomato sauce
- 1 cup kalamata olives, pitted and halved
- 1 tablespoon parsley, chopped

Directions:

In your instant pot, combine the turkey with the rest of the ingredients, put the lid on and cook on High for 25 minutes. Release the pressure naturally for 10 minutes, divide everything between plates and serve.

Nutrition: calories 263, fat 14, fiber 3, carbs 7, protein 16

Chicken, Carrots and Zucchini Mix

*Prep time: 10 minutes | **Cooking time:** 20 minutes | Servings: 4*

Ingredients:

- 4 chicken thighs
- 1 teaspoon avocado oil
- A pinch of salt and black pepper
- 1 celery stalk, chopped
- ¼ pound baby carrots, halved
- 2 zucchinis, sliced
- 2 tablespoons tomato paste
- 2 cups chicken stock
- 1 tablespoon parsley, chopped

Directions:

Set your instant pot on Sauté mode, add the oil, heat it up, add the chicken and brown for 2 minutes more. Add the rest of the ingredients, put the lid on and cook on High for 18 minutes. Release the pressure naturally for 10 minutes, divide the mix between plates and serve.

Nutrition: calories 263, fat 12, fiber 2, carbs 7, protein 18

Chicken and Avocado Salsa

*Prep time: 10 minutes | **Cooking time:** 35 minutes | Servings: 4*

Ingredients:

- 2 chicken breasts, skinless, boneless and cubed
- A pinch of salt and black pepper
- 1 tablespoon olive oil
- 1 tablespoon smoked paprika
- 1 cup chicken stock
- 2 avocados, peeled, pitted and cubed
- 1 cucumber, cubed
- 1 tablespoon basil, chopped
- 1 tablespoon balsamic vinegar

Directions:

In your instant pot, combine the chicken with salt, pepper, paprika and the stock, put the lid on and cook on Low for 35 minutes. Release the pressure naturally for 10 minutes and divide the chicken between plates. In a bowl, mix the avocados with the oil, and the rest of the ingredients, toss, divide next to the chicken and serve.

Nutrition: calories 201, fat 7, fiber 3, carbs 6, protein 8

Turkey Chili

Prep time: 10 minutes | Cooking time: 30 minutes | Servings: 4

Ingredients:

- ½ pound red beans,
- soaked overnight and drained
- 1 yellow onion, chopped
- 2 garlic cloves, minced
- 1 pound turkey breast, skinless, boneless and cubed
- 1 tablespoon chili powder
- 1 and ½ cups chicken stock
- 1 cup tomato sauce
- A pinch of salt and black pepper
- 1 tablespoon cilantro, chopped

Directions:

In your instant pot, mix the beans with the onion and the rest of the ingredients, put the lid on and cook on High for 30 minutes. Release the pressure naturally for 10 minutes, divide the chili into bowls and serve.

Nutrition: calories 263, fat 12, fiber 3, carbs 7, protein 15

Cocoa and Cumin Chicken

Prep time: 10 minutes | Cooking time: 20 minutes | Servings: 4

Ingredients:

- 1 yellow onion, sliced
- 4 chicken breasts, skinless, boneless and cubed
- 1 tablespoon balsamic vinegar
- 1 tablespoon cocoa powder
- 1 tablespoon cumin, ground
- 1 and ½ cups chicken stock
- A pinch of salt and black pepper
- 1 tablespoon olive oil
- 2 tablespoons tomato sauce

Directions:

Set your instant pot on Sauté mode, add the oil, heat it up, add the onion and the meat and brown for 2 minutes. Add the rest of the ingredients, toss, put the lid on and cook on High for 18 minutes. Release the pressure naturally for 10 minutes, divide everything between plates and serve.

Nutrition: calories 214, fat 14, fiber 2, carbs 6, protein 15

Duck Curry

Prep time: 10 minutes | Cooking time: 30 minutes | Servings: 4

Ingredients:

- 1 and ½ pound duck breasts, skinless, boneless and cubed
- 1 tablespoon olive oil
- 1 yellow onion, sliced
- 5 ounces canned coconut cream
- 1 tablespoon green curry paste
- ½ bunch coriander, chopped

Directions:

Set your instant pot on Sauté mode, add the oil, heat it up, add the onion, curry paste and the duck and brown for 5 minutes. Add the rest of the ingredients, put the lid on and cook on High for 25 minutes. Release the pressure naturally for 10 minutes, divide the curry into bowls and serve.

Nutrition: calories 231, fat 12, fiber 4, carbs 7, protein 15

Duck and Brown Onions Mix

Prep time: 10 minutes | Cooking time: 30 minutes | Servings: 4

Ingredients:

- 2 pounds duck pieces
- 2 tablespoons olive oil
- 2 brown onions, sliced
- 2 garlic cloves, minced
- 14 ounces chicken stock
- 1 cup tomato sauce
- 1 tablespoon sweet paprika
- 1 tablespoon parsley, chopped

Directions:

Set your instant pot on Sauté mode, add the oil, heat it up, add the onion, garlic and the duck pieces and brown for 5 minutes. Add the rest of the ingredients, put the lid on and cook on High for 25 minutes. Release the pressure naturally for 10 minutes, divide everything between plates and serve.

Nutrition: calories 263, fat 12, fiber 5, carbs 7, protein 16

Parmesan Duck Breast

Prep time: 10 minutes | Cooking time: 25 minutes | Servings: 4

Ingredients:

- 1 tablespoon olive oil
- 2 pounds duck breasts, skinless and boneless
- A pinch of salt and black pepper
- 1 cup chicken stock
- 1 yellow onion, chopped
- 1 tomato, cubed
- 1 cup cheddar cheese, shredded

Directions:

Set your instant pot on Sauté mode, add the oil, heat it up, add the onion and the duck breasts and brown for 5 minutes. Add the stock, salt, pepper and the tomato, put the lid on and cook on High for 20 minutes. Release the pressure fast for 5 minutes, sprinkle the cheese all over, leave everything aside for another 5 minutes, divide between plates and serve.

Nutrition: calories 242, fat 14, fiber 3, carbs 7, protein 14

Chicken and Green Onions Rice

Prep time: 10 minutes | Cooking time: 25 minutes | Servings: 4

Ingredients:

- 2 pounds chicken breasts, skinless, boneless and cubed
- 1 cup wild rice
- 2 tablespoons green onions
- 3 cups chicken stock
- 1 tablespoon hot sauce
- 1 tablespoon coriander, chopped
- A pinch of salt and black pepper

Directions:

In your instant pot, mix the chicken with the rice and the rest of the ingredients, put the lid on and cook on High for 25 minutes. Release the pressure naturally for 10 minutes, divide everything between plates and serve.

Nutrition: calories 232, fat 12, fiber 2, carbs 6, protein 15

Cream Cheese Duck Breast

Prep time: 10 minutes | Cooking time: 20 minutes | Servings: 4

Ingredients:

- 2 duck breasts, skinless, boneless and halved
- 1 cup chicken stock
- 1 and ½ cup cream cheese
- 1 tablespoon Italian seasoning
- 1 tablespoon spring onions, chopped
- 1 tablespoon cilantro, chopped
- A pinch of salt and black pepper

Directions:

In your instant pot, mix the duck with the stock, seasoning, salt and pepper, put the lid on and cook on High for 15 minutes. Release the pressure naturally for 10 minutes, set the pot on Sauté mode again, add the rest of the ingredients, toss gently, cook for 5-6 minutes more, divide between plates and serve.

Nutrition: calories 263, fat 14, fiber 4, carbs 6, protein 18

Turkey and Mushrooms Sauce

Prep time: 5 minutes | Cooking time: 25 minutes | Servings: 4

Ingredients:

- 1 big turkey breast, skin
- less, boneless and sliced
- ½ cup coconut cream
- 1 yellow onion, chopped
- 1 tablespoon olive oil
- 1 pound white mushrooms, sliced
- ½ cup chicken stock
- ¼ cup cilantro, chopped

Directions:

Set the instant pot on Sauté mode, add the oil, heat it up, add the onion and mushrooms and sauté for 3 minutes. Add the turkey and brown for 2 minutes more. Add the remaining ingredients, put the lid on and cook on High for 20 minutes. Release the pressure fast for 5 minutes, divide everything between plates and serve.

Nutrition: calories 262, fat 16, fiber 2, carbs 8, protein 16

Corn, Zucchinis and Chicken Mix

Prep time: 5 minutes | Cooking time: 25 minutes | Servings: 4

Ingredients:

- 1 and ½ cups corn
- 1 zucchini, sliced
- 2 chicken breasts, skinless, boneless and halved
- 1 yellow onion, sliced
- 1 tablespoon olive oil
- 1 cup chicken stock
- ½ cup tomato sauce
- A pinch of salt and black pepper

Directions:

Set the instant pot on Sauté mode, add the oil, heat it up, add the onion and sauté for 4 minutes. Add the chicken and the rest of the ingredients, put the lid on and cook on High for 20 minutes. Release the pressure fast for 5 minutes, divide everything between plates and serve.

Nutrition: calories 283, fat 16, fiber 2, carbs 6, protein 17

Chicken, Leeks and Lentils

Prep time: 10 minutes | Cooking time: 30 minutes | Servings: 4

Ingredients:

- 2 tablespoons
- olive oil
- 1 cup yellow onion, chopped
- 1 cup lentils, dried
- A pinch of salt and black pepper
- 1 pound chicken thighs, skinless, boneless and cubed
- 1 cup tomato sauce
- 2 teaspoons coriander, ground

Directions:

Set your instant pot on Sauté mode, add the oil, heat it up, add the onion and the chicken and brown for 5 minutes. Add the rest of the ingredients, put the lid on and cook on High for 25 minutes. Release the pressure naturally for 10 minutes, divide the mix between plates and serve.

Nutrition: calories 291, fat 17, fiber 3, carbs 7, protein 16

Chicken and Squash

Prep time: 10 minutes | Cooking time: 25 minutes | Servings: 4

Ingredients:

- 3 garlic cloves, minced
- 2 tablespoons avocado oil
- 2 red chilies, chopped
- 1 butternut squash, cubed
- 1 pound chicken breasts, skinless, boneless and cubed
- A pinch of salt and black pepper
- 1 cup chicken stock
- 2 tablespoons sweet paprika

Directions:

Set your instant pot on Sauté mode, add the oil, heat it up, add the garlic and the chilies and cook for 2 minutes. Add the meat and brown for 3 minutes more. Add the rest of the ingredients, put the lid on and cook on High for 20 minutes. Release the pressure naturally for 10 minutes, divide everything between plates and serve.

Nutrition: calories 226, fat 9, fiber 1, carbs 6, protein 12

Turkey and Turmeric Chickpeas

Prep time: 10 minutes | Cooking time: 30 minutes | Servings: 4

Ingredients:

- 1 yellow onion, chopped
- 2 tablespoons olive oil
- 4 garlic cloves, minced
- 1 and ½ teaspoon hot paprika
- 1 teaspoon turmeric powder
- 1 cup chickpeas, soaked overnight and drained
- 1 pound turkey breast, skinless, boneless and sliced
- A pinch of salt and black pepper
- 1 cup chicken stock

Directions:

Set your instant pot on Sauté mode, add the oil, heat it up, add the garlic and the onion and sauté for 2 minutes. Add the meat and brown for 3 minutes more. Add the rest of the ingredients, put the lid on and cook on High for 25 minutes. Release the pressure naturally for 10 minutes, divide the mix between plates and serve.

Nutrition: calories 283, fat 11, fiber 2, carbs 8, protein 15

Chicken and Spicy Kale

Prep time: 10 minutes | Cooking time: 20 minutes | Servings: 4

Ingredients:

- 2 pounds chicken breasts, skinless, boneless and cubed
- 1 yellow onion, chopped
- A pinch of salt and black pepper
- 1 tablespoon olive oil
- 2 cups kale, torn
- 1 teaspoon red pepper flakes
- 1 cup chicken stock

Directions:

Set your instant pot on Sauté mode, add the oil, heat it up, add the onion and the pepper flakes and cook for 2 minutes. Add the rest of the ingredients, put the lid on and cook on High for 18 minutes. Release the pressure naturally for 10 minutes, divide everything between plates and serve.

Nutrition: calories 272, fat 7, fiber 3, carbs 7, protein 14

Marjoram Chicken and Apricots

Prep time: 10 minutes | Cooking time: 20 minutes | Servings: 4

Ingredients:

- 1 pound chicken breast, skinless, boneless and cubed
- 1 tablespoon olive oil
- ½ teaspoon sweet paprika
- 1 teaspoon marjoram, dried
- 1 cup chicken stock
- 1 cup apricots, chopped
- A pinch of salt and black pepper

Directions:

Set your instant pot on Sauté mode, add the oil, heat it up, add the chicken and brown for 2 minutes. Add the rest of the ingredients, put the lid on and cook on High for 18 minutes. Release the pressure naturally for 10 minutes, divide everything between plates and serve.

Nutrition: calories 211, fat 9, fiber 5, carbs 6, protein 12

Thyme Duck and Chives

Prep time: 10 minutes | Cooking time: 20 minutes | Servings: 4

Ingredients:

- 2 duck breasts, boneless, skin scored and halved
- 1 tablespoon avocado oil
- 1 yellow onion, chopped
- 1 cup chicken stock
- A pinch of salt and black pepper
- 2 teaspoons thyme, dried
- 1 tablespoon chives, chopped

Directions:

Set the instant pot on Sauté mode, add the oil, heat it up, add the duck breasts skin side down and sear for 2 minutes. Add the rest of the ingredients except the chives, put the lid on and cook on High for 18 minutes. Release the pressure naturally for 10 minutes, divide everything between plates, sprinkle the chives on top and serve.

Nutrition: calories 293, fat 15, fiber 4, carbs 6, protein 14

Chicken and Zucchini Noodles

Prep time: 10 minutes | Cooking time: 20 minutes | Servings: 4

Ingredients:

- 2 chicken breasts, skinless, boneless and halved
- 3 celery stalks, chopped
- 1 and ½ cups chicken stock
- 1 tablespoon tomato sauce
- A pinch of salt and black pepper
- 2 zucchinis, cut with a spiralizer
- 1 teaspoon chili powder
- 1 tablespoon cilantro, chopped

Directions:

In your instant pot, mix the chicken with the other ingredients except the zucchini noodles and the cilantro, put the lid on and cook on High for 15 minutes Release the pressure naturally for 10 minutes, set the pot on Sauté mode again, add the zucchini noodles, cook for 5 minutes more, divide between plates and serve with cilantro sprinkled on top.

Nutrition: calories 223, fat 9, fiber 2, carbs 4, protein 11

Chicken and Cucumber Salad

Prep time: 10 minutes | Cooking time: 20 minutes | Servings: 4

Ingredients:

- 2 chicken breasts, skinless, boneless and halved
- 1 tablespoon sweet paprika
- 1 cup chicken stock
- 1 tablespoon olive oil
- 1 yellow onion, chopped
- ½ teaspoon cinnamon powder
- 2 cucumbers, sliced
- 1 avocado, peeled, pitted and cubed
- 1 tomato, cubed
- 1 tablespoon cilantro, chopped

Directions:

Set instant pot on Sauté mode, add the oil, heat it up, add the onion and the meat and brown for 5 minutes. Add the paprika, stock and the cinnamon, put the lid on and cook on High for 15 minutes. Release the pressure naturally for 10 minutes, and divide the chicken between plates. In a bowl, mix the cucumbers with the avocado, tomato and cilantro, toss, divide the mix next to the chicken and serve.

Nutrition: calories 210, fat 11, fiber 2, carbs 7, protein 14

Turkey and Pomegranate Mix

Prep time: 10 minutes | Cooking time: 30 minutes | Servings: 4

Ingredients:

- 1 big turkey breast, skinless, boneless and sliced
- 1 cup pomegranate seeds
- 1 cup chicken stock
- 1 tablespoon sweet paprika
- 1 tablespoon olive oil
- A pinch of salt and black pepper
- 1 tablespoon cilantro, chopped

Directions:

Set the instant pot on Sauté mode, add the oil, heat it up, add the meat and brown for 5 minutes. Add the rest of the ingredients, put the lid on and cook on High for 25 minutes. Release the pressure naturally for 10 minutes, divide everything between plates and serve.

Nutrition: calories 263, fat 8, fiber 2, carbs 7, protein 12

Garlic Chicken Mix

Prep time: 10 minutes | Cooking time: 20 minutes | Servings: 4

Ingredients:

- 2 chicken breasts, skinless, boneless and halved
- 1 cup tomato sauce
- 1 tablespoon basil, chopped
- ¼ cup sweet chili sauce
- 4 garlic cloves, minced
- ¼ cup chicken stock

Directions:

In your instant pot, combine the chicken with the rest of the ingredients, put the lid on and cook on High for 20 minutes. Release the pressure naturally for 10 minutes, divide everything between plates and serve.

Nutrition: calories 220, fat 8, fiber 2, carbs 7, protein 15

Chicken, Tomato and Bell Peppers

Prep time: 10 minutes | Cooking time: 25 minutes | Servings: 4

Ingredients:

- 2 chicken breasts, skinless, boneless and cubed
- 2 tablespoons olive oil
- 1 teaspoon Creole seasoning
- A pinch of cayenne pepper
- 1 cup tomato, cubed
- 1 cup mixed bell peppers, cubed
- 1 yellow onion, chopped
- 1 cup chicken stock

Directions:

Set the instant pot on Sauté mode, add the oil, heat it up, add the onion and the chicken and brown for 5 minutes. Add the other ingredients, put the lid on and cook on High for 20 minutes. Release the pressure naturally for 10 minutes, divide everything between plates and serve.

Nutrition: calories 282, fat 12, fiber 2, carbs 6, protein 18

Greek Chicken and Yogurt

Prep time: 5 minutes | Cooking time: 25 minutes | Servings: 4

Ingredients:

- 2 chicken breasts, skinless, boneless and halved
- 1 cup tomato sauce
- 2 teaspoons cumin, ground
- A pinch of salt and black pepper
- ¾ cup coconut cream
- 2 teaspoons garam masala
- 1 cup Greek yogurt
- ¼ cup cilantro, chopped

Directions:

In your instant pot, mix the chicken with the tomato sauce and the rest of the ingredients, put the lid on and cook on High for 25 minutes. Release the pressure fast for 5 minutes, divide everything between plates and serve.

Nutrition: calories 285, fat 16, fiber 4, carbs 8, protein 18

Chicken, Broccoli and Black Beans

Prep time: 10 minutes | Cooking time: 25 minutes | Servings: 4

Ingredients:

- 2 chicken breasts, skinless and boneless
- 1 tablespoon olive oil
- 1 and ½ cups chicken stock
- A pinch of salt and black pepper
- 1 cup broccoli florets
- 1 cup black beans, soaked overnight and drained
- 2 tablespoons tomato sauce

Directions:

Set your instant pot on Sauté mode, add the oil, heat it up, add the chicken and brown for 5 minutes. Add the stock and the rest of the ingredients, put the lid on and cook on High for 20 minutes. Release the pressure naturally for 10 minutes, divide everything between plates and serve.

Nutrition: calories 292, fat 17, fiber 2, carbs 7, protein 16

Chicken Wings and Scallions Sauce

Prep time: 10 minutes | Cooking time: 25 minutes | Servings: 4

Ingredients:

- 8 chicken wings
- A pinch of salt and black pepper
- 1 tablespoon olive oil
- 6 scallions, chopped
- ½ teaspoon garlic powder
- 1 tomato, chopped
- ¼ cup cilantro, chopped
- 2 cups chicken stock
- 8 ounces tomato sauce

Directions:

Set your instant pot on Sauté mode, add the oil, heat it up, add the scallions, garlic powder, salt and pepper and sauté for 5 minutes. Add the chicken wings and brown for 5 minutes more. Add the remaining ingredients, put the lid on and cook on High for 15 minutes. Release the pressure naturally for 10 minutes, divide everything between plates and serve.

Nutrition: calories 224, fat 11, fiber 2, carbs 9, protein 11

Chicken and Cayenne Tomatoes

Prep time: 10 minutes | Cooking time: 20 minutes | Servings: 4

Ingredients:

- 1 and ½ pounds chicken breast, skinless, boneless and cubed
- 1 cup tomatoes, cubed
- 1 tablespoon avocado oil
- A pinch of salt and black pepper
- 1 teaspoon cayenne pepper
- 1 cup chicken stock
- 1 tablespoon smoked paprika
- 1 tablespoon cilantro, chopped

Directions:

Set your instant pot on Sauté mode, add the oil, heat it up, add the meat and brown for 2-3 minutes. Add the rest of the ingredients, put the lid on and cook on High for 18 minutes. Release the pressure naturally for 10 minutes, divide everything between plates and serve.

Nutrition: calories 229, fat 9, fiber 4, carbs 7, protein 16

Turkey and Cauliflower Sauté

Prep time: 10 minutes | Cooking time: 35 minutes | Servings: 4

Ingredients:

- 1 yellow onion, chopped
- 2 pounds turkey breast, skinless, boneless and sliced
- 1 cup cauliflower florets
- 1 cup chicken stock
- 2 tablespoons olive oil
- 2 garlic cloves, minced
- A pinch of rosemary, dried
- A pinch of salt and black pepper

Directions:

Set your instant pot on Sauté mode, add the oil, heat it up, add the onion, cauliflower, garlic, rosemary, salt and pepper, toss and sauté for 10 minutes. Add the turkey and the stock, put the lid on and cook on High for 25 minutes. Release the pressure naturally for 10 minutes, divide the mix between plates and serve.

Nutrition: calories 262, fat 12, fiber 4, carbs 7, protein 16

Turkey and Mushrooms Meatballs

Prep time: 10 minutes | Cooking time: 30 minutes | Servings: 4

Ingredients:

- ¼ cup parmesan, grated
- 1 pound turkey meat, ground
- 4 garlic cloves, minced
- 1 red onion, chopped
- 10 white mushrooms, sliced
- ¼ cup parsley, chopped
- ½ cup almond meal
- 1 egg, whisked
- A pinch of salt and black pepper
- 1 and ½ cups tomato sauce
- 2 tablespoons olive oil

Directions:

In a bowl, mix the turkey meat with the other ingredients except the sauce and the oil, stir well and shape medium meatballs out of this mix. Set the instant pot on Sauté mode, add the oil, heat it up, add the meatballs and brown them for 2 minutes on each side. Add the sauce, put the lid on and cook on High for 25 minutes. Release the pressure naturally for 10 minutes, divide everything between plates and serve.

Nutrition: calories 361, fat 9, fiber 8, carbs 12, protein 8

Chicken, Bacon and Artichokes

Prep time: 10 minutes | Cooking time: 25 minutes | Servings: 4

Ingredients:

- 1 cup bacon, cooked and crumbled
- 2 chicken breasts, skinless, boneless and halved
- 2 cups canned artichokes, drained and chopped
- 1 cup chicken stock
- 1 tablespoon chives, chopped
- 2 tablespoons tomato paste

Directions:

In your instant pot, mix the chicken with the rest of the ingredients, put the lid on and cook on High for 25 minutes. Release the pressure naturally for 10 minutes, divide everything between plates and serve.

Nutrition: calories 221, fat 12, fiber 2, carbs 6, protein 11

Lime Turkey Wings

Prep time: 10 minutes | Cooking time: 30 minutes | Servings: 4

Ingredients:

- 1 yellow onion, chopped
- 2 turkey wings, halved
- 1 tablespoon avocado oil
- 2 tablespoons lime juice
- 1 tablespoon lime zest, grated
- 4 garlic cloves, minced
- 1 cup chicken stock
- A pinch of salt and black pepper

Directions:

Set your instant pot on sauté mode, add the oil, heat it up, add the onion and sauté for 2 minutes. Add the turkey and the rest of the ingredients, put the lid on and cook on High for 28 minutes. Release the pressure naturally for 10 minutes, divide everything between plates and serve.

Nutrition: calories 231, fat 11, fiber 3, carbs 7, protein 18

Pomegranate and Cranberries Turkey

Prep time: 10 minutes | Cooking time: 30 minutes | Servings: 4

Ingredients:

- 2 tablespoons avocado oil
- 1 big turkey breast, skinless, boneless and sliced
- A pinch of salt and black pepper
- 1 cup cranberries
- 1 cup pomegranate juice
- 1 cup walnuts, chopped
- 1 bunch thyme, chopped

Directions:

Set your instant pot on sauté mode, add the oil, heat it up, add the meat and brown for 5 minutes. Add the rest of the ingredients, put the lid on and cook on High for 25 minutes. Release the pressure naturally for 10 minutes, divide everything between plates and serve.

Nutrition: calories 252, fat 12, fiber 2, carbs 7, protein 17

Chicken and Thyme Brussels Sprouts

Prep time: 10 minutes | Cooking time: 25 minutes | Servings: 4

Ingredients:

- 2 chicken breasts, skinless, boneless and halved
- 1 tablespoon olive oil
- A pinch of salt and black pepper
- 2 thyme springs, chopped
- 2 cups Brussels sprouts, halved
- 1 cup chicken stock

Directions:

Set your instant pot on sauté mode, add the oil, heat it up, add the meat and brown for 5 minutes. Add the rest of the ingredients, put the lid on and cook on High for 20 minutes. Release the pressure naturally for 10 minutes, divide everything between plates and serve.

Nutrition: calories 207, fat 9, fiber 3, carbs 7, protein 16

Creamy Chicken and Peas Casserole

Prep time: 10 minutes | Cooking time: 30 minutes | Servings: 4

Ingredients:

- 2 pounds chicken breast, skinless, boneless and cubed
- A pinch of salt and black pepper
- 1 tablespoon sweet paprika
- 1 tablespoon Italian seasoning
- 1 cup veggie stock
- 1 cup coconut cream
- 1 cup peas
- 1 cup cheddar, shredded

Directions:

Pour the stock in the instant pot and add the chicken pieces. Add salt, pepper, seasoning, paprika and peas and toss a bit. Add the cream on top, put the lid on and cook on High for 20 minutes. Release the pressure fast for 5 minutes, sprinkle the cheese all over, put the lid back on and cook on High for 10 minutes more. Release the pressure fast for 5 minutes again, divide the casserole between plates and serve.

Nutrition: calories 221, fat 11, fiber 2, carbs 7, protein 14

Balsamic Turkey and Onions

Prep time: 10 minutes | Cooking time: 30 minutes | Servings: 4

Ingredients:

- 2 and ½ pounds turkey breast, skinless, boneless and sliced
- A pinch of salt and black pepper
- 2 tablespoons balsamic vinegar
- 1 tablespoon olive oil
- 1 cup chicken stock
- 2 cups red onions, sliced
- 2 tablespoons cilantro, chopped

Directions:

Set your instant pot on Sauté mode, add the oil, heat it up, add the onions and the balsamic vinegar and sauté for 5 minutes. Add the meat and brown for 5 minutes more. Add the rest of the ingredients, put the lid on and cook on High for 20 minutes. Release the pressure naturally for 10 minutes, divide the mix between plates and serve.

Nutrition: calories 221, fat 12, fiber 2, carbs 5, protein 17

Parm Chicken and Fennel

Prep time: 10 minutes | Cooking time: 25 minutes | Servings: 4

Ingredients:

- 2 chicken breasts, skinless, boneless and halved
- 2 tablespoons olive oil
- 2 tablespoons ginger, grated
- 2 fennel bulbs, sliced
- 1 tablespoon basil, chopped
- 1 cup chicken stock

Directions:

Set your instant pot on sauté mode, add the oil, heat it up, add the ginger and the meat and brown for 5 minutes. Add the rest of the ingredients, put the lid on and cook on High for 20 minutes. Release the pressure naturally for 10 minutes, divide everything between plates and serve.

Nutrition: calories 221, fat 11, fiber 3, carbs 8, protein 16

Chicken, Potatoes and Bell Peppers

Prep time: 10 minutes | Cooking time: 30 minutes | Servings: 4

Ingredients:

- 2 chicken breasts, skinless, boneless and halved
- 1 yellow onion, chopped
- 2 potatoes, cubed
- 2 green bell peppers, cubed
- 4 garlic cloves, minced
- A pinch of salt and black pepper
- 1 cup chicken stock
- ¼ cup tomato puree

Directions:

In your instant pot, mix the chicken with the onion and the rest of the ingredients, put the lid on and cook on High for 30 minutes. Release the pressure naturally for 10 minutes, divide everything between plates and serve.

Nutrition: calories 221, fat 14, fiber 3, carbs 6, protein 13

Duck and Rice Mix

Prep time: 10 minutes | Cooking time: 30 minutes | Servings: 4

Ingredients:

- 1 tablespoon ginger, grated
- 4 garlic cloves, minced
- 1 cup coconut milk
- 1 cup wild rice
- 3 cups chicken stock
- 2 duck breasts, skinless, boneless and cubed
- 1 teaspoon five spice
- A pinch of salt and black pepper
- 1 tablespoon capers, drained and chopped

Directions:

In your instant pot, mix the duck with the rice and the rest of the ingredients, put the lid on and cook on High for 30 minutes. Release the pressure naturally for 10 minutes, divide everything between plates and serve.

Nutrition: calories 251, fat 17, fiber 2, carbs 7, protein 14

Chicken and Vinegar Potatoes

Prep time: 10 minutes | Cooking time: 25 minutes | Servings: 4

Ingredients:

- 1 cup chicken stock
- 2 tablespoons olive oil
- 2 pounds chicken breasts, skinless, boneless and halved
- ¼ cup balsamic vinegar
- 3 tablespoons mustard
- 1 and ½ pounds red potatoes, cubed
- A pinch of salt and black pepper

Directions:

Set your instant pot on sauté mode, add the oil, heat it up, add the chicken and brown for 5 minutes. Add the rest of the ingredients, put the lid on and cook on High for 20 minutes. Release the pressure naturally for 10 minutes, divide between plates and serve.

Nutrition: calories 251, fat 13, fiber 4, carbs 7, protein 12

Creamy Garlic Chicken Mix

Prep time: 10 minutes | Cooking time: 25 minutes | Servings: 4

Ingredients:

- 2 pounds chicken thighs, skinless, boneless and cubed
- 1 tablespoon ginger, grated
- 2 red onions, chopped
- 2 tablespoons olive oil
- A pinch of salt and black pepper
- 1 cup coconut cream
- 1 tablespoon curry powder

Directions:

Set your instant pot on sauté mode, add the oil, heat it up, add the onion, ginger and the chicken and brown for 5 minutes. Add the rest of the ingredients, put the lid on and cook on High for 20 minutes. Release the pressure naturally for 10 minutes, divide the mix between plates and serve.

Nutrition: calories 220, fat 17, fiber 3, carbs 7, protein 15

Chicken and Glazed Carrots

Prep time: 10 minutes | Cooking time: 25 minutes | Servings: 4

Ingredients:

- 1 teaspoon chili powder
- 2 tablespoons balsamic vinegar
- 1 teaspoon sweet paprika
- A pinch of salt and black pepper
- 2 tablespoons olive oil
- 2 pounds chicken breasts, skinless, boneless and cubed
- ½ cup chicken stock

Directions:

Set your instant pot on sauté mode, add the oil, heat it up, add the meat and brown for 5 minutes. Add the rest of the ingredients, put the lid on and cook on High for 20 minutes. Release the pressure naturally for 10 minutes, divide the mix between plates and serve.

Nutrition: calories 251, fat 16, fiber 2, carbs 7, protein 15

Turkey and Quinoa Mix

Prep time: 10 minutes | Cooking time: 30 minutes | Servings: 4

Ingredients:

- 1 turkey breast, skinless and boneless
- 1 tablespoon tomato paste
- 2 cups chicken stock
- 1 cup quinoa
- 1 teaspoon basil, dried
- A pinch of salt and black pepper

Directions:

In your instant pot, mix the turkey breasts with the tomato paste and the rest of the ingredients, put the lid on and cook on Low for 30 minutes. Release the pressure naturally for 10 minutes, divide everything between plates and serve.

Nutrition: calories 241, fat 12, fiber 4, carbs 7, protein 15

Duck and Lentils

Prep time: 10 minutes | Cooking time: 25 minutes | Servings: 4

Ingredients:

- 2 duck breasts, boneless, halved and skin scored
- 1 red onion, chopped
- 2 tablespoons olive oil
- 8 ounces lentils
- 1 tablespoon parsley, chopped
- 3 cups chicken stock
- A pinch of salt and black pepper

Directions:

Set your instant pot on sauté mode, add the oil, heat it up, add the onion and the meat skin side down and brown for 5 minutes. Add the rest of the ingredients, put the lid on and cook on High for 20 minutes. Release the pressure naturally for 10 minutes, divide everything between plates and serve.

Nutrition: calories 273, fat 12, fiber 2, carbs 6, protein 13

Chicken and Tomato Chickpeas Mix

Prep time: 10 minutes | Cooking time: 25 minutes | Servings: 4

Ingredients:

- 2 tablespoons olive oil
- 1 yellow onion, chopped
- 1 tablespoon smoked paprika
- 2 cups canned chickpeas, drained
- 2 cups tomatoes, chopped
- 2 cups chicken stock
- 2 tablespoons oregano, chopped
- A pinch of salt and black pepper
- 2 chicken breasts, skinless, boneless and halved

Directions:

Set your instant pot on sauté mode, add the oil, heat it up, add the onion and the chicken and brown for 5 minutes. Add the paprika, chickpeas and the remaining ingredients, put the lid on and cook on High for 20 minutes. Release the pressure naturally for 10 minutes, divide everything between plates and serve.

Nutrition: calories 231, fat 16, fiber 3, carbs 5, protein 14

Curry Chicken and Squash

Prep time: 5 minutes | Cooking time: 35 minutes | Servings: 4

Ingredients:

- 3 garlic cloves, minced
- 2 tablespoons olive oil
- 2 tablespoons green curry paste
- 2 cups squash, cubed
- 2 chicken breasts, skinless, boneless and halved
- A pinch of salt and black pepper
- 1 cup chicken stock
- ½ cup basil, chopped

Directions:

Set your instant pot on sauté mode, add the oil, heat it up, add the garlic and the meat and brown for 5 minutes. Add the curry paste and the rest of the ingredients, put the lid on and cook on Low for 30 minutes. Release the pressure fast for 5 minutes, divide the mix between plates and serve.

Nutrition: calories 271, fat 14, fiber 3, carbs 6, protein 16

Chicken and Black Eyed Peas

Prep time: 10 minutes | Cooking time: 30 minutes | Servings: 4

Ingredients:

- 1 pound breasts, skinless, boneless and cubed
- A pinch of salt and black pepper
- 1 cup black eyed peas
- 1 teaspoon sweet paprika
- 2 tablespoons avocado oil
- 1 yellow onion, cut into wedges
- 2 cups chicken stock

Directions:

In your instant pot, combine the chicken with salt, pepper and the remaining ingredients, put the lid on and cook on High for 30 minutes. Release the pressure naturally for 10 minutes, divide the mix between plates and serve.

Nutrition: calories 221, fat 12, fiber 2, carbs 5, protein 17

Sesame Turkey and Sprouts

Prep time: 10 minutes | Cooking time: 25 minutes | Servings: 4

Ingredients:

- 1 tablespoon olive oil
- 1 yellow onion, chopped
- 2 garlic cloves, minced
- 1 teaspoon sweet paprika
- 1 tablespoon white sesame seeds, toasted
- A pinch of salt and black pepper
- 1 turkey breast, skinless, boneless and cubed
- 1 cup Brussels sprouts, halved
- 1 cup chicken stock

Directions:

Set the instant pot on sauté mode, add the oil, heat it up, add the onion and the garlic and sauté for 5 minutes. Add the meat and the rest of the ingredients except the sesame seeds, put the lid on and cook on High for 20 minutes. Release the pressure naturally for 10 minutes, divide the mix between plates and serve with the sesame seeds sprinkled on top.

Nutrition: calories 227, fat 12, fiber 3, carbs 7, protein 18

Instant Pot Vegetable Recipes

Lime Artichokes

Prep time: 5 minutes | Cooking time: 20 minutes | Servings: 4

Ingredients:

- 4 artichokes, trimmed
- 1 tablespoon lime zest, grated
- 2 cups chicken stock
- ½ cup lime juice
- A pinch of salt and black pepper

Directions:

In your instant pot, combine the artichokes with the lime zest and the rest of the ingredients, put the lid on and cook on High for 20 minutes. Release the pressure fast for 5 minutes, divide everything between plates and serve.

Nutrition: calories 121, fat 2, fiber 1, carbs 5, protein 6

Balsamic Artichoke

Prep time: 5 minutes | Cooking time: 20 minutes | Servings: 4

Ingredients:
- 4 big artichokes, trimmed
- A pinch of salt and black pepper
- ¼ cup chicken stock
- 2 teaspoons balsamic vinegar
- 1 teaspoon basil, chopped

Directions:

In your instant pot, combine the artichokes with salt, pepper and the rest of the ingredients, put the lid on and cook on High for 20 minutes. Release the pressure fast for 5 minutes, divide the artichokes between plates and serve.

Nutrition: calories 120, fat 1, fiber 2, carbs 4, protein 2

Coconut Artichokes

Prep time: 5 minutes | Cooking time: 20 minutes | Servings: 4

Ingredients:
- 4 artichokes, trimmed
- ½ cup chicken stock
- 8 ounces coconut, shredded
- 1 teaspoon onion powder

Directions:

In your instant pot, combine the artichokes with the stock, coconut and onion powder, put the lid on and cook on High for 20 minutes. Release the pressure fast for 5 minutes, divide the artichokes between plates and serve.

Nutrition: calories 110, fat 2, fiber 2, carbs 4, protein 3

Cheese Artichokes

Prep time: 5 minutes | Cooking time: 20 minutes | Servings: 2

Ingredients:
- 2 artichokes, trimmed
- 1 bay leaf
- 1 cup chicken stock
- 1 tablespoon chili powder
- 2 garlic cloves, chopped
- 1 cup mozzarella, shredded

Directions:

In your instant pot, combine the artichokes with the rest of the ingredients except the mozzarella, put the lid on and cook on High for 20 minutes. Release the pressure fast for 5 minutes, divide the artichokes between plates and serve with the mozzarella sprinkled on top.

Nutrition: calories 140, fat 2, fiber 2, carbs 5, protein 2

Artichokes and Bacon

Prep time: 5 minutes | Cooking time: 20 minutes | Servings: 4

Ingredients:

- 4 artichokes, trimmed
- 2 bacon slices, cooked and chopped
- 1 cup chicken stock
- A pinch of salt and black pepper
- 1 tablespoon smoked paprika
- 1 tablespoon chives, chopped

Directions:

In your instant pot, mix the artichokes with the paprika, stock, salt and pepper, put the lid on and cook on High for 20 minutes. Release the pressure fast for 5 minutes, divide the artichokes between plates, sprinkle the bacon and the chives on top and serve.

Nutrition: calories 120, fat 2, fiber 3, carbs 5, protein 6

Cajun Asparagus

Prep time: 4 minutes | Cooking time: 5 minutes | Servings: 4

Ingredients:

- 1 teaspoon olive oil
- A pinch of red pepper flakes, crushed
- 1 bunch asparagus, trimmed
- ½ tablespoon Cajun seasoning
- A pinch of salt and black pepper
- 1 cup chicken stock

Directions:

In your instant pot, mix all the ingredients, put the lid on and cook on High for 5 minutes. Release the pressure fast for 4 minutes, divide the asparagus between plates and serve.

Nutrition: calories 142, fat 2, fiber 2, carbs 4, protein 3

Asparagus and Capers

Prep time: 4 minutes | Cooking time: 5 minutes | Servings: 4

Ingredients:

- 1 bunch asparagus, trimmed
- 2 tablespoons balsamic vinegar
- 1 tablespoon parsley, chopped
- A pinch of salt and black pepper
- 1 cup chicken stock
- 2 tablespoons capers, drained and chopped

Directions:

In your instant pot, mix the asparagus with the vinegar and the rest of the ingredients, put the lid on and cook on High for 5 minutes. Release the pressure fast for 4 minutes, divide everything between plates and serve.

Nutrition: calories 120, fat 2, fiber 2, carbs 4, protein 2

Asparagus and Goat Cheese

Prep time: 5 minutes | Cooking time: 5 minutes | Servings: 4

Ingredients:

- 1 bunch asparagus, trimmed
- A pinch of salt and black pepper
- 1 cup water
- 1 cup goat cheese, crumbled

Directions:

Add the water to the instant pot, add the steamer basket, add the asparagus, put the lid on and cook on High for 5 minutes. Release the pressure fast for 5 minutes, divide the asparagus between plates, sprinkle salt, pepper and the goat cheese on top and serve.

Nutrition: calories 134, fat 2, fiber 3, carbs 4, protein 5

Asparagus and Orange Sauce

Prep time: 5 minutes | Cooking time: 5 minutes | Servings: 4

Ingredients:

- 1 and ½ pounds asparagus, trimmed
- 2 teaspoons orange zest, grated
- 1 cup orange juice
- 1 teaspoon chili powder
- A pinch of salt and black pepper
- 2 scallions, chopped

Directions:

In your instant pot, combine all the ingredients, put the lid on and cook on High for 5 minutes. Release the pressure fast for 5 minutes, divide the asparagus and orange sauce between plates and serve.

Nutrition: calories 121, fat 3, fiber 2, carbs 3, protein 3

Green Beans and Beets

Prep time: 10 minutes | Cooking time: 20 minutes | Servings: 4

Ingredients:

- 1 and ½ cups chicken stock
- 4 beets, peeled and cubed
- 1 red onion, sliced
- 1 pound green beans, trimmed and halved
- A pinch of salt and black pepper
- 1 tablespoon dill, chopped
- 1 tablespoon balsamic vinegar

Directions:

In your instant pot, combine the beets with the green beans and the rest of the ingredients, put the lid on and cook on High for 20 minutes. Release the pressure naturally for 10 minutes, divide everything between plates and serve.

Nutrition: calories 162, fat 3, fiber 1, carbs 4, protein 5

Brussels Sprouts and Garlic

*Prep time: 10 minutes | **Cooking time:** 20 minutes | Servings: 4*

Ingredients:

- 1 pound Brussels sprouts
- 1 cup chicken stock
- 2 green onions, chopped
- 4 garlic cloves, minced
- A pinch of salt and black pepper
- 1 tablespoon dill, chopped

Directions:

In your instant pot, mix the sprouts with the stock and the rest of the ingredients, put the lid on and cook on High for 20 minutes. Release the pressure naturally for 10 minutes, divide the mix between plates and serve.

Nutrition: calories 142, fat 2, fiber 1, carbs 3, protein 4

Bell Peppers and Rice

*Prep time: 10 minutes | **Cooking time:** 20 minutes | Servings: 4*

Ingredients:

- 1 pound red bell peppers, cut into wedges
- 1 cup white rice, already cooked
- 2 cup veggie stock
- 1 tablespoon chives, chopped
- 1 tablespoon walnuts, chopped

Directions:

In your instant pot, mix the bell peppers with the rice and the rest of the ingredients, put the lid on and cook on High for 20 minutes. Release the pressure naturally for 10 minutes, divide the mix between plates and serve.

Nutrition: calories 152, fat 2, fiber 2, carbs 4, protein 5

Garlic Peppers Mix

*Prep time: 10 minutes | **Cooking time:** 15 minutes | Servings: 4*

Ingredients:

- 1 pound mixed bell peppers, cut into thick strips
- ½ cup veggie stock
- 3 garlic cloves, minced
- A pinch of cayenne pepper
- A pinch of salt and black pepper
- 1 tablespoon cilantro, chopped

Directions:

In your instant pot, combine the bell peppers with the stock and the rest of the ingredients, put the lid on and cook on High for 15 minutes. Release the pressure naturally for 10 minutes, divide the mix between plates and serve.

Nutrition: calories 121, fat 2, fiber 2, carbs 4, protein 5

Bell Peppers and Pine Nuts
Prep time: 5 minutes | Cooking time: 15 minutes | Servings: 4

Ingredients:
- 1 pound mixed bell peppers, cut into wedges
- 1 cup veggie stock
- ¼ cup pine nuts, toasted
- 1 tablespoon olive oil
- 1 tablespoon spring onions, chopped

Directions:
In your instant pot, combine the bell peppers with the rest of the ingredients, put the lid on and cook on High for 15 minutes. Release the pressure naturally for 10 minutes, divide the mix between plates and serve.

Nutrition: calories 110, fat 2, fiber 2, carbs 4, protein 4

Bacon and Mustard Bell Peppers
Prep time: 5 minutes | Cooking time: 15 minutes | Servings: 4

Ingredients:
- 1 pound mixed bell peppers, cut into strips
- A pinch of salt and black pepper
- ½ cup bacon, cooked and chopped
- 1 tablespoon mustard
- 1 cup chicken stock

Directions:
In your instant pot, combine the bell peppers with the rest of the ingredients, put the lid on and cook on High for 15 minutes. Release the pressure naturally for 5 minutes, divide the mix between plates and serve.

Nutrition: calories 151, fat 2, fiber 3, carbs 5, protein 4

Beets and Parmesan
Prep time:10 minutes | Cooking time: 30 minutes | Servings: 4

Ingredients:
- 1 pound beets, peeled and cubed
- Juice of 1 lime
- A pinch of salt and black pepper
- 1 cup chicken stock
- 3 tablespoons parmesan, grated

Directions:
In your instant pot, combine the beets with the rest of the ingredients except the parmesan, put the lid on and cook on High for 30 minutes. Release the pressure naturally for 10 minutes, divide the beets between plates, sprinkle the parmesan on top and serve.

Nutrition: calories 126, fat 1, fiber 2, carbs 4, protein 4

Potatoes and Cheddar
Prep time: 10 minutes | Cooking time: 30 minutes | Servings: 4

Ingredients:

- 1 and ½ pounds sweet potatoes, peeled and cut into wedges
- 1 cup cheddar cheese, grated
- 1 and ½ tablespoons tomato sauce
- 1 cup beef stock
- A pinch of salt and black pepper
- 1 tablespoon dill, chopped

Directions:

In your instant pot, mix the potatoes with the rest of the ingredients except the cheese, toss, put the lid on and cook on High for 20 minutes. Release the pressure naturally for 10 minutes, divide the mix between plates, sprinkle the cheddar on top and serve.

Nutrition: calories 162, fat 8, fiber 2, carbs 4, protein 7

Creamy Beets
Prep time: 10 minutes | Cooking time: 30 minutes | Servings: 4

Ingredients:

- 4 beets, peeled and cubed
- 2 spring onions, chopped
- 1 cup beef stock
- 1 cup coconut cream
- A pinch of salt and black pepper
- 2 tablespoons parsley flakes

Directions:

In your instant pot, mix the beets with the spring onions and the rest of the ingredients, put the lid on and cook on High for 30 minutes. Release the pressure naturally for 10 minutes, divide the mix between plates and serve.

Nutrition: calories 182, fat 4, fiber 2, carbs 4, protein 5

Garlic Celeriac
Prep time: 10 minutes | Cooking time: 15 minutes | Servings: 4

Ingredients:

- 1 celeriac, cut into sticks
- 1 tablespoon avocado oil
- 4 garlic cloves, minced
- 1 cup chicken stock
- A pinch of salt and black pepper
- 1 tablespoon dill, chopped

Directions:

Set your instant pot on Sauté mode, add the oil, heat it up, add the garlic and brown for 2 minutes. Add the celeriac and the rest of the ingredients, put the lid on and cook on High for 13 minutes more. Release the pressure naturally for 10 minutes, divide the mix between plates and serve.

Nutrition: calories 188, fat 2, fiber 2, carbs 4, protein 5

Creamy Zucchini

Prep time: 10 minutes | Cooking time: 10 minutes | Servings: 4

Ingredients:

- 2 tablespoons balsamic vinegar
- 4 zucchinis, sliced
- A pinch of salt and black pepper
- 1 cup coconut cream
- 1 teaspoon turmeric powder
- 1 tablespoon dill, chopped

Directions:

In your instant pot, mix the zucchinis with the rest of the ingredients, put the lid on and cook on High for 10 minutes. Release the pressure naturally for 10 minutes, divide the mix between plates and serve.

Nutrition: calories 162, fat 2, fiber 2, carbs 5, protein 6

Spicy Zucchinis

Prep time: 10 minutes | Cooking time: 10 minutes | Servings: 4

Ingredients:

- 4 zucchinis, roughly cubed
- ¼ cup chicken stock
- 1 tablespoon chili powder
- ½ teaspoon cayenne pepper
- ½ teaspoon red pepper flakes

Directions:

In your instant pot, mix the zucchinis with the rest of the ingredients, put the lid on and cook on High for 10 minutes. Release the pressure naturally for 10 minutes, divide the mix between plates and serve.

Nutrition: calories 162, fat 4, fiber 3, carbs 5, protein 7

Celery Sauté

Prep time: 10 minutes | Cooking time: 15 minutes | Servings: 4

Ingredients:

- 4 celery stalks, roughly chopped
- A pinch of salt and black pepper
- 1 tablespoon tomato sauce
- ½ cup chicken stock
- 1 tablespoon parsley, chopped

Directions:

In your instant pot, mix the celery with the rest of the ingredients, put the lid on and cook on High for 15 minutes. Release the pressure naturally for 10 minutes, divide the mix between plates and serve.

Nutrition: calories 121, fat 2, fiber 2, carbs 4, protein 2

Micro Greens Sauté

Prep time: 5 minutes | Cooking time: 4 minutes | Servings: 4

Ingredients:

- 2 cups micro greens
- 1 tablespoon tomato sauce
- A pinch of salt and black pepper
- ¼ cup chicken stock
- 1 tablespoon parsley, chopped

Directions:

In your instant pot, mix all the ingredients, put the lid on and cook on High for 4 minutes. Release the pressure naturally for 5 minutes, divide the mix between plates and serve.

Nutrition: calories 100, fat 1, fiber 2, carbs 2, protein 1

Dill Okra Mix

Prep time: 10 minutes | Cooking time: 10 minutes | Servings: 4

Ingredients:

- 2 cups okra
- A pinch of salt and black pepper
- 1 cup tomato sauce
- 1 tablespoon sweet paprika
- 2 tablespoon dill, chopped

Directions:

In your instant pot, mix the okra with salt, pepper and the rest of the ingredients, put the lid on and cook on High for 10 minutes. Release the pressure naturally for 10 minutes, divide the mix between plates and serve.

Nutrition: calories 121, fat 2, fiber 2, carbs 4, protein 4

Balsamic Cauliflower

Prep time: 10 minutes | Cooking time: 12 minutes | Servings: 4

Ingredients:

- 1 pound cauliflower florets
- 2 garlic cloves, minced
- 1 cup chicken stock
- A pinch of salt and black pepper
- 1 cup tomato sauce
- 1 tablespoon balsamic vinegar
- 1 tablespoon dill, chopped

Directions:

In your instant pot, mix the cauliflower with the rest of the ingredients except the dill, put the lid on and cook on High for 12 minutes. Release the pressure naturally for 10 minutes, divide the cauliflower between plates, sprinkle the dill on top and serve.

Nutrition: calories 123, fat 1, fiber 2, carbs 3, protein 2

Cauliflower and Collard Greens

Prep time: 10 minutes | Cooking time: 12 minutes | Servings: 6

Ingredients:
- 1 pound collard greens, trimmed
- 1 pound cauliflower florets
- 1 cup coconut cream
- 1 tablespoon chili powder
- A pinch of salt and black pepper
- 1 tablespoon chives, chopped

Directions:

In your instant pot, combine the cauliflower with the collard greens and the rest of the ingredients except the chives, put the lid on and cook on High for 12 minutes. Release the pressure naturally for 10 minutes, divide the mix between plates, sprinkle the chives on top and serve.

Nutrition: calories 122, fat 2, fiber 2, carbs 5, protein 3

Balsamic Collard Greens

Prep time: 10 minutes | Cooking time: 20 minutes | Servings: 4

Ingredients:
- 1 bunch collard greens, trimmed
- ½ cup chicken stock
- 2 tablespoons tomato puree
- A pinch of salt and black pepper
- 1 tablespoon balsamic vinegar

Directions:

In your instant pot, mix the collard greens with the stock and the rest of the ingredients, put the lid on and cook on High for 20 minutes. Release the pressure naturally for 10 minutes, divide the mix between plates and serve.

Nutrition: calories 130, fat 2, fiber 2, carbs 4, protein 6

Collard Greens and Apples Mix

Prep time: 10 minutes | Cooking time: 20 minutes | Servings: 4

Ingredients:
- 1 sweet onion, chopped
- 3 garlic cloves, minced
- 2 and ½ pounds collard greens, chopped
- A pinch of salt and black pepper
- 1 cup chicken stock
- 1 cup green apple, cored and cubed
- 1 tablespoon cilantro, chopped

Directions:

In your instant pot, combine the collard greens with the sweet onion and the rest of the ingredients, put the lid on and cook on High for 20 minutes. Release the pressure naturally for 10 minutes, divide the mix between plates and serve.

Nutrition: calories 140, fat 2, fiber 2, carbs 5, protein 7

Dill Endives and Chives
Prep time: 10 minutes | Cooking time: 12 minutes | Servings: 4

Ingredients:
- 4 endives, trimmed and halved
- A pinch of salt and black pepper
- 1 cup chicken stock
- 1 tablespoon chives, chopped
- 1 tablespoon dill, chopped

Directions:

In your instant pot, mix the endives with the rest of the ingredients, put the lid on and cook on High for 12 minutes. Release the pressure naturally for 10 minutes, divide the mix between plates and serve.

Nutrition: calories 114, fat 2, fiber 2, carbs 4, protein 4

Nutmeg Endives
Prep time: 10 minutes | Cooking time: 12 minutes | Servings: 4

Ingredients:
- 4 endives, trimmed
- A pinch of salt and black pepper
- ½ cup coconut milk
- ½ teaspoon nutmeg, ground

Directions:

In your instant pot, combine the endives with the rest of the ingredients, put the lid on and cook on High for 12 minutes. Release the pressure naturally for 10 minutes, divide the mix between plates and serve.

Nutrition: calories 124, fat 2, fiber 1, carbs 3, protein 4

Fennel and Okra Mix
Prep time: 10 minutes | Cooking time: 15 minutes | Servings: 4

Ingredients:
- 2 fennel bulbs, trimmed and sliced
- A pinch of salt and black pepper
- 1 cup okra
- Juice of ½ lemon
- ½ cup veggie stock
- 2 tablespoons parsley, chopped

Directions:

In your instant pot, mix the fennel with the okra and the rest of the ingredients, put the lid on and cook on High for 15 minutes. Release the pressure naturally for 10 minutes, divide the mix between plates and serve.

Nutrition: calories 121, fat 1, fiber 1, carbs 4, protein 5

Creamy Fennel
Prep time: 10 minutes | Cooking time: 20 minutes | Servings: 4

Ingredients:
- 2 fennel bulbs, sliced
- 2 spring onions, chopped
- 2 cups coconut cream
- 2 ounces parmesan, grated
- A pinch of salt and black pepper
- 1 tablespoon parsley, chopped

Directions:

In your instant pot, combine the fennel with the cream and the rest of the ingredients except the parmesan and the parsley, put the lid on and cook on High for 20 minutes. Release the pressure naturally for 10 minutes, divide the mix between plates, sprinkle the parmesan and the parsley on top and serve.

Nutrition: calories 200, fat 7, fiber 2, carbs 4, protein 6

Eggplant and Parsnips
Prep time: 5 minutes | Cooking time: 12 minutes | Servings: 4

Ingredients:
- 1 big eggplant, peeled and sliced
- 2 garlic cloves, minced
- A pinch of salt and black pepper
- 1 tablespoon sweet paprika
- 1 teaspoon cumin, ground
- 2 parsnips, sliced
- 1 cup tomato sauce

Directions:

In your instant pot, mix the eggplant with the parsnips and the rest of the ingredients, put the lid on and cook on High for 12 minutes. Release the pressure fast for 5 minutes, divide the mix between plates and serve.

Nutrition: calories 124, fat 2, fiber 2, carbs 4, protein 5

Eggplant and Olives
Prep time: 10 minutes | Cooking time: 12 minutes | Servings: 4

Ingredients:
- 4 cups eggplant, cubed
- 1 tablespoon olive oil
- 1 red onion, chopped
- 1 cup black olives, pitted and sliced
- 1 teaspoon chili powder
- A pinch of salt and black pepper
- ½ cup chicken stock

Directions:

Set the instant pot on Sauté mode, add the oil, heat it up, add the onion and sauté for 2 minutes. Add the eggplant and the rest of the ingredients, put the lid on and cook on High for 12 minutes. Release the pressure naturally for 10 minutes, divide the mix between plates and serve.

Nutrition: calories 135, fat 5, fiber 2, carbs 3, protein 4

Lemon Eggplants and Chives
Prep time: *10 minutes* | ***Cooking time:*** *10 minutes* | ***Servings:*** *4*

Ingredients:

- 1 pound eggplant, cut into medium chunks
- 2 tablespoons sweet paprika
- 1 teaspoon coriander, ground
- A pinch of salt and black pepper
- ½ cup chicken stock
- ¼ cup lemon juice
- 1 tablespoon chives, chopped

Directions:

In your instant pot, mix the eggplant with salt, pepper and the rest of the ingredients except the chives, put the lid on and cook on High for 10 minutes. Release the pressure naturally for 10 minutes, divide the mix between plates, sprinkle the chives on top and serve.

Nutrition: calories 128, fat 3, fiber 2, carbs 4, protein 5

Eggplants and Watercress Mix
Prep time: *10 minutes* | ***Cooking time:*** *12 minutes* | ***Servings:*** *4*

Ingredients:

- 2 eggplants, cubed
- 1 cup cherry tomatoes, halved
- 2 tablespoons lime juice
- 1 bunch watercress, trimmed
- ½ cup chicken stock
- 1 tablespoon ginger, grated

Directions:

In your instant pot, combine the eggplants with the rest of the ingredients, put the lid on and cook on High for 12 minutes. Release the pressure naturally for 10 minutes, divide the mix between plates and serve.

Nutrition: calories 146, fat 4, fiber 2, carbs 4, protein 6

Garlic Tomatoes and Watercress
Prep time: *10 minutes* | ***Cooking time:*** *12 minutes* | ***Servings:*** *4*

Ingredients:

- 1 pound cherry tomatoes, halved
- 2 garlic cloves, chopped
- 1 tablespoon olive oil
- 1 red chili pepper, chopped
- ¾ cup veggie stock
- 1 bunch watercress, trimmed
- 1 tablespoon cilantro, chopped

Directions:

Set your instant pot on Sauté mode, add the oil, heat it up, add the garlic and the chili pepper, stir and cook for 2 minutes. Add the tomatoes and the rest of the ingredients, put the lid on and cook on High for 10 minutes. Release the pressure naturally for 10 minutes, divide the mix between plates and serve.

Nutrition: calories 146, fat 4, fiber 2, carbs 4, protein 7

Eggplant and Rice Mix
Prep time: 10 minutes | Cooking time: 15 minutes | Servings: 4

Ingredients:

- 1 and ½ cups cauliflower rice
- 1 red onion, chopped
- 2 cups chicken stock
- 1 tablespoon olive oil
- 2 eggplants, cubed
- 1 teaspoon hot paprika
- A pinch of salt and black pepper
- ½ teaspoon thyme, dried

Directions:

Set your instant pot on Sauté mode, add the oil, heat it up, add the onion and sauté for 2 minutes. Add the cauliflower rice and the rest of the ingredients, put the lid on and cook on High for 13 minutes. Release the pressure naturally for 10 minutes, divide the mix into bowls and serve.

Nutrition: calories 134, fat 2, fiber 2, carbs 5, protein 5

Kale and Watercress Mix
Prep time: 5 minutes | Cooking time: 12 minutes | Servings: 4

Ingredients:

- 3 garlic cloves, chopped
- 1 tablespoon avocado oil
- 1 pound kale, trimmed
- 1 bunch watercress
- 1 tablespoon lime zest, grated
- 1 tablespoon lime juice
- 1 tablespoon capers, drained and chopped
- ½ cup tomato sauce

Directions:

Set the instant pot on Sauté mode, add the oil, heat it up, add the garlic, lime zest, lime juice, capers and tomato sauce, stir and simmer for 5 minutes. Add the rest of the ingredients, put the lid on and cook on High for 10 minutes. Release the pressure fast for 5 minutes, divide the mix into bowls and serve.

Nutrition: calories 129, fat 4, fiber 2, carbs 3, protein 2

Balsamic Kale and Peppers
Prep time: 10 minutes | Cooking time: 10 minutes | Servings: 4

Ingredients:

- 1 pound kale, chopped
- 1 pound mixed bell peppers, cut into strips
- 1 yellow onion, thinly sliced
- 1 cup chicken stock
- 4 garlic cloves, chopped
- 1 tablespoon balsamic vinegar
- A pinch of salt and black pepper
- ¼ teaspoon red pepper flakes

Directions:

In your instant pot, combine the kale with the bell peppers, and the rest of the ingredients, put the lid on and cook on High for 10 minutes. Release the pressure naturally for 10 minutes, divide the kale and peppers mix into bowls and serve.

Nutrition: calories 119, fat 2, fiber 2, carbs 4, protein 5

Instant Pot Dessert Recipes

Zucchini and Carrots Bread
Prep time: 10 minutes | Cooking time: 50 minutes | Servings: 6

Ingredients:

- 3 cups zucchinis, grated
- 1 and ½ cups carrots, grated
- 1 cup coconut sugar
- 1 tablespoon vanilla
- 2 eggs, whisked
- 2 cups almond flour
- 1 tablespoon baking powder
- Cooking spray
- 1 cup water

Directions:

In a bowl mix the zucchinis with the carrots, sugar and the rest of the ingredients except the water and the cooking spray and stir well. Grease a loaf pan that fits the instant pot with the cooking spray and pour the zucchini and carrots mix. Add the water to the instant pot, add the steamer basket, put the loaf pan inside, put the lid on and cook on High for 50 minutes. Release the pressure naturally for 10 minutes, cool the bread down, slice and serve.

Nutrition: calories 152, fat 5, fiber 2, carb 6, protein 3

Pear and Apple Bread
Prep time: 10 minutes | Cooking time: 45 minutes | Servings: 6

Ingredients:

- ¾ cup coconut sugar
- 1/3 cup avocado oil
- 1 teaspoon vanilla extract
- 1 egg, whisked
- 1 cup pears, cored and cubed
- 1 cup apples, cored and cubed
- 1 teaspoon baking powder
- 1 and ½ cups coconut flour
- 1/3 cup cashew milk
- 2 cups water
- Cooking spray

Directions:

In a bowl, mix the coconut sugar with the oil, vanilla and the rest of the ingredients except the water and the cooking spray and stir well. Grease a loaf pan that fits the instant pot with the cooking spray and pour the apples and pears mix inside. Add the water to your instant pot, add the steamer basket, add the loaf pan inside, put the lid on and cook on High for 45 minutes. Release the pressure naturally for 10 minutes, cool the bread down, slice and serve.

Nutrition: calories 220, fat 4, fiber 2, carbs 4, protein 6

Banana Cake
Prep time: 10 minutes | Cooking time: 30 minutes | Servings: 4

Ingredients:

- 2 egg, whisked
- ½ cup coconut sugar
- 2 tablespoons avocado oil
- 1 cup almond milk
- 4 tablespoons almond flour
- 2 bananas, peeled and mashed
- ½ teaspoon baking powder
- Cooking spray
- 1 cup water

Directions:

In a bowl, mix the eggs with the sugar and the rest of the ingredients except the cooking spray and the water and stir well. Grease a cake pan with the cooking spray and pour the banana mix inside. Add the water to the pot, add steamer basket, add the cake pan inside, put the lid on and cook on High for 30 minutes. Release the pressure naturally for 10 minutes, cool the cake down, slice and serve.

Nutrition: calories 262, fat 7, fiber 2, carbs 5, protein 8

Cinnamon Apple Mix

Prep time: 10 minutes | Cooking time: 20 minutes | Servings: 4

Ingredients:

- 2 teaspoons cinnamon powder
- 4 apples, cored and cut into chunks
- 1 tablespoon coconut sugar
- ½ cup apple juice

Directions:

In your instant pot, mix the apples with the rest of the ingredients, put the lid on and cook on Low for 20 minutes. Release the pressure naturally for 10 minutes, divide the mix between plates and serve.

Nutrition: calories 120, fat 2, fiber 2, carbs 4, protein 3

Pears and Raisins Mix

Prep time: 10 minutes | Cooking time: 15 minutes | Servings: 4

Ingredients:

- 4 pears, cored and cut into wedges
- 1 cup apple juice
- ¼ cup raisins
- ½ cup coconut sugar
- 1 teaspoon vanilla extract

Directions:

In your instant pot, combine the pears with the rest of the ingredients, put the lid on and cook on High for 15 minutes. Release the pressure naturally for 10 minutes, divide the mix between plates and serve.

Nutrition: calories 162, fat 2, fiber 2, carbs 4, protein 5

Creamy Chocolate Ramekins

Prep time: 5 minutes | Cooking time: 5 minutes | Servings: 4

Ingredients:

- 2 cups coconut cream
- 4 ounces dark chocolate, cut into chunks
- 1 teaspoon coconut sugar
- 2 cups water

Directions:

Divide the cream into 4 ramekins, add the chocolate and sprinkle the coconut sugar on top. Put the water in your instant pot, add the steamer basket, add the ramekins inside, put the lid on and cook on High for 5 minutes. Release the pressure fast for 5 minutes, whisk the cream in each ramekin and serve.

Nutrition: calories 172, fat 2, fiber 3, carbs 4, protein 5

Cranberries and Cocoa Cream
*Prep time: 10 minutes | **Cooking time:** 20 minutes | Servings: 4*

Ingredients:
- 4 ounces cranberries, chopped
- 2 cups water
- 4 ounces coconut cream
- 1 cup coconut sugar
- 1 teaspoon ginger powder
- 1 teaspoon cinnamon powder
- 1 tablespoon cocoa powder

Directions:
In a bowl, mix the cranberries with the cream and the rest of the ingredients, whisk well and divide into 4 ramekins. Add the water to your instant pot, add the steamer basket, add the ramekins inside, put the lid on and cook on High for 20 minutes. Release the pressure naturally for 10 minutes, and serve the cream right away.

Nutrition: calories 200, fat 5, fiber 3, carbs 4, protein 5

Squash and Carrots Pudding
*Prep time: 10 minutes | **Cooking time:** 25 minutes | Servings: 4*

Ingredients:
- 1 butternut squash, peeled and grated
- 2 eggs, whisked
- 2 cups water
- 1 cup almond milk
- ¾ cup coconut sugar
- 2 carrots, peeled and grated
- 1 teaspoon cinnamon powder
- Cooking spray

Directions:
In a bowl, mix the squash with the eggs and the rest of the ingredients except the water and the cooking spray and whisk well. Grease a pudding pan with the cooking spray and pour the squash and carrots mix inside. Add the water to the instant pot, add the steamer basket, put the pudding pan inside, put the lid on and cook on High for 25 minutes. Release the pressure naturally for 10 minutes, cool the pudding down and serve.

Nutrition: calories 200, fat 5, fiber 2, carbs 5, protein 6

Tapioca and Quinoa Pudding
*Prep time: 10 minutes | **Cooking time:** 10 minutes | Servings: 4*

Ingredients:
- 2 and ½ cups coconut milk
- 1/3 cup tapioca pearls, rinsed
- ½ cup quinoa
- ½ cup coconut sugar
- 1 teaspoon cinnamon powder

Directions:
In your instant pot, mix the coconut milk with tapioca and the rest of the ingredients, stir, put the lid on and cook on High for 10 minutes. Release the pressure naturally for 10 minutes, divide the pudding into bowls and serve.

Nutrition: calories 172, fat 4, fiber 2, carbs 4, protein 5

Almond and Apples Bowls

Prep time: 10 minutes | Cooking time: 20 minutes | Servings: 4

Ingredients:

- 1 cup almonds, chopped
- 2 eggs, whisked
- 1 cup coconut milk
- ¾ cup coconut sugar
- 1 teaspoon vanilla extract
- 1 cup apples, cored and cubed

Directions:

In your instant pot, mix the almonds with the eggs and the rest of the ingredients, put the lid on and cook on Low for 20 minutes. Release the pressure naturally for 10 minutes, divide the mix into bowls and serve.

Nutrition: calories 172, fat 2, fiber 2, carbs 4, protein 6

Coconut Grapes Cream

Prep time: 10 minutes | Cooking time: 15 minutes | Servings: 4

Ingredients:

- 2 cups grapes, halved
- 1 cup coconut cream
- 1 tablespoon cinnamon powder
- ½ cup coconut sugar
- 1 cup water

Directions:

In a bowl, mix the grapes with the rest of the ingredients, stir and divide into 4 ramekins. Add the water to the instant pot, add the steamer basket, put the ramekins inside, put the lid on and cook on High for 15 minutes. Release the pressure naturally for 10 minutes and serve the cream cold.

Nutrition: calories 172, fat 3, fiber 2, carbs 6, protein 6

Orange Cream

Prep time: 10 minutes | Cooking time: 15 minutes | Servings: 4

Ingredients:

- 2 cups coconut cream
- 1 teaspoon vanilla extract
- 4 tablespoons coconut sugar
- ¼ cup orange juice
- Zest of 1 orange, grated
- 1 cup water

Directions:

In a bowl, mix the cream with the vanilla extract and the rest of the ingredients except the water, whisk well and divide into 4 ramekins. Add the water to the instant pot, add the steamer basket, put the ramekins inside, put the lid on and cook on High for 15 minutes. Release the pressure naturally for 10 minutes and serve right away.

Nutrition: calories 162, fat 2, fiber 2, carbs 4, protein 6

Egg Pudding

Prep time: 5 minutes | *Cooking time:* 20 minutes | *Servings:* 4

Ingredients:
- 4 egg yolks, whisked
- 1 teaspoon baking powder
- 2 cups coconut cream
- ½ teaspoon vanilla extract
- 1 cup coconut sugar
- ½ cup raisins
- 1 cup water

Directions:

In a bowl mix the egg yolks with the cream and the rest of the ingredients except the water, whisk well and divide into 4 ramekins. Add the water to the pot, add the steamer basket, add the ramekins inside, put the lid on and cook on High for 20 minutes. Release the pressure fast for 5 minutes, and serve the pudding cold.

Nutrition: calories 200, fat 4, fiber 2, carbs 5, protein 4

Cinnamon Apples Stew

Prep time: 10 minutes | *Cooking time:* 10 minutes | *Servings:* 4

Ingredients:
- 4 apples, cored and cut into wedges
- 1 teaspoon vanilla extract
- 1 tablespoon cinnamon powder
- 1 cup apple juice
- ½ cup orange juice
- 2 tablespoons coconut sugar

Directions:

In your instant pot, mix the apples with the vanilla and the rest of the ingredients, put the lid on and cook on High for 10 minutes. Release the pressure naturally for 10 minutes, divide the mix into bowls and serve.

Nutrition: calories 182, fat 4, fiber 2, carbs 4, protein 6

Lime Pear Bowls

Prep time: 10 minutes | *Cooking time:* 10 minutes | *Servings:* 4

Ingredients:
- 4 pears, cored and cut into wedges
- Juice of 1 lime
- Zest of 1 lime, grated
- 1 cup apple juice
- ½ teaspoon vanilla extract

Directions:

In your instant pot, mix the pears with lime juice and the rest of the ingredients, put the lid on and cook on High for 10 minutes. Release the pressure naturally for 10 minutes, divide the mix into bowls and serve.

Nutrition: calories 162, fat 2, fiber 2, carbs 4, protein 6

Apple and Cauliflower Rice Pudding
Prep time: 10 minutes | Cooking time: 15 minutes | Servings: 4

Ingredients:
- 2 cups cauliflower rice
- 1 cup apples, cored and cubed
- 3 cups almond milk
- 3 tablespoon coconut sugar
- 1 teaspoon vanilla extract
- 1 tablespoon cinnamon powder

Directions:

In your instant pot, mix the cauliflower rice with the apples and the rest of the ingredients, put the lid on and cook on High for 15 minutes. Release the pressure naturally for 10 minutes, divide the rice into bowls and serve.

Nutrition: calories 172, fat 2, fiber 3, carbs 6, protein 6

Cream Cheese Pudding
Prep time: 10 minutes | Cooking time: 20 minutes | Servings: 4

Ingredients:
- 2 cups cream cheese, soft
- 2 cups coconut cream
- 3 tablespoons coconut sugar
- 4 eggs, whisked
- 1 teaspoon baking soda
- 1 teaspoon lemon zest, grated
- 1 cup water

Directions:

In a bowl, whisk the cream cheese with the coconut cream and the rest of the ingredients except the water, whisk really well and divide into 4 ramekins. Put the water in your instant pot, add the steamer basket, put the ramekins inside, put the lid on and cook on High for 20 minutes. Release the pressure naturally for 10 minutes and serve the puddings warm.

Nutrition: calories 200, fat 5, fiber 2, carbs 4, protein 6

Sweet Zucchini Pudding
Prep time: 10 minutes | Cooking time: 20 minutes | Servings: 4

Ingredients:
- 1 cup zucchinis, grated
- 1 egg, whisked
- 1 teaspoon baking soda
- 2 cups cashew milk
- 3 tablespoons coconut sugar
- 1 cup coconut cream
- 1 teaspoon vanilla extract
- 1 cup water

Directions:

In a bowl, mix the zucchinis with the milk and the rest of the ingredients except the water, whisk well and pour into a pudding pan. Put the water in the instant pot, add the steamer basket, put the pudding pan inside, put the lid on and cook on High for 20 minutes. Release the pressure naturally for 10 minutes and serve the pudding cold.

Nutrition: calories 162, fat 3, fiber 2, carbs 4, protein 3

Lemon Cream
Prep time: 10 minutes | Cooking time: 15 minutes | Servings: 4

Ingredients:

- 2 cups coconut cream
- 1 tablespoon lemon zest, grated
- 1 tablespoon lemon juice
- 2 eggs, whisked
- 1 teaspoon vanilla extract
- 1 cup raisins
- 1 cup water

Directions:

In a bowl, mix the cream with the rest of the ingredients except the water, whisk well and divide into ramekins. Put the water in the instant pot, add the steamer basket, put the ramekins inside, put the lid on and cook on High for 15 minutes. Release the pressure naturally for 10 minutes and serve.

Nutrition: calories 162, fat 2, fiber 2, carbs 4, protein 4

Orange Jam
Prep time: 10 minutes | Cooking time: 40 minutes | Servings: 6

Ingredients:

- Juice of 2 limes
- 1 tablespoon lime zest, grated
- 2 cups coconut sugar
- 1 pound oranges, peeled and cut into segments
- 3 cups water

Directions:

In your instant pot, mix the oranges with the rest of the ingredients, put the lid on and cook on Low for 40 minutes. Release the pressure naturally for 10 minutes, blend the mix using an immersion blender, divide into jars and serve.

Nutrition: calories 162, fat 1, fiber 2, carbs 3, protein 6

Strawberries Cream
Prep time: 10 minutes | Cooking time: 20 minutes | Servings: 4

Ingredients:

- 1 pound strawberries, chopped
- Zest of 1 lemon
- 2 cups coconut cream
- 1 tablespoon cocoa powder
- 1 teaspoon vanilla extract
- 1 cup water

Directions:

In a bowl, mix the strawberries with the rest of the ingredients except the water, whisk well and divide into 4 ramekins. Put the water in the instant pot, add the steamer basket, add the ramekins inside, put the lid on and cook on High for 20 minutes. Release the pressure naturally for 10 minutes and serve the cream cold.

Nutrition: calories 100, fat 1, fiber 2, carbs 4, protein 3

Sweet Carrot and Raisins Cream

Prep time: 10 minutes | Cooking time: 20 minutes | Servings: 4

Ingredients:

- 1 and ½ pounds carrots, peeled and grated
- 2 tablespoons lime juice
- 1 cup coconut sugar
- 1 and ½ cups coconut cream
- 1 teaspoon cinnamon powder
- 1 and ½ cups water

Directions:

In a bowl, mix the carrots with the lime juice and the rest of the ingredients except the water, whisk well and divide into 4 ramekins. Put the water in the instant pot, add the steamer basket, put the ramekins inside, put the lid on and cook on High for 20 minutes. Release the pressure naturally for 10 minutes, and serve the cream cold.

Nutrition: calories 124, fat 2, fiber 2, carbs 4, protein 5

Pears and Grapes Stew

Prep time: 10 minutes | Cooking time: 15 minutes | Servings: 4

Ingredients:

- 4 pears, cored and cut into quarters
- 2 cups grapes, halved
- ¼ cup apple juice
- 1 teaspoon vanilla extract

Directions:

In your instant pot, mix the pears with the grapes and the rest of the ingredients, put the lid on and cook on High for 15 minutes. Release the pressure naturally for 10 minutes, divide the sweet stew into bowls and serve.

Nutrition: calories 129, fat 2, fiber 2, carbs 4, protein 7

Ginger Peach Cream

Prep time: 10 minutes | Cooking time: 15 minutes | Servings: 4

Ingredients:

- 4 cups peaches, peeled and cubed
- 2 tablespoons coconut sugar
- 1 tablespoon ginger, grated
- 2 cups coconut cream
- 1 teaspoon vanilla extract
- 1 cup water

Directions:

In a bowl, mix the peaches with the sugar, ginger and the rest of the ingredients except the water, whisk and divide into 4 ramekins. Put the water in the instant pot, add the steamer basket, put the ramekins inside, put the lid on and cook on High for 15 minutes. Release the pressure naturally for 10 minutes, and serve the cream cold.

Nutrition: calories 120, fat 1, fiber 1, carbs 4, protein 6

Blackberry Stew
*Prep time: 10 minutes | **Cooking time:** 15 minutes | Servings: 4*

Ingredients:
- 12 ounces blackberries
- 2 tablespoons lemon juice
- 2 tablespoons coconut sugar
- 1 and ½ cups orange juice
- 1 teaspoon vanilla extract

Directions:
In your instant pot, mix the blackberries with the rest of the ingredients, put the lid on and cook on High for 15 minutes. Release the pressure naturally for 10 minutes, divide the mix into bowls and serve.

Nutrition: calories 110, fat 2, fiber 2, carbs 4, protein 5

Apple Compote
*Prep time: 10 minutes | **Cooking time:** 15 minutes | Servings: 6*

Ingredients:
- 3 cups apples, cored and cubed
- 2 tablespoons lime juice
- 1 cup water
- ¾ cup coconut sugar
- 1 teaspoon vanilla extract

Directions:
In your instant pot, mix the apples with the rest of the ingredients, put the lid on and cook on High for 15 minutes. Release the pressure naturally for 10 minutes, divide the compote into bowls and serve.

Nutrition: calories 152, fat 1, fiber 2, carbs 4, protein 5

Grapes Lime Compote
*Prep time: 10 minutes | **Cooking time:** 15 minutes | Servings: 6*

Ingredients:
- 1 and ½ cups grapes, halved
- 2 tablespoons lime juice
- 2 cups apple juice
- 3 tablespoons coconut sugar

Directions:
In your instant pot, mix the grapes with the rest of the ingredients, put the lid on and cook on High for 15 minutes. Release the pressure naturally for 10 minutes, divide the mix into bowls and serve.

Nutrition: calories 110, fat 2, fiber 2, carbs 5, protein 5

Apricots and Raisins Bowls

Prep time: 10 minutes | Cooking time: 15 minutes | Servings: 4

Ingredients:

- 2 cups apricots, cubed
- ¼ cup coconut cream
- ½ cup raisins
- ¼ cup coconut sugar
- 2 tablespoons coconut butter
- 1 teaspoon almond extract

Directions:

In your instant pot, mix the apricots with the cream and the rest of the ingredients, put the lid on and cook on High for 15 minutes. Release the pressure naturally for 10 minutes, divide everything into bowls and serve.

Nutrition: calories 158, fat 4, fiber 1, carbs 5, protein 2

Blueberries Cream

Prep time: 10 minutes | Cooking time: 15 minutes | Servings: 4

Ingredients:

- 2 cups blueberries
- 1 cup coconut cream
- 4 tablespoons coconut sugar
- 1 teaspoon vanilla extract

Directions:

In your instant pot, mix the blueberries with the rest of the ingredients, put the lid on and cook on High for 15 minutes. Release the pressure naturally for 10 minutes, divide the cream into bowls and serve.

Nutrition: calories 152, fat 2, fiber 2, carbs 4, protein 4

Dates and Apples Bowls

Prep time: 10 minutes | Cooking time: 15 minutes | Servings: 4

Ingredients:

- 4 apples, cored and cut into chunks
- 1 and ½ cups apple juice
- ½ cup dates, pitted
- 1 teaspoon cinnamon powder
- 1 teaspoon vanilla extract

Directions:

In your instant pot, mix the apples with the apple juice and the rest of the ingredients, put the lid on and cook on High for 15 minutes. Release the pressure naturally for 10 minutes, divide the mix into bowls and serve.

Nutrition: calories 110, fat 1, fiber 2, carbs 4, protein 6

Greek Banana Cake

Prep time: 10 minutes | Cooking time: 30 minutes | Servings: 4

Ingredients:

- 1 and ½ cups coconut flour
- 1 teaspoon baking powder
- ½ teaspoon cinnamon powder
- 2 eggs, whisked
- 1 cup Greek yogurt
- ½ cup coconut sugar
- ¼ cup apple juice
- 3 bananas, peeled and mashed
- 2 tablespoons coconut flakes
- Cooking spray
- 2 cups water

Directions:

In a bowl, mix the flour with the baking powder and the rest of the ingredients except the cooking spray and the water, and whisk really well. Grease a cake pan with the cooking spray and pour the cake mix in it. Add the water to the instant pot, add the steamer basket, put the cake pan inside, put the lid on and cook on High for 30 minutes. Release the pressure naturally for 10 minutes, cool the cake down, slice and serve.

Nutrition: calories 200, fat 6, fiber 2, carbs 5, protein 6

Walnuts Bread

Prep time: 10 minutes | Cooking time: 25 minutes | Servings: 4

Ingredients:

- 1 cup almond milk
- 3 eggs, whisked
- 1 tablespoon vanilla extract
- 2 cups coconut sugar
- 2 cups walnuts, chopped
- 2 cups almonds flour
- ¼ teaspoon baking powder
- 1 teaspoon cinnamon powder
- 2 cups water
- Cooking spray

Directions:

In a bowl, mix the milk with the eggs and the rest of the ingredients except the cooking spray and the water and whisk well. Grease a loaf pan with the cooking spray and pour the bread mix in it. Add the water to the instant pot, add the steamer basket, put the loaf pan inside, put the lid on and cook on High for 25 minutes. Release the pressure naturally for 10 minutes, cool the bread down, slice and serve.

Nutrition: calories 200, fat 5, fiber 2, carbs 5, protein 6

Strawberry Cheesecake

Prep time: 10 minutes | Cooking time: 50 minutes | Servings: 5

Ingredients:

For the crust:

- 2 tablespoons coconut butter, melted
- ½ cup graham crackers, crumbled

For the filling:

- 1 cup coconut cream
- 1 cup strawberries, chopped
- ½ cup coconut sugar
- 12 ounces cream cheese, soft
- 1 and ½ teaspoon vanilla extract
- 2 eggs, whisked
- Cooking spray
- 1 cup water

Directions:

Grease a spring form pan with cooking spray and leave it aside. In a bowl, mix the crackers with butter, stir, spread in the bottom of the pan and keep in the freezer for now. In a bowl, mix the cream with the strawberries and the rest of the ingredients except the water, whisk well and pour over the crust. Add the water to the instant pot, add the steamer basket, put the cake pan inside, put the lid on and cook on High for 50 minutes. Release the pressure naturally for 10 minutes, and serve the cheesecake cold.

Nutrition: calories 200, fat 4, fiber 2, carbs 6, protein 6

Pineapple and Cauliflower Rice Pudding

Prep time: 10 minutes | Cooking time: 20 minutes | Servings: 6

Ingredients:

- 2 cups coconut milk
- 1 cup cauliflower rice
- ½ cup pineapple, peeled and cubed
- ¼ cup coconut cream
- 2 eggs, whisked
- ½ cup coconut sugar
- ½ teaspoon vanilla extract

Directions:

In your instant pot, mix the cauliflower rice with the milk and the other ingredients, put the lid on and cook on High for 20 minutes. Release the pressure naturally for 10 minutes, divide the pudding into bowls and serve.

Nutrition: calories 162, fat 3, fiber 2, carbs 5, protein 6

Coconut Custard

Prep time: 10 minutes | Cooking time: 15 minutes | Servings: 6

Ingredients:

- 2 egg yolks
- 3 eggs, whisked
- 2 cups coconut milk
- 1/3 cup coconut sugar
- 1 tablespoon coconut butter, melted
- ½ cup coconut cream
- 1 tablespoon cinnamon powder
- ½ cup coconut flakes
- 1 teaspoon vanilla extract

Directions:

In your instant pot, mix the eggs with egg yolks and the rest of the ingredients, whisk, put the lid on and cook on High for 15 minutes. Release the pressure naturally for 10 minutes, divide the mix in bowls and serve really cold.

Nutrition: calories 128, fat 5, fiber 1, carbs 2, protein 6

Cardamom Apple Pudding

Prep time: 10 minutes | Cooking time: 20 minutes | Servings: 4

Ingredients:

- 3 cups apples, cored and cubed
- ½ cup almond milk
- 1 and ½ cups coconut cream
- 2 eggs, whisked
- 1/3 cup coconut sugar
- 2 teaspoons vanilla extract
- ¼ teaspoon cardamom, ground
- 2 cups water

Directions:

In a bowl, mix the apples with the milk and the rest of the ingredients except the water, whisk well and divide the mix into 4 ramekins. Put the water in the instant pot, add the steamer basket, put the ramekins inside, put the lid on and cook on High for 20 minutes. Release the pressure naturally for 10 minutes, cool the puddings down and serve.

Nutrition: calories 187, fat 4, fiber 2, carbs 4, protein 6

Chocolate Rice Pudding

Prep time: 10 minutes | Cooking time: 20 minutes | Servings: 4

Ingredients:
- 2 and ½ cups almond milk
- 1 and ¼ cups white rice
- ¼ cup coconut sugar
- 1/3 cup coconut butter, soft
- 1 teaspoon vanilla extract
- ¼ cup dark chocolate, chopped and soft

Directions:

In your instant pot, mix the rice with the milk and the rest of the ingredients, put the lid on and cook on High for 20 minutes. Release the pressure naturally for 10 minutes, stir the pudding, divide into bowls and serve.

Nutrition: calories 200, fat 7, fiber 2, carbs 4, protein 6

Rhubarb Cream

Prep time: 10 minutes | Cooking time: 15 minutes | Servings: 4

Ingredients:
- 1 cup coconut cream
- 2 cups rhubarb, chopped
- 3 tablespoon coconut sugar
- 1 teaspoon vanilla extract
- 2 eggs, whisked
- 1 cup water

Directions:

In a bowl, mix the cream with the rhubarb, sugar, eggs and vanilla, whisk really well and divide into 4 ramekins. Add the water to the instant pot, add the steamer basket, put the ramekins inside, put the lid on and cook on High for 15 minutes. Release the pressure naturally for 10 minutes, and serve the cream cold.

Nutrition: calories 142, fat 2, fiber 2, carbs 4, protein 6

Mango Cake

Prep time: 10 minutes | Cooking time: 40 minutes | Servings: 4

Ingredients:
- 1 cup mango, peeled and cubed
- ¾ cup almond flour
- ½ cup cashew butter, soft
- 1 cup water
- 1 and ½ cups coconut sugar
- ½ teaspoon baking powder
- 3 eggs, whisked
- 1 teaspoon vanilla extract

Directions:

In a bowl, beat the eggs really well. Add the flour, the butter and the rest of the ingredients except the water and whisk well. Line a cake pan with parchment paper and pour the cake mix in it. Add the water to the instant pot, add the steamer basket, put the cake pan inside, put the lid on and cook on High for 40 minutes. Release the pressure naturally for 10 minutes, cool the cake down, slice and serve.

Nutrition: calories 182, fat 4, fiber 2, carbs 7, protein 5

Nutmeg Pumpkin Pudding

Prep time: 10 minutes | *Cooking time:* 35 minutes | *Servings:* 6

Ingredients:

- 2 cups water
- Cooking spray
- ½ cup coconut sugar
- 2 eggs, whisked
- 1 cup coconut cream
- ½ cup almond flour
- 1 teaspoon nutmeg, ground
- ½ teaspoon baking soda
- 2/3 cup coconut butter, melted
- 1 and ½ cups pumpkin flesh

Directions:

In a bowl, mix the sugar with the eggs and the rest of the ingredients except the cooking spray and the water and whisk really well. Grease a pudding pan with the cooking spray and pour the pumpkin mix in it. Put the water in the instant pot, add the steamer basket, put the pudding pan inside, put the lid on and cook on High for 35 minutes. Release the pressure naturally for 10 minutes, cool the pudding down, divide between dessert plates and serve.

Nutrition: calories 200, fat 7, fiber 3, carbs 6, protein 7

Cooking can be so exhausting sometimes due to the lack of free time or cooking skills. The cookbook you've discovered today will put an end to the ordeal of spending long hours in the kitchen and complex cooking methods.

These great recipes collection brought to you reveals how much fun it actually is to cook different meals for you and your loved ones.

All you really need is a useful tool to help you out and the best one you can use these days is the instant pot.

This innovative kitchen appliance allows you to cook tasty and delicious culinary feasts for everyone in a matter of minutes and with minimum effort.

The instant pot has so many fans all over the world and it can soon become you new favorite kitchen appliance. All you have to do is to get a copy of this original cooking journal and to start cooking some incredible, rich and flavored dishes.

Start a great culinary journey and experience this innovative way of cooking! Try the instant pot and make some healthy and easy dishes in the comfort of your own home!

Made in the USA
Lexington, KY
14 May 2019